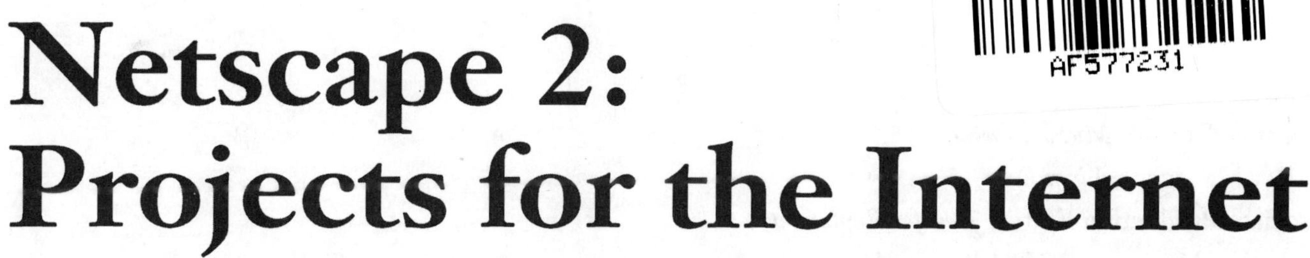

Netscape 2: Projects for the Internet

Gillian Hall
Arizona State University

H. David Crockett
Portland State University

The Benjamin/Cummings Publishing Company, Inc.

Menlo Park, California • Reading, Massachusetts
New York • Don Mills, Ontario • Harlow, U.K. • Amsterdam
Bonn • Paris • Milan • Madrid • Sydney • Singapore • Tokyo
Seoul • Taipei • Mexico City • San Juan, Puerto Rico

Sponsoring Editor: *Maureen A. Allaire*
Associate Editor: *Kathy G. Yankton*
Editorial Assistant: *Heide Chavez*
Executive Editor: *Michael Payne*
Project Manager: *Adam Ray*
Associate Production Editor: *Jennifer Englander*
Marketing Manager: *Melissa Baumwald*
Custom Publishing Operations Specialist: *Michael Smith*
Manufacturing Supervisor: *Janet Weaver*
Composition and Film Buyer: *Vivian McDougal*
Copy Editor: *Barbara Conway*
Proofreader: *Roseann Viano*
Indexer: *Nancy Kopper*

ISBN 0-8053-2195-0 bundled version
ISBN 0-8053-2283-3 stand alone version

1 3 4 5 6 7 8 9 10—VG—00 99 98 97 96

Ordering from the SELECT System

For more information on ordering and pricing policies for the SELECT System of microcomputer applications texts and their supplements, please contact your Addison-Wesley • Benjamin/Cummings sales representative or call our SELECT Hotline at 800/854-2595.

The Benjamin/Cummings Publishing Company, Inc.
2725 Sand Hill Road
Menlo Park, CA 94025
http://www.aw.com/bc/is/
bc.is@aw.com

Getting Started

Welcome to the *SELECT Lab Series.* We invite you to explore how you can take advantage of the newest Windows 95 features of the most popular software applications using this up-to-date learning package.

Greater access to ideas and information is changing the way people work. With Windows 95 applications you have greater integration capabilities and access to Internet resources than ever before. The *SELECT Lab Series* helps you take advantage of these valuable resources with special assignments devoted to the Internet and additional connectivity resources which can be accessed through our web site, **http://www.aw.com/bc/is.**

The key to using software is making the software work for you. The *SELECT Lab Series* will help you learn to use software as a productivity tool by guiding you step-by-step through case-based projects similar to those you will encounter at school, work, or home. When you are finished with this learning package, you will be fully prepared to use the resources this software offers. Your success is our success.

A Guided Tour

To facilitate the learning process, we have developed a consistent organizational structure for each module in the *SELECT Lab Series.*

You begin using the software almost immediately. A brief **Overview** introduces the software package and the basic application functions. **Getting Help** covers the on-line Help feature in each package. **A Note to the Student** explains any special conventions or system configurations observed in a particular module.

Each module contains six to eight **Projects,** an **Operations Reference** of all the operations covered in each module, an extensive **Glossary** of **key terms,** and an **Index.**

The following figures introduce the elements you will encounter as you use each SELECT module.

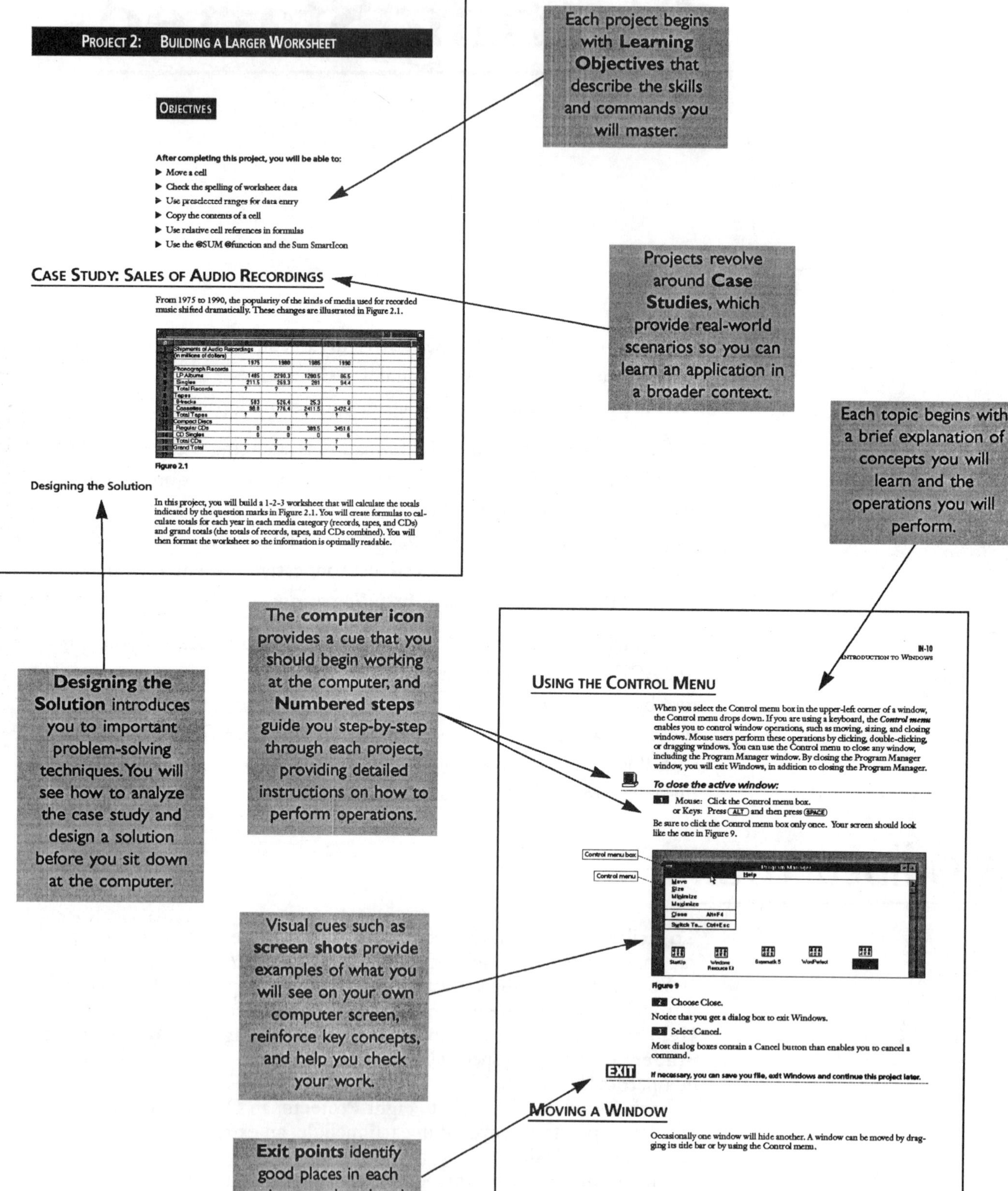
Each project begins with **Learning Objectives** that describe the skills and commands you will master.
Projects revolve around **Case Studies**, which provide real-world scenarios so you can learn an application in a broader context.
Each topic begins with a brief explanation of concepts you will learn and the operations you will perform.
The **computer icon** provides a cue that you should begin working at the computer, and **Numbered steps** guide you step-by-step through each project, providing detailed instructions on how to perform operations.
Designing the Solution introduces you to important problem-solving techniques. You will see how to analyze the case study and design a solution before you sit down at the computer.
Visual cues such as **screen shots** provide examples of what you will see on your own computer screen, reinforce key concepts, and help you check your work.
Exit points identify good places in each project to take a break.
PROJECT 2: BUILDING A LARGER WORKSHEET
OBJECTIVES
After completing this project, you will be able to:
▶ Move a cell
▶ Check the spelling of worksheet data
▶ Use preselected ranges for data entry
▶ Copy the contents of a cell
▶ Use relative cell references in formulas
▶ Use the @SUM @function and the Sum SmartIcon
CASE STUDY: SALES OF AUDIO RECORDINGS
From 1975 to 1990, the popularity of the kinds of media used for recorded music shifted dramatically. These changes are illustrated in Figure 2.1.
Figure 2.1
Designing the Solution
In this project, you will build a 1-2-3 worksheet that will calculate the totals indicated by the question marks in Figure 2.1. You will create formulas to calculate totals for each year in each media category (records, tapes, and CDs) and grand totals (the totals of records, tapes, and CDs combined). You will then format the worksheet so the information is optimally readable.
IN-10
INTRODUCTION TO WINDOWS
USING THE CONTROL MENU
When you select the Control menu box in the upper-left corner of a window, the Control menu drops down. If you are using a keyboard, the *Control menu* enables you to control window operations, such as moving, sizing, and closing windows. Mouse users perform these operations by clicking, double-clicking, or dragging windows. You can use the Control menu to close any window, including the Program Manager window. By closing the Program Manager window, you will exit Windows, in addition to closing the Program Manager.
To close the active window:
1 Mouse: Click the Control menu box.
or Keys: Press ALT and then press SPACE
Be sure to click the Control menu box only once. Your screen should look like the one in Figure 9.
Control menu box
Control menu
Figure 9
2 Choose Close.
Notice that you get a dialog box to exit Windows.
3 Select Cancel.
Most dialog boxes contain a Cancel button than enables you to cancel a command.
EXIT
If necessary, you can save you file, exit Windows and continue this project later.
MOVING A WINDOW
Occasionally one window will hide another. A window can be moved by dragging its title bar or by using the Control menu.

Key Terms are boldfaced and italicized and appear throughout each project.

WRD-12
Word for Windows

Opening a New Document

Word for Windows normally opens with a blank window and is ready to create a new document. If someone was using the computer before you, however, the window may already contain text. In that case, you will need to open a blank window for your new document. (If Word for Windows is not running already, start it by double-clicking the Word for Windows icon on the Windows desktop.)

To open a blank window for a new document:

1 Select New on the File menu or press ALT + F7 and then type n

The New dialog box appears, as shown in Figure 1.1. This dialog box allows you to select from a variety of ***templates*** and ***wizards***. ***Templates*** are preformatted skeleton documents ranging from memos to newsletters. ***Wizards*** ask a series of questions about a document format and then use that information to build a document for you to use. Right now, you need the default general-purpose template named Normal.

Figure 1.1

2 If Normal does not appear in the Template box, type Normal

3 Select OK.

Tip You can open a new document with a click of the mouse.
Use the New document button on the standard toolbar to open a Normal document with a single click.

The document area of the screen will be blank except for the blinking vertical ***insertion point*** (|), ***the end-of-document mark*** (__), and possibly a ***paragraph mark*** (¶). The ***insertion point*** marks the position where text will be inserted or deleted when you type at the keyboard. The ***end-of-document mark*** shows where the document ends; you cannot insert characters after the end-of-document mark. A ***paragraph mark*** indicates the end of a paragraph and forces the beginning of a new line. The paragraph mark may not show on your screen. If not, you will learn shortly how to make it visible.

Margin figures show on-screen tools that are often convenient alternatives to menu commands presented in the numbered steps.

Tips, Reminders, Cautions, and **Quick Fixes** appear throughout each project to highlight important, helpful, or pertinent information about each application.

Study Questions (Multiple Choice, Short Answer, and For Discussion) may be used as self-tests or homework assignments.

Short Answer
1. What are the two main services offered by My Computer?
2. What objects are considered physical locations in My Computer?
3. Why is a directory structure sometimes called a tree?
4. How do you run a program from My Computer?
5. How do you create a new folder?
6. Will copying a file result in the original being changed in any way?
7. Why should you drag and drop objects using mouse button 2?
8. Will renaming a file cause a second copy of that file to be generated?

For Discussion
1. Why was the ability to create folders for file management on the PC. so important?
2. My Computer will open a new window every time the user double-clicks on a drive or folder o... How could this create a problem?
3. Why should you expect there to be some sort of access restrictions on network drives?

Review Exercises

Examining the File System
Use My Computer to examine the root folders of your computer's local hard drive(s). If the computer ... part of a network, take a look at the network drives as well. Get some practice resizing, moving, and cl... the many windows that will be created during this exercise. Draw a tree that shows how information i... organized on your system and network—make note of the major folders in the root directories, and lo... for other folders within these. You don't have to list the thousands of individual files!

Launching Programs from My Computer
Use My Computer to explore your student data diskette. Without using the Find command, look for ... program file AirMail and use My Computer to run the program. After closing AirMail, look on your l... hard drive(s) for a folder called Program Files. This is a standard directory on Windows 95 systems, though it may not be present, or may have a different name, on your system. Use My Computer to op... the Program Files folder, and examine what's inside. There are probably more folders within Program Files; if an Accessories folder is present, open it and then use My Computer to launch MS Paint or W... Pad.

Assignments

Drag-and-Drop Manipulation of Files and Folders
In this assignment, you will use My Computer to "juggle" files and folders. This will provide extensive practice with window management and using the mouse for drag-and-drop operations.

Open the Temp folder on your student data diskette. Create a folder within it called Reports. Open the Reports folder and create three new text documents called Rain Forest, Desert, and Coral Reef. Using drag-and-drop, *move* the Reports folder (which will include the files you just created) to the Text folder of the student data diskette. Select the two files Rain Forest and Coral Reef and, again using drag-and-drop, *copy* them to the Work subdirectory. Rename the file Desert to Tundra. Finally, delete the Reports folder (which will also delete the files it contains).

Review Exercises present hands-on tasks to help you build on skills acquired in the projects.

Assignments require critical thinking and encourage synthesis and integration of project skills.

The Next Step

Access has many functions that are part of the ... You've already seen the Now() function in sev... If you're interested in extending your knowle... good place to start is the manual.

There are several other Report Wizards we... reports have no Detail band. Tabular reports ... forms. The AutoReport Wizard will attempt ... that makes the most sense—at least, to the W... Word Mail Merge, exports data in a format th... Merge feature can read. This is handy for pro...

Experiment with fonts and print styles, an...

Each project ends with **The Next Step** which discusses the concepts from the project and proposes other uses and applications for the skills you have learned, a **Summary,** and a list of **Key Terms and Operations.**

Summary and Exercises

Summary

- Access includes ReportWizards for single-column, grouped, and tabular formats, as well as mailing labels. Wizards are also included that generate automatic reports and export data to Microsoft Word's Mail Merge format
- To build a report with fields from two or more tables, you can query by example to create a view first, and then create the report based on that view.
- Grouping lets you create reports with records collated according to the values in one or more fields.
- Grouping also lets you create subtotals for groups as well as a grand total for the report.
- You can display today's date with the Now() function.
- You can change the format in which the date is printed.
- The mailing label ReportWizard handles standard Avery label layouts.
- To insert text characters in a mailing label, you must use the text buttons provided by the ReportWizards.
- The UCase() function is helpful when you want to make sure report output is entirely upper case.

Key Terms and Operations

Key Terms
group
group footer
group header
inner join
Now()
outer join
page footer
page header
report footer
report header
UCase()

Operations
Create a new report
Page Preview
Report Design
Sample Preview

FOLLOWING THE NUMBERED STEPS

To make the application modules easy to use in a lab setting, we have standardized the presentation of hands-on computer instructions as much as possible. The numbered step sections provide detailed, step-by-step instructions to guide you through the practical application of the conceptual material presented. Both keystroke and mouse instructions are used according to which one is more appropriate to complete a task. The instructions in the module assume that you know how to operate the keyboard, monitor, and printer.

Tip When you are using a mouse, unless indicated otherwise, you should assume that you are clicking the left button on the mouse. Several modules provide instructions for both mouse and keyboard users. When separate mouse and keyboard steps are given, be sure to follow one method or the other, but not both.

Each topic begins with a brief explanation of concepts. A computer icon or the ► symbol and a description of the task you will perform appear each time you are to begin working on the computer.

For Example:

To enter the address:

1 Type **`123 Elm Street`** and press (ENTER)

Notice that the keys you are to press and the text you are to type stand out. The text you will type appears in a special typeface to distinguish it from regular text. The key that you are to press mimics the labels of the keys on your keyboard.

When you are to press two keys or a key and a character simultaneously, the steps show the keys connected either with a plus sign or a bar.

For Example: (SHFT)+(TAB)
(CTRL)+C

When you are to press keys sequentially, the keys are not connected and a space separates them.

For Example: (CTRL) (PGDN)
(HOME) (HOME) (↑)

Be sure to press each key firmly, but quickly, one after the other. Keys begin repeating if you hold them down too long.

In some instances margin figures of single icons or buttons will appear next to the numbered steps. Margin figures provide visual cues to important tools that you can select as an alternative to the menu command in the numbered step.

For typographical conventions and other information unique to the application, please see *A Note to the Student* in the Overview of each module.

The *SELECT* Lab Series—A Connected Learning Resource

The *SELECT Lab Series* is a complete learning resource for success in the Information Age. Our application modules are designed to help you learn fast and effectively. Based around projects that reflect your world, each module helps you master key concepts and problem-solving techniques for using the software application you are learning. Through our web site you can access dynamic and current information resources that will help you get up to speed on the Information Highway and keep up with the ever changing world of technology.

Explore our web site **http://www.aw.com/bc/is** to discover:

- **B/C Link Online:** Our on-line newsletter which features the latest news and information on current computer technology and applications.
- **Student Opportunities and Activities:** Benjamin/Cummings' web site connects you to important job opportunities and internships.
- **What's New:** Access the latest news and information topics.
- **Links:** We provide relevant links to other interesting resources and educational sites.

The TechSuite

This module may be part of our new custom bundled system—the **Benjamin/Cummings TechSuite.** Your instructor can choose any combination of concepts texts, applications modules, and software to meet the exact needs of your course. The TechSuite meets your needs by offering you one convenient package at a discount price.

Supplements

Each module has a corresponding Instructor's Manual with a Test Bank and Transparency Masters. For each project in the student text, the Instructor's Manual includes Expanded Student Objectives, Answers to Study Questions, and Additional Assessment Techniques. The Test Bank contains two separate tests (with answers) consisting of multiple choice, true/false, and fill-in questions that are referenced to pages in the student's text. Transparency Masters illustrate 25 to 30 key concepts and screen captures from the text.

The Instructor's Data Disk contains student data files, answers to selected Review Exercises, answers to selected Assignments, and the test files from the Instructor's Manual in ASCII format.

ACKNOWLEDGMENTS

The Benjamin/Cummings Publishing Company would like to thank the following reviewers for their valuable contributions to the *SELECT Lab Series.*

Joseph Aieta
Babson College

Tom Ashby
Oklahoma CC

Bob Barber
Lane CC

Robert Caruso
Santa Rosa Junior College

Robert Chi
California State
Long Beach

Jill Davis
State University of New
York at Stony Brook

Fredia Dillard
Samford University

Peter Drexel
Plymouth State College

Ralph Duffy
North Seattle CC

David Egle
University of Texas,
Pan American

Jonathan Frank
Suffolk University

Patrick Gilbert
University of Hawaii

Maureen Greenbaum
Union County College

Sally Ann Hanson
Mercer County CC

Sunil Hazari
East Carolina University

Bruce Herniter
University of Hartford

Lisa Jackson
Henderson CC

Cynthia Kachik
Santa Fe CC

Bennett Kramer
Massasoit CC

Charles Lake
Faulkner State
Junior College

Ron Leake
Johnson County CC

Randy Marak
Hill College

Charles Mattox, Jr.
St. Mary's University

Jim McCullough
Porter and Chester
Institute

Gail Miles
Lenoir-Rhyne College

Steve Moore
University of
South Florida

Anthony Nowakowski
Buffalo State College

Gloria Oman
Portland State University

John Passafiume
Clemson University

Leonard Presby
William Paterson
College

Louis Pryor
Garland County CC

Michael Reilly
University of Denver

Dick Ricketts
Lane CC

Dennis Santomauro
Kean College of
New Jersey

Pamela Schmidt
Oakton CC

Gary Schubert
Alderson-Broaddus College

T. Michael Smith
Austin CC

Cynthia Thompson
Carl Sandburg College

Marion Tucker
Northern Oklahoma
College

JoAnn Weatherwax
Saddleback College

David Whitney
San Francisco State
University

James Wood
Tri-County
Technical College

Minnie Yen
University of Alaska,
Anchorage

Allen Zilbert
Long Island University

Contents

PROJECT 6: CREATING YOUR OWN WEB PAGE 173

OPERATIONS REFERENCE 205

GLOSSARY 209

INDEX 211

Overview

Objectives

After completing this Overview, you should be able to:

- Understand some basic Internet concepts, issues, and terminology
- Understand the role of the World Wide Web in the Internet
- Understand why Web browsers are important Internet tools
- Start the Netscape Navigator Web browser application
- Customize the appearance of the Netscape window
- Get online Help
- Exit Netscape Navigator

Over the past few years, the ***Internet*** has gradually become a household word. Advertisers, broadcasters, educators, magazines, and others routinely offer their Internet addresses as places to get more information on their products and services. For users of the Internet, those addresses are rapidly becoming more important than phone numbers. By the time you finish this course, you will understand why!

Today you cannot watch television, listen to the radio, or read a magazine or newspaper without encountering references to the Internet. In fact many magazines, newspapers, and television programs now publish their wares on the Internet. Imagine reading the daily newspaper or the latest edition of your favorite magazine on your computer screen. That concept may seem far fetched, but it is reality. Many people are doing just that right now.

The Internet provides people with easier access to more information than has ever been possible before. From the IRS and the Library of Congress to universities, businesses, and individuals just like you, it seems everyone is scrambling to publish and access information on the Internet.

This situation can make the uninitiated a little tense when the word *Internet* comes up in conversation. Not to worry. If this course will be your first experience with the Internet, you will find it to be a much friendlier place to visit than did the Internet pioneers just a few years ago. You have chosen an ideal point in the evolution of this thing we call the Internet to get your feet wet. It has never been easier or more fun than it is today!

What Is the Internet?

The Internet got its start in 1969 as ***ARPAnet***, a computer network designed by the U.S. Defense Department to ensure that the Defense Department computers could communicate with each other. For obvious reasons, the emphasis was to design a network over which information could travel even if certain network connections or computers in the network "died". So the robust, decentralized communication protocol (called ***Internet Protocol***, or IP) which still exists today was first developed in the interest of U.S. national security.

For many years only government officials, and a few scientists and academics, had access to ARPAnet. The communication protocols developed for ARPAnet, however, were shared with the outside world, and it wasn't long before universities and other organizations began putting together their own IP-based networks. Then in the late 1980s the National Science Foundation, NASA, and the Department of Energy provided funding that enabled IP-based networks to interconnect. This event gave rise to what we now know as the Internet—a collection of interconnected computer networks.

Remember all that talk about the Information Superhighway? Well in the last few years, government and (mostly) nongovernment money has been funding a massive communications line ***backbone*** for connecting major portions of the Internet in the U.S. The idea is to create the analog for "freeways" on the Internet where there currently exists an immense tangle of "country roads." In addition non-IP networks are currently connecting to the Internet via ***gateways***, devices that connect networks whose communication protocols are different. So in the same way that ARPAnet and other IP-based networks have been absorbed into the Internet, other networks and computers of all kinds all over the world are rapidly becoming just another part of what we call the Internet.

How Does It Work?

As illustrated in Figure 0.1, the Internet is basically a collection of computers all over the world linked with telephonelike connections. If you have a computer at home with a modem, you know your computer can communicate with other computers over a regular phone line. The communication is pretty slow, however, even with a fast modem. This is why the lines used for the Internet are much more powerful than those most of us have in our homes. These powerful lines are commonly referred to as ***digital lines***. They are provided by the telephone company just like regular phone lines and are increasingly easy to come by.

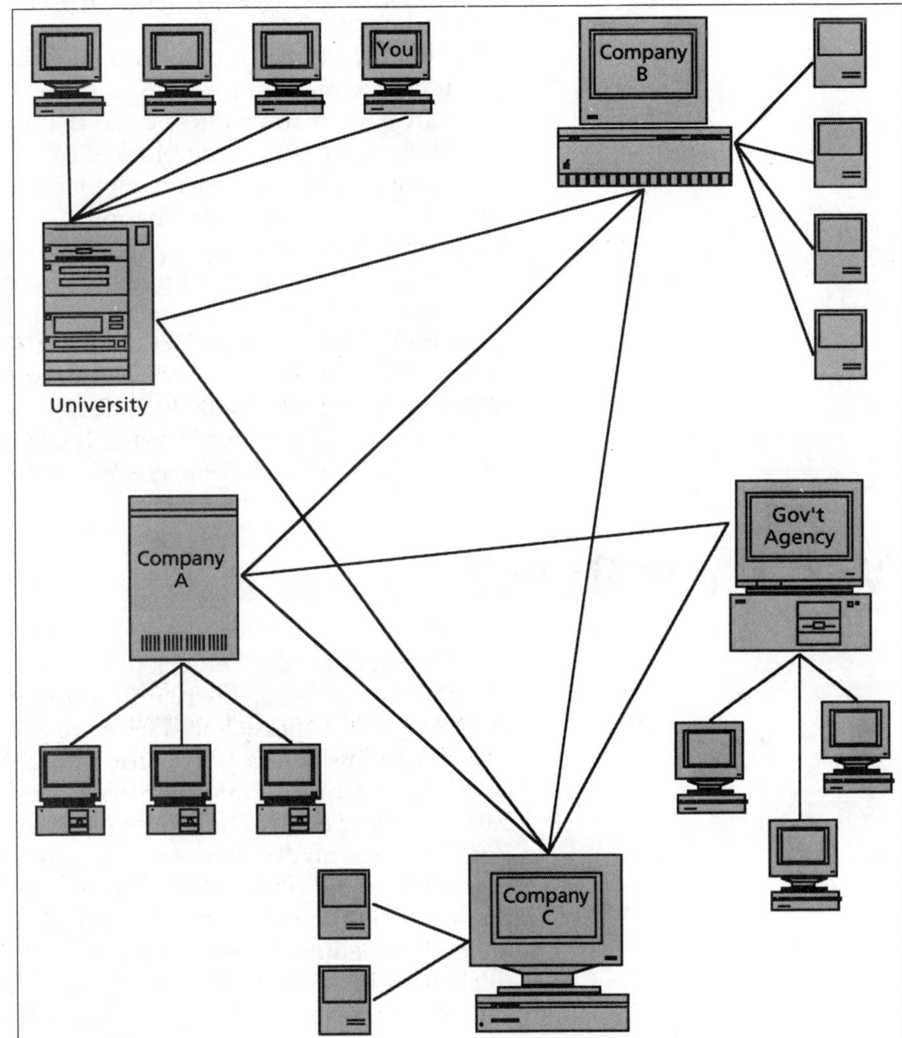

Figure 0.1

Stuart Harris and Gayle Kidder used a wonderful analogy in their book, *Netscape Quick Tour*, for explaining how the Internet works. Here's our version. Imagine that the Internet is an immensely complex network of canals (instead of computers and communication lines). When anyone wants to send a message, they simply pop a message in a bottle, stick on an address label, walk to the nearest canal, and drop the bottle in the water. That's it. Except that your message must fit in the bottle. Messages too big to fit in one bottle must be divided between many bottles and thrown in the canal separately. There may be thousands of different routes your message could take to get to its destination, but the bottle (of course) has no knowledge of any of them—it's just bobbing along, taken wherever the current is headed.

Now imagine that at each canal junction there is a person with a net. This person, like each computer system on the Internet, knows which canals in the immediate area are blocked by barges, hopelessly clogged with bottles, or flowing relatively clearly. The person with the net fishes out all the bottles approaching the junction and checks the addresses. This person keeps bottles addressed to individuals who live around the junction and notifies those people by sending a messenger. The bottles addressed to other areas are thrown into a canal that is headed in generally the right direction and/or that is not blocked or clogged. This process is repeated every time a bottle approaches a junction, thereby ensuring that every bottle finally reaches its destination.

None of the people at any canal junction knows anything about the condition of the network of canals beyond their immediate vicinity, and yet messages arrive at their destinations reliably.

This idea, that a network could function without someone somehow maintaining control over the entire network, was totally new when it was conceived in the late 1960s. It is the idea on which the entire Internet is based. It is the reason the Internet is a complex, disorganized, and often chaotic jumble of interconnectedness. It is also why the Internet works!

WHO'S THE BOSS?

The Internet of today belongs to no one. It is operated and administered by everyone involved. There is no one governing body, no board of directors, and no president. There are only shareholders—all those individuals, businesses, universities, governments, and other organizations that administer computers with access to the Internet. Each Internet participant has control only over its own computer or computer network. For example, you decide whether and when your home computer is connected to the Internet. Your university decides whether or not it will participate in the Internet; it also decides what information it will make available for public access and what information it will make available only to people with special passwords. Your university may set policies regarding what type of material is appropriate for Internet access on its own computers, but it cannot control the kind of information you access on other computers, say in Australia.

So the Internet is relatively disorganized and unregulated worldwide. It is feared by some governments as it represents an amazingly efficient way in which people with revolutionary ideas can disseminate information, communicate, and coordinate. The Internet is embraced by people in countries like the U.S. who seem to have an unquenchable thirst for information. This embrace may be conditional, however. There is a movement afoot to regulate the kind of information people in the U.S. may share via the Internet. Such regulation would require us to consider and define terms such as *privacy*, *obscenity*, and *accessibility*. These are words with which the U.S. government has grappled in its First Amendment interpretations for many decades.

The topic of Internet regulation is a particularly sticky one. The historical nature of the Internet has been one of open-mindedness and generosity. Computer administrators all over the world have done and continue to do their best to share as much information as possible. Individuals also play an important role in what you will find on the

Internet. In fact, most of the material currently on the Internet was put there by the over 20 million individuals with Internet access. This means you will find information that amazes, bores, enlightens, confuses, enrages, offends, and delights you. The Internet is currently a gigantic worldwide public forum where absolutely anything goes. Lively discussions regarding whether or not this is wise, proper, safe, or appropriate promise to go on for years.

Of course, there is also a widespread and vocal movement to fight Internet regulation. In your travels on the Internet, you will sometimes encounter a blue ribbon. This symbol indicates support for free speech on the Internet.

What Is the World Wide Web?

The ***World Wide Web*** (often just called the Web) didn't exist prior to 1989. The Web is a very new and rapidly growing segment of the Internet developed for the sole purpose of making access to information on the Internet easier and faster. Back in the 1980s, when the Internet had made it possible to access hundreds of thousands of documents all over the world, the idea emerged of somehow linking documents in order to make related information easier to find.

Linked Documents

The idea of linking related documents is something like the age-old footnote or endnote. In books you sometimes encounter a word or phrase followed by a superscript number. This is one way of saying, "Look at the bottom of the page (or in the back of the book) for the corresponding number, and you will find more information about this." Instead of just referencing related documents as endnotes and footnotes often do, Web pages are actually linked to other documents using *hypertext links* and, more recently, *hypermedia links* instead of footnotes.

Hypertext links allow you to click on a highlighted word or phrase in one document and be instantly transported to the referenced document. This works because the clickable link actually contains information you cannot see about the exact location and name of another document. So when you click such a link, the referenced document is loaded and dispalyed on your screen. The referenced document might also contain hypertext links. So, by using these links, you are able to move through the Web in a literally weblike fashion by simply pointing and clicking. In just a few moments, you may travel the world, looking at documents residing on computers in North America, Europe, Australia, and beyond.

Hypermedia links go a step beyond hypertext in that it facilitates links to pictures, sounds, and movies in addition to text. Thanks to recent advances in microcomputer technology that allow the easy display of sound, motion video, and graphics, the Web has truly become hypermedia.

What Is a Web Page?

So now you understand how documents on the Web are linked. But what are those documents? In its early days the Web was simply a new way of looking at the Internet rather than a new part of the Internet. The Web provided an easier way to view information that was already there. But as the idea of the Web caught on, special documents called ***Web pages*** began to proliferate. Unlike all other documents, Web pages are specifically designed to be accessed and displayed over the World Wide Web. Each Web page has a unique address called the ***Uniform Resource Locator*** (***URL***) which allows computers all over the world to locate it.

The term *page* was coined due to the similarity between the onscreen appearance of Web documents to the pages of a magazine. That is where the similarity ends, however. Unlike a magazine page, a Web page does not have a fixed width, length, or physical location. In fact, a Web page is actually an encoded data document that can be read and interpreted by a *Web browser* like Netscape. The data document tells Netscape things like "place this picture here," "make this a header," "use this font and graphic here," and "link this text to this other Web page." Netscape uses the encoded information in the Web page data document to display the Web page itself. What you see on your screen is the actual Web page—an interpretation of a set of ***Hypertext Markup Language*** (***HTML***) instructions contained in a Web page data document.

That is all the casual Web user needs to know about the anatomy of Web pages. Because *you* are destined to become a fully qualified "Web surfer," however, you will learn a bit more about Web pages in this and upcoming projects!

WHAT ARE WEB BROWSERS?

When the first strands of the Internet were strung together, the command-line language used by Unix-based computers was the only way to access information on the Internet, and only a few academics, scientists, and military folks spoke that language with any fluency. Everyone else was to be summarily excluded from access to the increasing wealth of information available on the Internet until a friendlier method of Internet interaction was developed. The emergence of the Web was a step in the right direction. Its basic concept of document linking via hypertext would soon put an end to the necessity of laborious search and find operations. However, the Internet was still a cold and hostile environment for most of us. It was almost completely devoid of the user-friendly point-and-click interfaces that were quickly becoming the standard in so many other areas of human-computer interaction.

In 1993 the U.S. Government designed an application to make the Web easily accessible and understandable, and a product called NCSA Mosaic emerged from the National Center for Supercomputing Applications (NCSA) in Illinois. (Interestingly, although Mosaic was a product of a U.S. Government lab, it was actually designed almost entirely by undergraduates at Urbana-Champaign.) Mosaic was the first Windows-based ***Web browser***, and it was received with tremendous enthusiasm by everyone interested in the Internet. Being a product of a U.S. Government lab, it was also free, which was nice too.

The popularity and power of the Web browser did not escape the notice of alert entrepreneurs. Netscape Communications Corporation immediately hired the talented team of programmers who developed Mosaic. Their marching orders were to design a bigger, better, more complete Web browser. The result was Netscape, a Web browser which includes built-in helper applications and features providing point-and-click access to all major services available on the Internet.

Following close on the heels of Netscape has come a host of other Web browsing tools. In addition, older non-Windows text-based Web browsers such as Lynx continue to be used. Netscape, however, has become overwhelmingly popular as an Internet access tool. It is for this reason that you will be using Netscape for most of the Internet projects in this book.

> ***Tip*** While life holds few guarantees, the Internet, and therefore the World Wide Web, offers one guarantee: Nothing ever stays the same! Although we have done our best to provide the most current view of Internet and Web locations referenced in this book, it is almost a certainty that there will have been lots of changes by the time you read this. Do not be disconcerted if your screen sometimes looks different than the figures in this text. Remember, the Internet is constantly changing!

STARTING NETSCAPE NAVIGATOR

In this book we assume you are using a computer running Windows 3.1. If you are using another type of computer like a Macintosh, your procedure for starting up the program will be different than the one presented here. It is important to note, however, that Netscape is designed to look and feel the same on any computer platform. This means that if you are using Netscape on a non-Windows machine, like a Macintosh, you can still use this book. The Netscape windows, icons, and menus on Macintosh computers are nearly identical to those on computers running Windows.

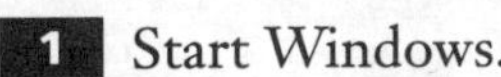

To start Netscape Navigator:

1. Start Windows.

2. Double-click the Netscape icon in the Program Manager window. You may need to open an Applications group window first, depending on the way the system and desktop is organized. Check with your instructor or lab assistant if you need help with this step.

> ***Tip*** When you see a button or icon next to a numbered step, you can select the button or icon on the screen in place of the command in the numbered step.

As shown in Figure 0.2, the Netscape Navigator startup screen appears and remains while your computer establishes its connection to the network. The startup screen disappears when the network connection has been confirmed. It is replaced by the Netscape window displaying the Netscape ***home page***, like the one shown in Figure 0.3, or a home page selected by your school.

Figure 0.2

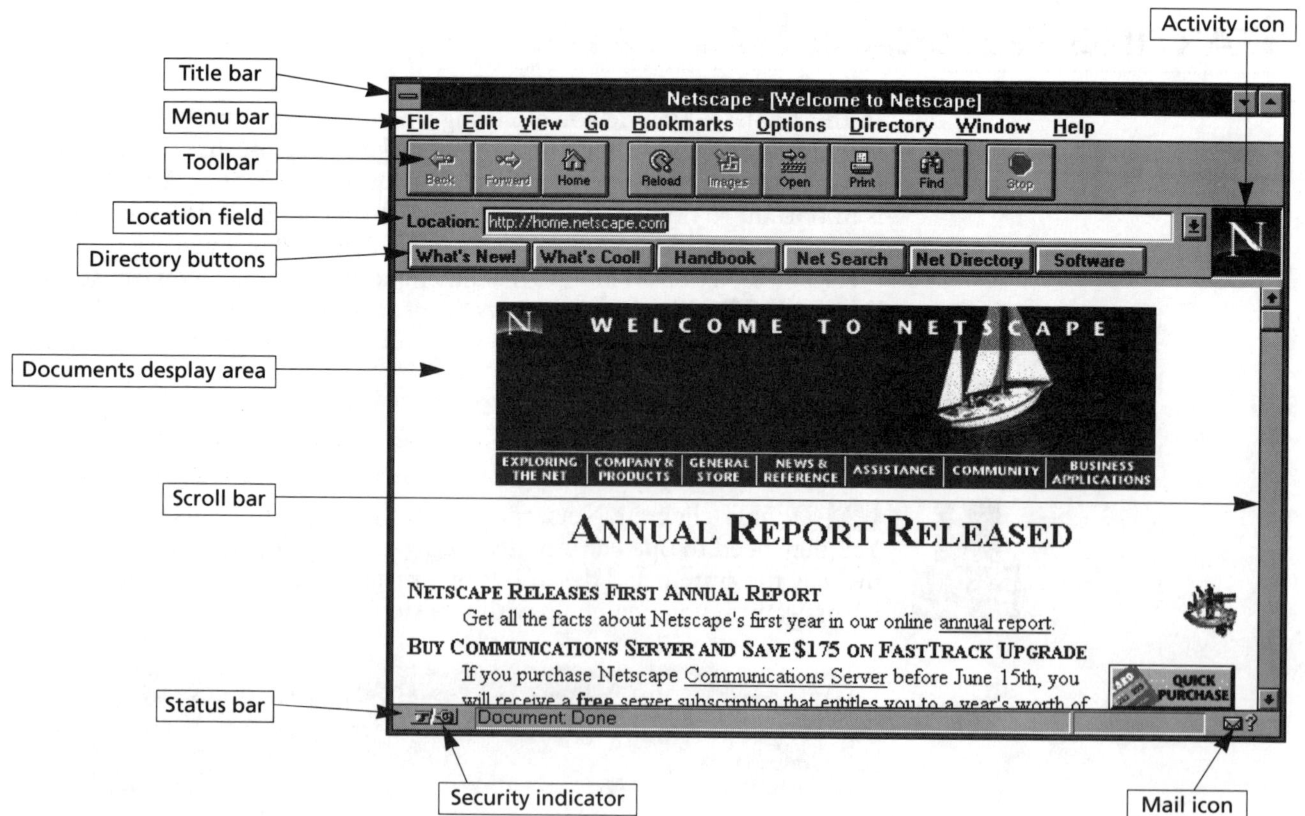

Figure 0.3

The Netscape Window

The Netscape Navigator window is much like those of other Windows applications. As shown in Figure 0.3, it contains a title bar, menu bar, toolbar, scroll bars, and status bar. These are all features you will find in nearly all Windows applications. The Netscape window also has an area where documents are displayed, a Location field, and a selection of buttons for accessing Web pages maintained by Netscape Corporation for its users.

Activity icon: displays animated shooting stars when Netscape is busy downloading a document or file.

Title bar: contains the title of the application (Netscape) and the document file you are currently viewing (for example, *Welcome to Netscape* or the name of your university's home page).

Menu bar: gives you access to Netscape commands.

Toolbar: contains buttons that allow you to perform many commonly used Netscape commands with one click of the mouse.

Directory buttons: take you to Netscape-maintained Web pages designed to assist users in locating Internet resources, software, and online help.

Location field: allows you to enter the Internet address of the document you would like to view.

Scroll bars: give you a way to move around in the currently displayed document.

Status bar: gives information about Netscape's current status in transferring Internet documents to your computer and/or a description of on-screen activity.

Security indicator: provides a graphical representation of the security level of the currently displayed document.

Mail icon: a clickable button that opens the Mail window. It also provides graphical information regarding mail and news message status.

You can customize Netscape's appearance on your screen to suit your preferences. The toolbar, Location field, and directory buttons can all be removed. You can also change screen colors and fonts.

To remove the toolbar:

1 Choose Options from the menu bar.
The Show Toolbar option is checked by default.

2 Choose the Show Toolbar option, as shown in Figure 0.4.
The Netscape window is displayed without the toolbar, as shown in Figure 0.5.

To restore the toolbar, you simply repeat the above steps.

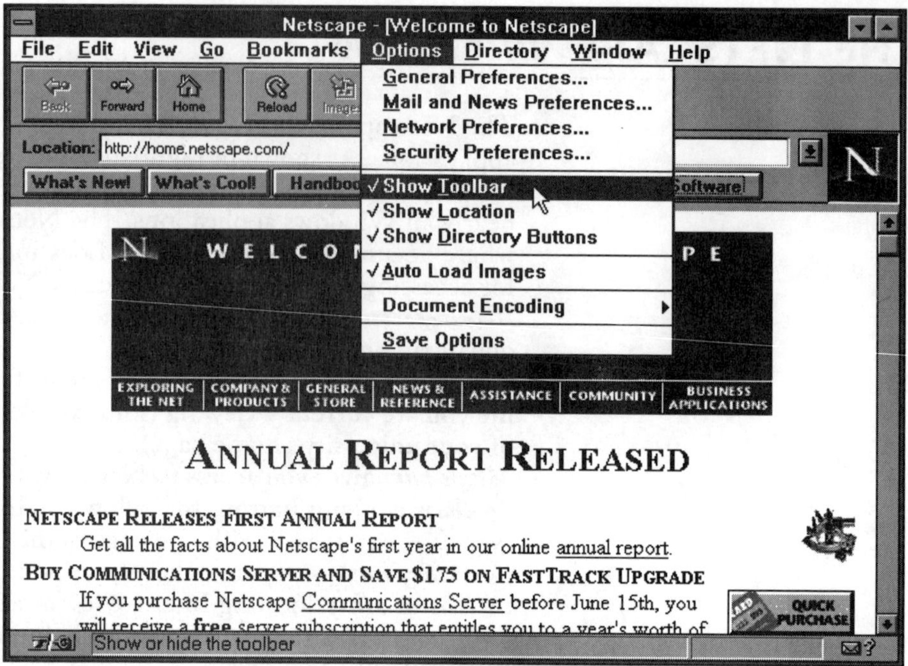

Figure 0.4

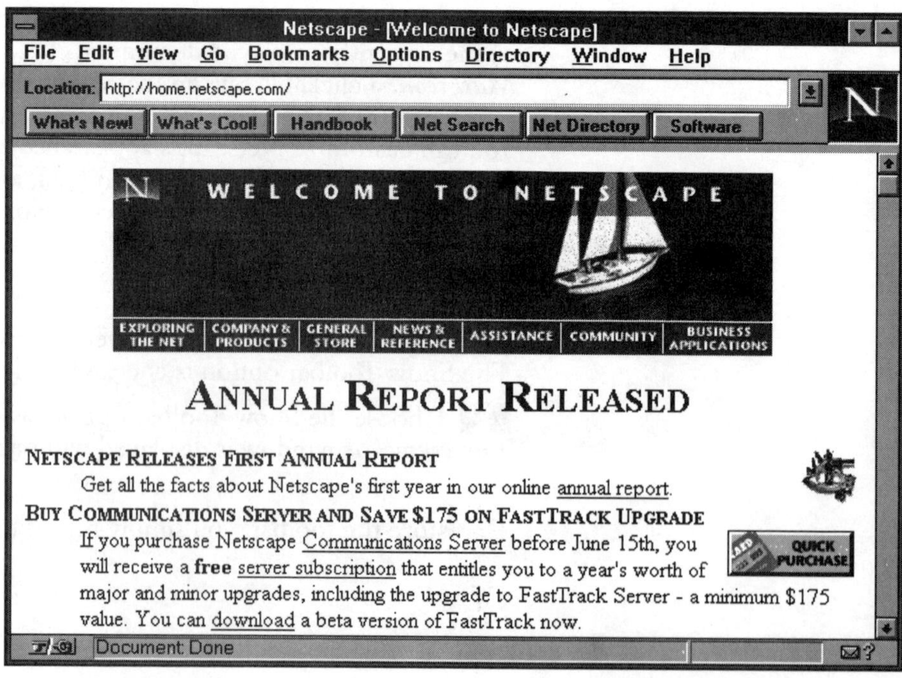

Figure 0.5

To remove the Location field:

1 Choose Options from the menu bar.
The Show Location option is checked by default.

2 Choose the Show Location option.
The Netscape window is displayed without the Location field, as shown in Figure 0.6.

To restore the Location field, you simply repeat the above steps.

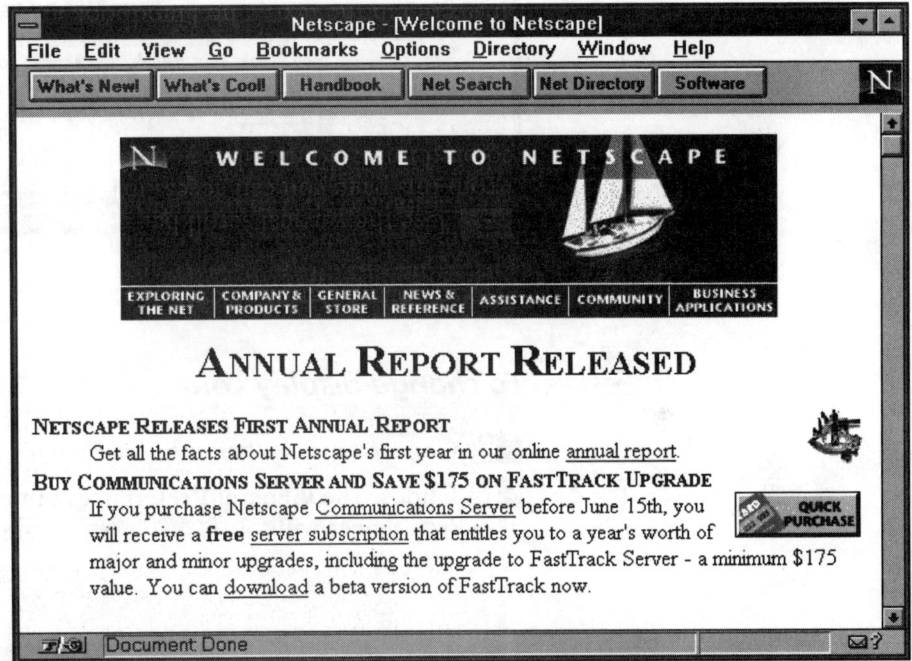

Figure 0.6

To remove the directory buttons:

1 Choose Options from the menu bar.
The Show Directory Buttons option is checked by default.

2 Choose the Show Directory Buttons option.
The Netscape window is displayed without the directory buttons, as shown in Figure 0.7.

To restore the directory buttons, you simply repeat the above steps.

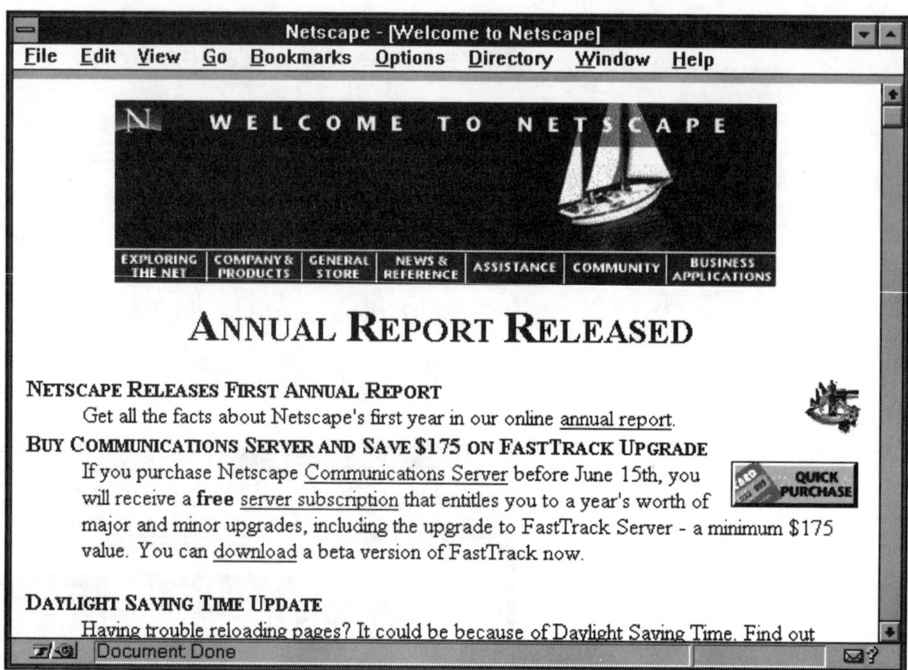

Figure 0.7

To change display colors:

1. Choose Options from the menu bar.
2. Choose the General Preferences option.

The Preferences window is displayed, as shown in Figure 0.8.

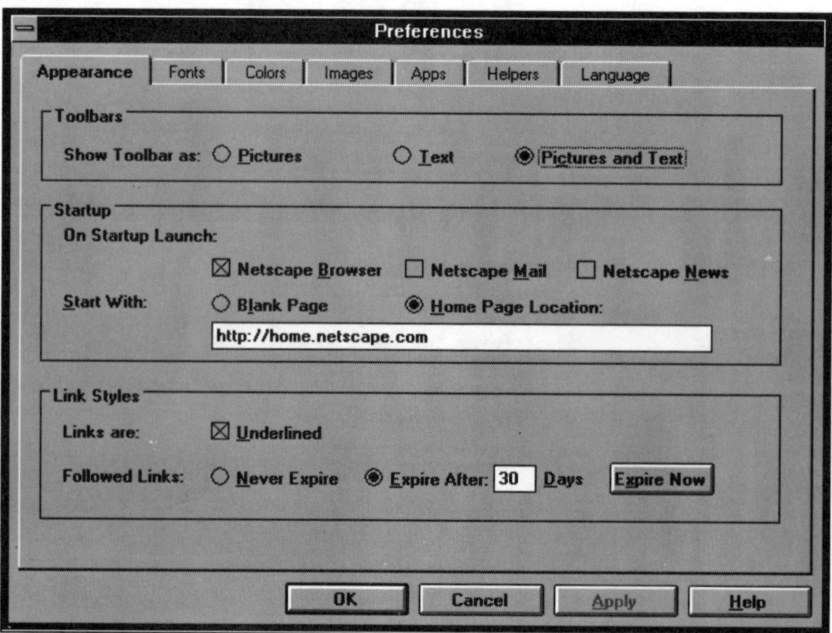

Figure 0.8

3 Select the Colors tab to display the Colors Preferences screen, as shown in Figure 0.9.

Notice that the current display colors are shown in the Color Preferences screen. From this screen you can select your own color preferences for links, text, and the background of Web pages. Links are discussed in detail Project 1. For now all you need to know is that links are special text on Web pages that are usually displayed in a different color from regular text so that they are easy to spot.

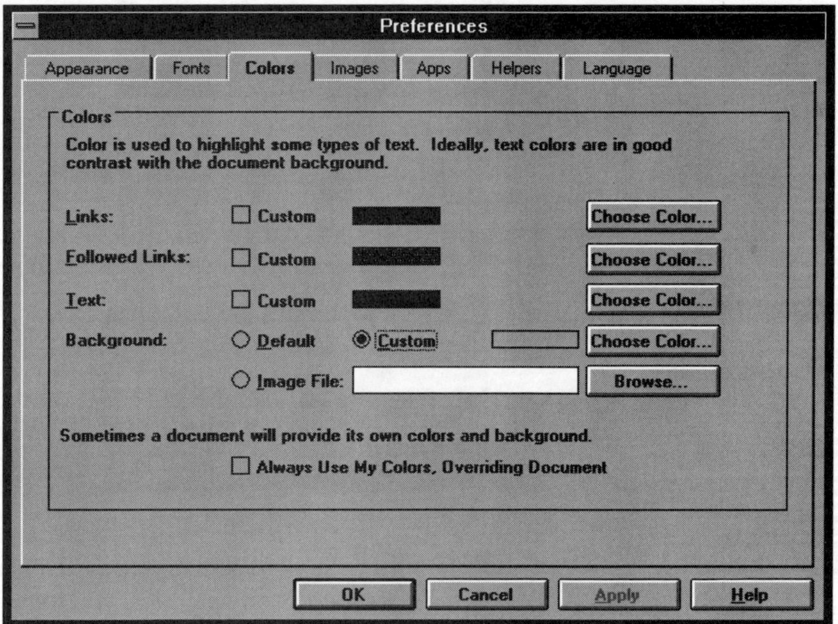

Figure 0.9

4 Select the Choose Color button for Links on the Colors Preferences screen.

The colors from which you may choose are displayed in the Color palette shown in Figure 0.10. Notice this palette also allows you to define your own custom colors using the Define Custom Colors button.

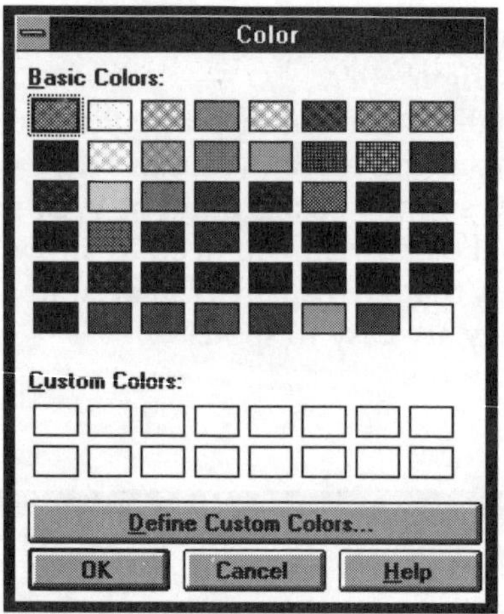

Figure 0.10

5 Select a color from the Basic Colors palette.

6 Select the OK button on the Color palette.

> ***Note*** Many Web pages have predifined colors that will override your color selections.

7 Select the box labeled Always Use My Colors, Overriding Document to make sure color the changes you make will be displayed on the current document.

8 Select the OK button on the Colors Preferences screen.
Can you find the links on the currently displayed document? They now appear in the color you selected.

Repeat these steps to select new colors for each of the remaining screen parts. Remember to choose colors that contrast well with the document background and that are easy on the eyes.

To change fonts:

1 Choose Options from the menu bar.

2 Choose the General Preferences option.

3 Select the Fonts tab to display the Fonts Preferences screen, as shown in Figure 0.11.
The current display fonts are shown on the Fonts Preferences screen. From this screen you can select your own font preferences for text that Netscape will display in a proportional font and for text that Netscape will display in a fixed font.

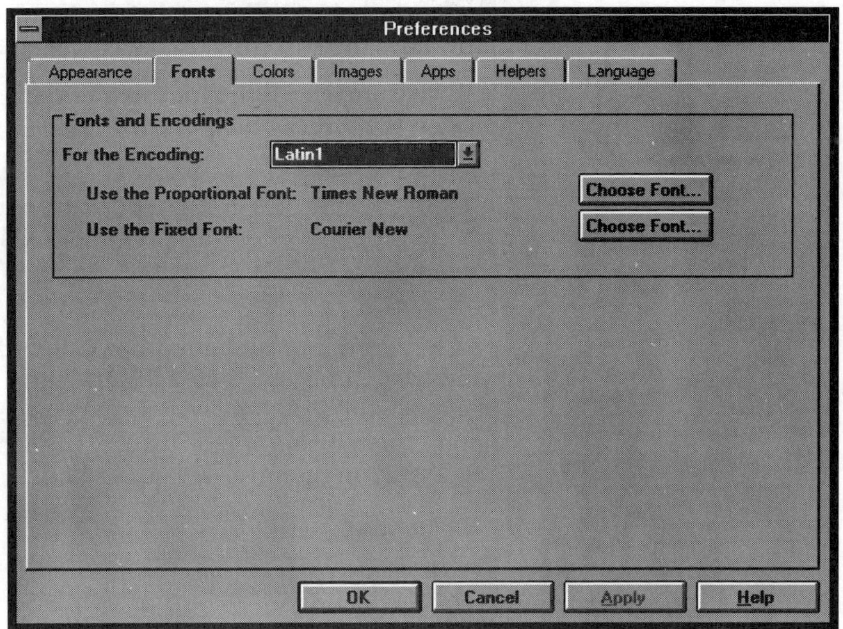

Figure 0.11

4 Select the Choose Font button for the Proportional Font on the Font Preferences screen.

The fonts from which you may choose are displayed in the Choose Base Font window shown in Figure 0.12. Notice that you can select both the font and the size and that a sample of your selection is displayed in the Sample area of the window.

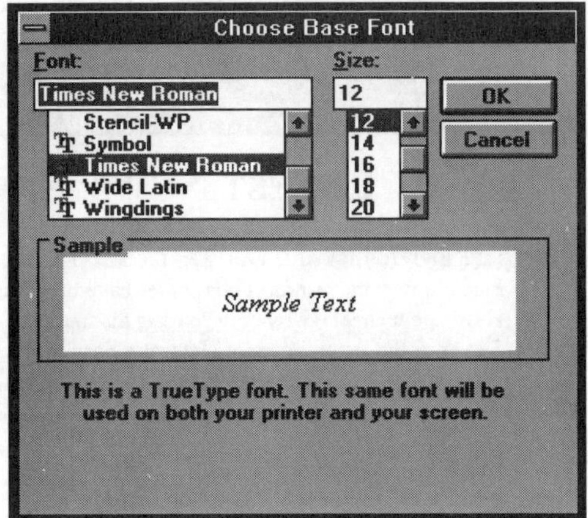

Figure 0.12

5 Select a new font from the menu of fonts displayed.

6 Select the OK button on the Choose Base Font window.

7 Select the OK button on the Fonts Preferences screen. How does the currently displayed document look?

Experiment with the font setting until you find a font and size that looks nice on the screen and is easy to read.

> ***Tip*** 10-point Times is a popular choice for the proportional font, and 10-point Courier is often selected as a fixed font. Both of these fonts are available on most computers.

The remaining configuration options displayed on the Preferences window are Images, Apps, Helpers, and Language. These options go beyond configuring the way the Netscape window is displayed, so we will ignore them for now. Don't worry though, we'll get back to some of these configuration options later in this book!

To save options:

1 Select the Options menu.

2 Select Save Options as shown in Figure 0.13.

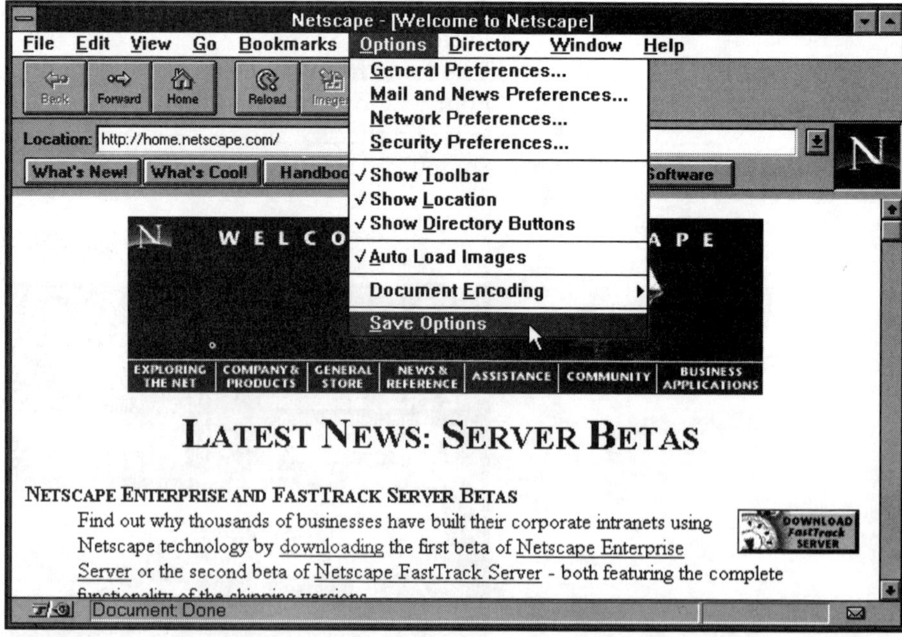

Figure 0.13

If you are working from school, it is likely that you are using a networked version of Netscape. This means that the changes you make to the way in which the Netscape window is displayed will be discarded after you end your current session, even if you save them. If you are working from home or with a local copy of Netscape, of course, your options preferences will be saved.

EXIT If necessary, you can take a break at this point. When you come back, just start up Netscape Navigator and proceed.

GETTING ONLINE HELP

Like most other Windows applications, Netscape offers a Help menu to assist you with questions or problems that may arise while you use the application. Unlike other Windows applications, however, Netscape's help facilities are available ***online***. This means that the help screens provided by Netscape are actually Web pages located on some other computer. The advantage to offering online help as opposed to the traditional help facilities of other applications is that Netscape Corporation can continuously update the available information. For example, they can post answers to questions frequently asked by users.

To access online help:

1 Choose Help from the menu bar.
As shown in Figure 0.14, a number of options appear in the Help menu. The ones you will probably find most useful are Handbook and Frequently Asked Questions (FAQs).

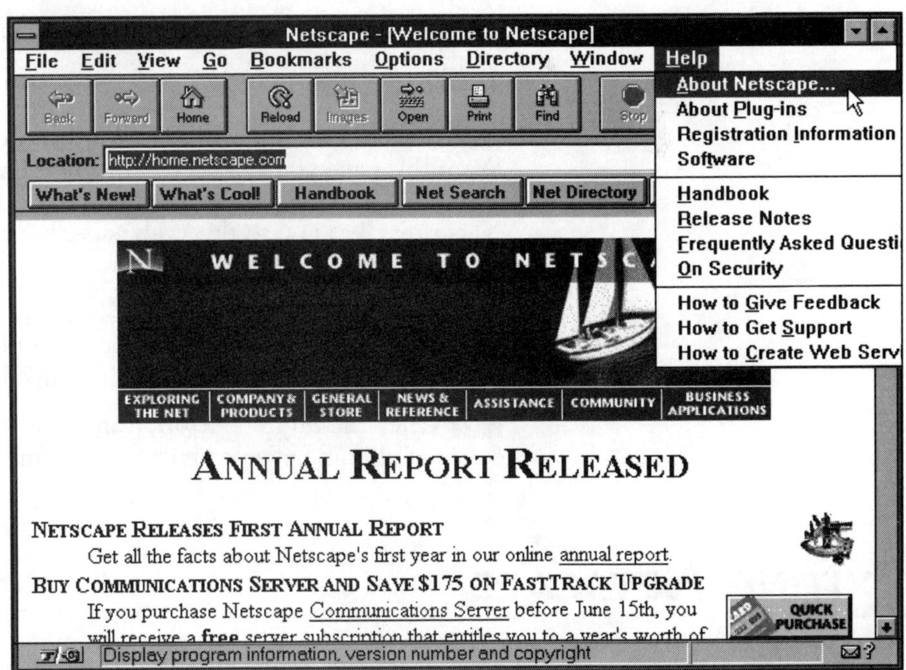

Figure 0.14

2 Choose the Handbook option.
Netscape takes you to the Netscape Navigator Handbook shown in Figure 0.15, a Web page maintained by Netscape Corporation for its users.

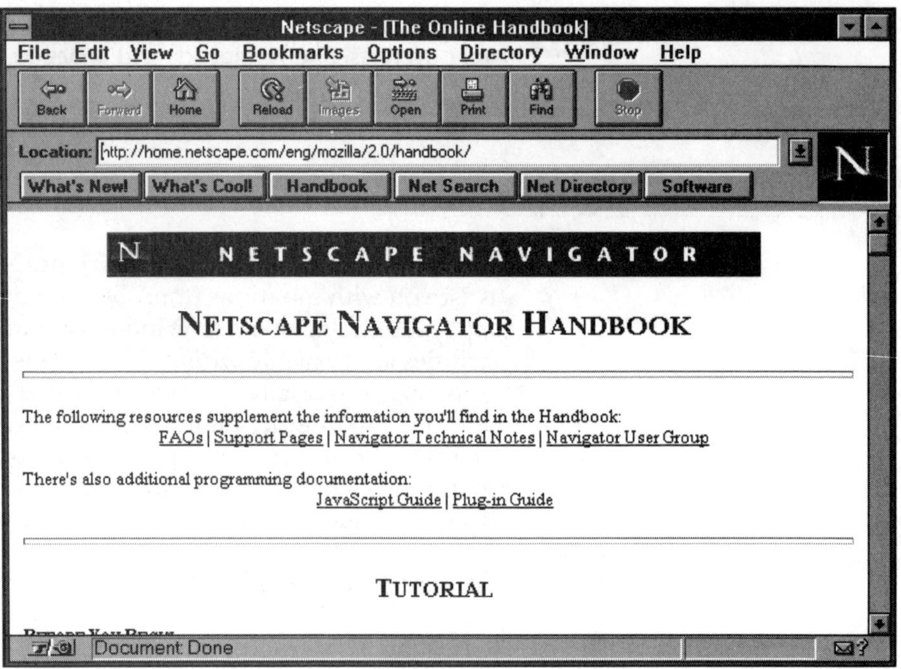

Figure 0.15

> ***Tip*** Another way to access the Netscape Navigator Handbook page is to select the Handbook button.

3 Use the vertical scroll bar to view the entire page.
From this page you can access information about any text displayed as colored links. (Remember your color selection?) Simply click a link, and Netscape takes you to the Web page that covers that topic.

4 Explore the Handbook by clicking on links that interest you.
As you work your way through this book, you may have questions not answered in the text. The Handbook and Frequently Asked Questions options under the Help menu will be invaluable resources for you.

5 Click the Home button in the toolbar to return to your system's designated home page when you have finished examining the Handbook.

EXITING NETSCAPE

Most Windows application use the same command to exit, so if you have used any other Windows applications, you already know how to exit Netscape.

To exit Netscape:

1 Choose Exit from the File menu, as shown in Figure 0.16.

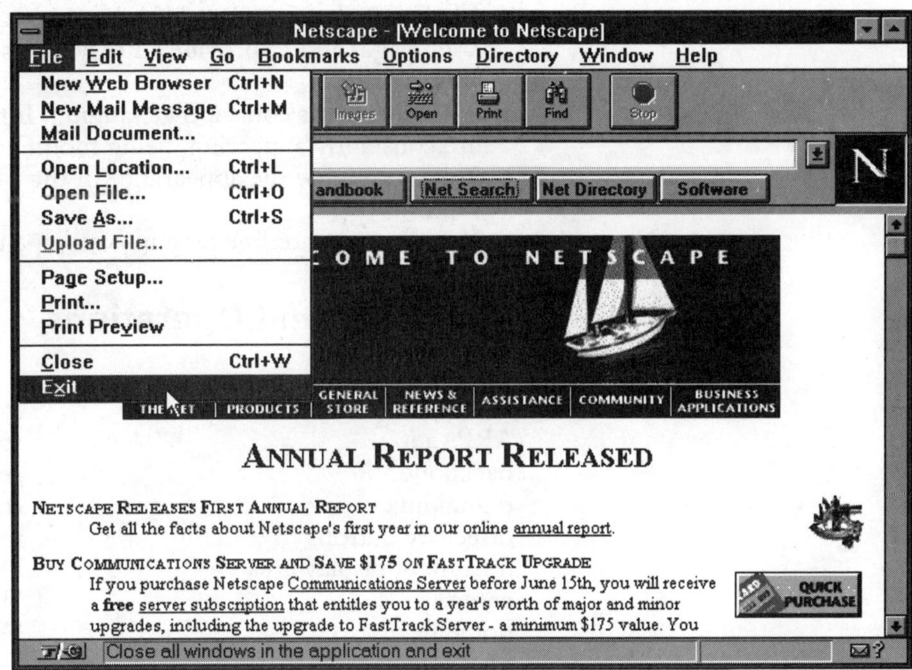

Figure 0.16

This concludes the Overview. You can either take a well-deserved break or go on and work through the Study Questions.

Summary and Exercises

Summary

- The Internet is a collection of computers all over the world interconnected by powerful telephonelike lines called digital or ISDN lines.
- The Internet began as ARPAnet, a U.S. Defense Department project initiated in the late 1960s.
- Although there is discussion in the country regarding regulating some aspects of the Internet, there is no one organization in charge of the Internet.
- The architecture of the Internet is completely decentralized, with no one person controlling the entire Internet.
- The World Wide Web (the Web) is the newest, fastest growing segment of the Internet.
- The Web was developed to make accessing information on the Internet easier and faster.
- A Web page is a special document designed specifically to be displayed by a Web browser like Netscape. Web pages are created using Hypertext Markup Language (HTML).
- The location of Web pages on the Internet is designated by the Uniform Resource Locator (URL), a unique standardized address.

- Netscape Navigator is a Web browser application designed to display Web pages and to provide an easy-to-use interface for navigating the Internet.
- The Internet is constantly changing. Internet documents like Web pages are constantly appearing, being modified, and disappearing.
- You can modify the appearance of the Netscape window using the Options menu.
- You can access online help in Netscape using the Help menu.

Key Terms and Operations

Key Terms

activity icon
ARPAnet
backbone
digital line
directory buttons
document display area
gateway
home page
hypermedia links
hypertext links
Hypertext Markup Language (HTML)
Internet
Internet protocol (IP)
Location field
mail icon
menu bar
online Help
scroll bar
status bar
security indicator
title bar
toolbar
Uniform Resource Locator (URL)
Web browser
Web page
World Wide Web (the Web)

Operations

Start Netscape
Select General Preferences
Set display Options
Access online Help
Exit Netscape

Study Questions

Multiple Choice

1. The World Wide Web is a segment of the Internet that
   a. allows related documents to be linked.
   b. is constantly changing.
   c. makes accessing information on the Internet easier.
   d. All of the above.

2. On a Web page a hypertext link is a
   a. program used to download text files from the Internet.
   b. pointer to a related Internet document.
   c. very fast text editor.
   d. connection between two words.

3. When the Internet first started out, it was called
   a. WorldNet.
   b. DECnet.
   c. ARPAnet.
   d. Mosaic.

4. The Internet is controlled entirely by
   a. the U.S. Defense Department.
   b. an elected board of directors.

4. The Internet is controlled entirely by
   a. the U.S. Defense Department.
   b. an elected board of directors.
   c. the National Science Foundation.
   d. no one.

5. Netscape Navigator is an application called a
   a. Web cruiser.
   b. Net crawler.
   c. Web browser.
   d. None of the above.

Short Answer

1. The ____________ at the bottom of the Netscape window gives information about Netscape's current status.

2. A URL is a unique __________ used to locate documents on the Web.

3. The Internet is constantly ______________.

4. The __________________ is the most recent segment of the Internet to arise and the fastest growing.

5. The Information Superhighway is a term used for the telephone line ____________ being developed to increase the efficiency of the Internet in the U.S.

For Discussion

1. Should there be a governing body overseeing the Internet and setting policies, standards, and rules? Why? Why not?

2. What are five aspects of the Netscape window that you can customize using the Options menu?

PROJECT 1: GETTING STARTED WITH NETSCAPE

Objectives

After completing this project, you should be able to:

- Use Netscape navigational icons
- Navigate using links
- Revisit sites using the history feature
- Control loading and display of Web pages and images
- Print a Web page

CASE STUDY: STARTING A JOB SEARCH

Assume you are finishing your undergraduate degree and are preparing to enter the job market following graduation. You have consulted the placement services office at your university and are convinced that there must be more job opportunities in your field than those you found there. When you ask if there are other sources you might consult for employment opportunities in your field, a placement services representative suggests you try the Web.

Intrigued, you asked what advantages the World Wide Web might offer. You learn that information available on the Web may be more complete and will almost certainly be more timely than almost any other source. You have heard others refer to the Web as an apparently inexhaustible source of information and are anxious to give it a try, especially if it will provide up-to-the-minute information about employers who are hiring in your field.

An Internet Solution

In this Project you will gain the important skills of getting around on the Web and returning to Web locations you have visited. Netscape Navigator provides an easy-to-use interface for accessing Web sites and moving from one Web site to another. As we discussed earlier, there are other Web browsers available. However, Netscape's user-friendly point-and-click interface has made it the browser of choice for most Web surfers.

NAVIGATING USING NETSCAPE

Before you can begin exploring the Web, often referred to as surfing, you must first start your Web browser—in this case, Netscape. This procedure is covered in the Overview if you need a refresher.

With Netscape open take a look at the toolbar located just below the main menu. Netscape's toolbar is a set of icons you can use to perform commonly used functions. The toolbar contains most of the tools you will need to navigate from one Web site to another. These navigational tools are Back, Forward, Home, and Open, as shown in Figure 1.1. In this section you will use all of these buttons and learn how they help you to get around on the Web.

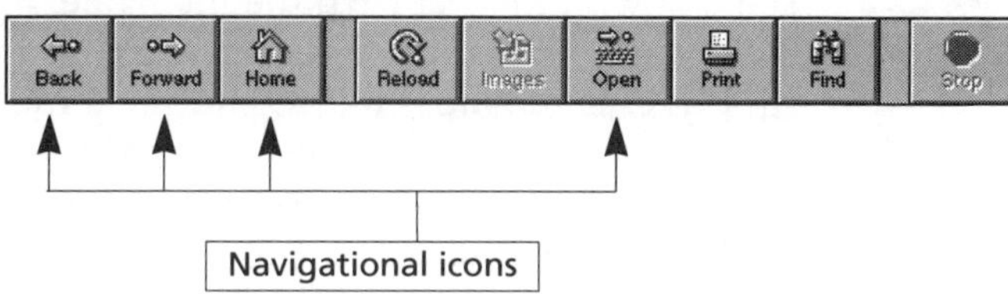

Figure 1.1

Finding Yourself on the Web

When you start Netscape, you are dropped off somewhere on the Web. You may find yourself delivered at the Netscape Welcome page or you might be looking at your university's home page. The Web location where Netscape goes on startup is often referred to as the startup location and is determined by the specific Netscape setup you are using. As shown in Figure 1.2, the address of your current location on the Web is displayed in the Location field just below the toolbar.

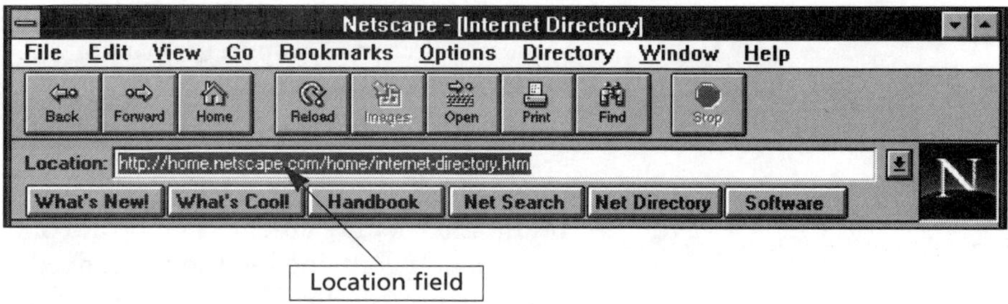

Figure 1.2

The address displayed in the Location field is in a standard format and is called the Uniform Resource Locator (URL). URLs can be quite long and may seem complicated. Actually, the standard format of URLs makes them fairly easy to understand. As shown in the example in Figure 1.3, URLs are composed of three parts: *protocol*, *domain name*, and *file name*.The ***protocol*** is the part preceding the two forward slashes and designates the type of Internet document. The ***domain name*** is the part after the two forward slashes and before the next slash. It designates the computer on which the file is located. The ***file name*** is everything after that and specifies the local directory path and file name. With minor modifications, some of which are shown in Table 1.1, this format holds true for all URLs.

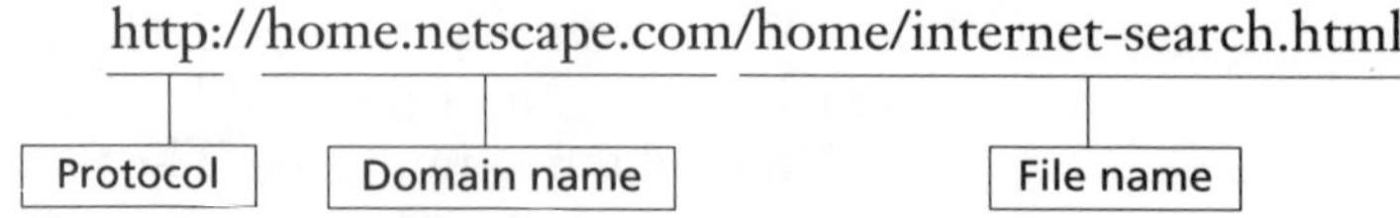

Figure 1.3

Let's take a closer look at the each part of the URL shown in Figure 1.3, starting with the last part, the file name: home/internet-search.html. This is the name of the file (internet-search.html) complete with directory path (in this case the file is located in the home directory). The .html file extension indicates that the file is written using the Hypertext Markup Language (HTML). This is the hallmark of a true Web page and gives Web pages their distinctive look when viewed using Netscape.

> ***Note*** Unlike DOS directory paths which use backward slashes (\) to delineate directories, URLs employ forward slashes (/) or *uphill* slashes. This is because the URL is written for the UNIX operating system, and UNIX uses forward slashes to delineate directories in directory paths. Notice also that file names in URLs are often longer than the standard DOS format. This can also be blamed on UNIX which allows file and directory names to be long enough to be meaningful!

The middle part of the URL is the domain name: home.netscape.com. The domain name is the computer system where the document is located. Domain names are used to identify every single computer on the Internet. Each part of the domain name is separated by a dot (.) and tells you something about the location of the computer. In this example, com indicates that the computer is part of a commercial organization (as opposed to edu, which indicates a college or university); netscape is the name of the organization; finally, home is the name of the computer at Netscape where the document is located.

The first part of the URL is called the protocol, which indicates the type of the Internet document. The protocol tells Netscape how to interpret the information contained in the referenced document. In this example the protocol is http: (for Hypertext Transfer Protocol), which indicates that this URL points to a document created using HTML. In other words, it is a Web page. You will eventually encounter a number of Internet document types on the Web. Table 1.1 lists some of these document types and their URL protocols and formats.

Table 1.1

Document type	URL protocol and format
FTP	ftp://*domain.name/complete.file.name*
Gopher	gopher://*domain.name:port*
Telnet	telnet://*domain.name:port*
World Wide Web	http://*domain.name/directory/path/filename.html*

Going Places Using URLs

There are many ways to jump to another Web page from the startup location. If you know the URL of the location you'd like to visit, the quickest way to get there is by entering that address. As with most functions, there are several ways to enter a URL in Netscape. First you'll try out the Open button on the Netscape toolbar.

To use the Open button:

1 Select Open from the Netscape toolbar, as shown in Figure 1.1. The Open Location dialog box as shown in Figure 1.4 appears.

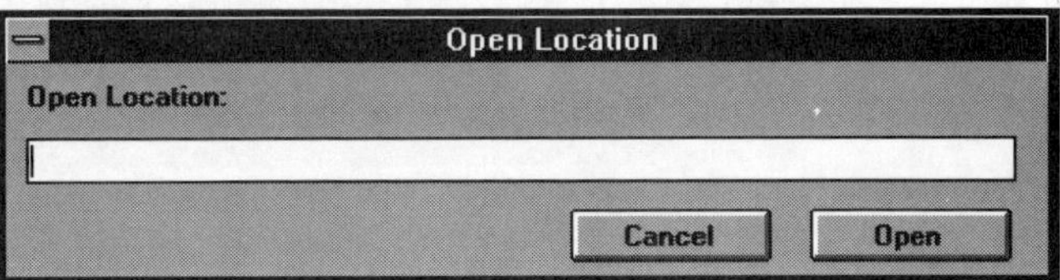

Figure 1.4

> ***Tip*** There are other ways to access the Open Location dialog box. You can select File/Open Location from the main menu, or you can press CTRL + L

2 Type the following URL in the Open Location field:
`http://home.netscape.com/home/internet-search.html`

3 Select Open.

Netscape will attempt to connect to the host specified in the URL (home.netscape.com) and, if successful, will open the file you specified in the path (home/internet-search.html) using the given protocol (http:). Watch the status bar at the bottom of the Netscape window to see what Netscape is up to. You will see messages like "Connect," "Contacting host," "Transferring data," "Waiting for reply," and "Reading file" flash by as the document you requested is located and prepared for display on your screen. If all goes well, you will soon find yourself looking at the Net Search page, as shown in Figure 1.5.

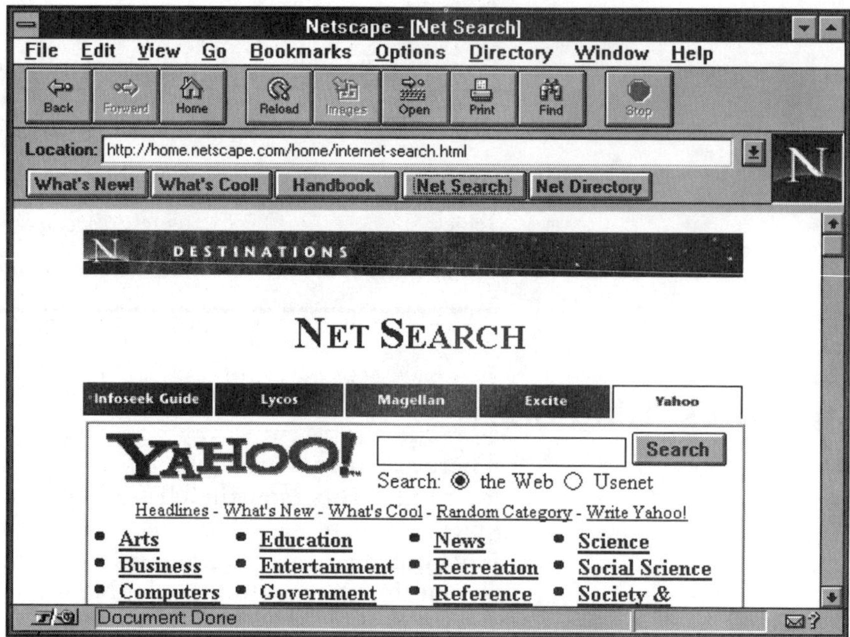

Figure 1.5

Don't Panic if your screen doesn't look just like the one shown in Figure 1.5. Remember, the Web is constantly changing, and it's very likely the Net Search page has changed in the short time since this book was printed.

Another way of using URLs to visit Web sites is to enter the desired location directly in the Location field under the toolbar.

To use the Location field:

1 Click in the Location field, and completely select the URL displayed.

2 Type the following URL in the Location field:
`http://update.wsj.com`
Notice that when you enter text in the Location field, the prompt changes from "Location:" to "Go to:" as shown in Figure 1.6.

Figure 1.6

3 Press ENTER

Netscape once again takes you to the Web page specified in the URL you entered. This time the address you entered is for the Wall Street Journal home page shown in Figure 1.7.

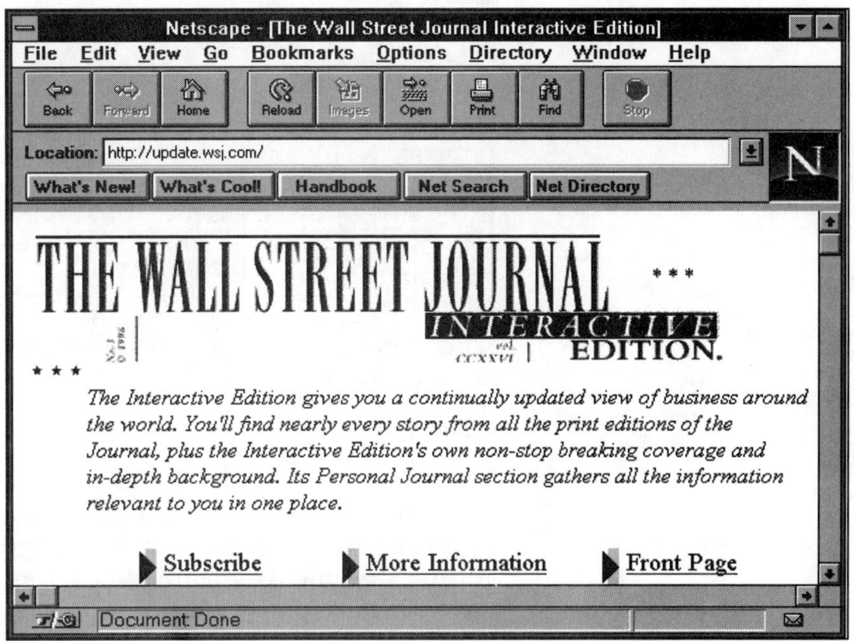

Figure 1.7

Going Places You've Already Been

When visiting locations on the Web, you may want to return to places you have already been. That is where the Back button comes in. The Back button allows you to retrace your steps through the Web. Each time you choose it, the Back button takes you to the Web page you were visiting immediately before the one currently displayed on the screen.

Figure 1.8 illustrates your travels through the Web so far. You can use this figure to help you understand the navigational tools demonstrated in this section.

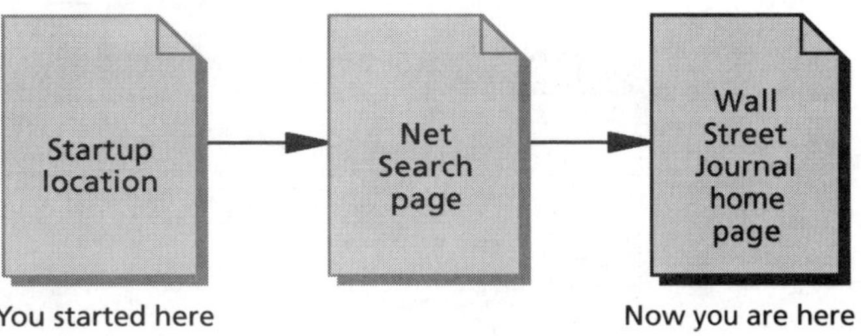

Figure 1.8

To use the Back button:

1 Select Back from the Netscape toolbar.
You return to the last location you visited, the Net Search page.

2 Select Back again.
Netscape takes you back to the startup page where you began, as shown in Figure 1.9.

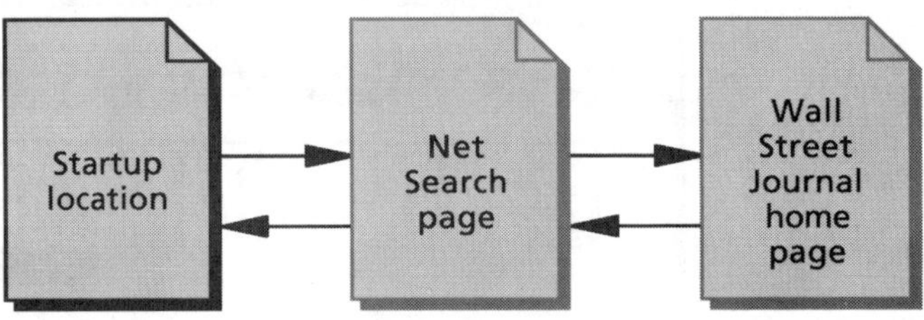

Figure 1.9

Whenever you retrace your steps using the Back button, you can then use the Forward button to return to pages from which you've backed up. You just used the Back button to go from the Wall Street Journal page to the Net Search page to the startup location, which is where you are now. What will happen if you now select the Forward button?

To use the Forward button:

1 Select Forward from the Netscape toolbar. You return to the Web page from which you last backed up: the Net Search page.

2 Select Forward again.
Netscape takes you forward again to the Wall Street Journal home page, as shown in Figure 1.10. Notice that the Forward button is no longer available. This means you have reached the farthest point in your Web travels so far.

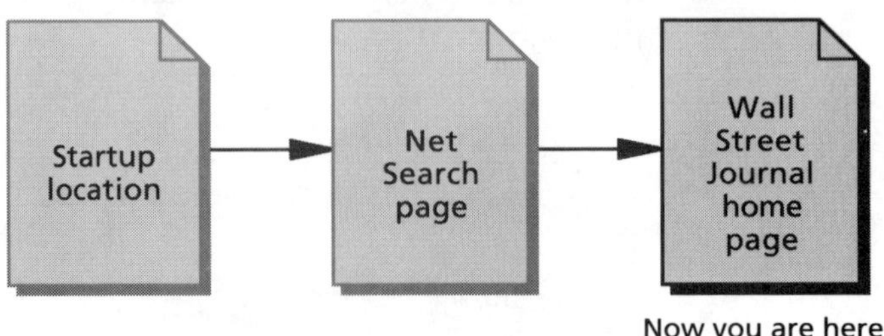

Figure 1.10

Tip There are other ways to go back and forward. You can choose Back and Forward from the Go menu. You can press ALT + ← (Back) and ALT + → (Forward). Finally, you can click the right mouse button for a small dialog box containing the options Back and Forward.

After visiting a number of Web sites, returning to your starting point using the Back button can become tedious. The Home button allows you to return to the startup location in one easy step.

To go home:

1 Select Home from the Netscape toolbar. As shown in Figure 1.11, you return to the Web page from which you started.

Tip You can also go home by selecting Home from the Go menu.

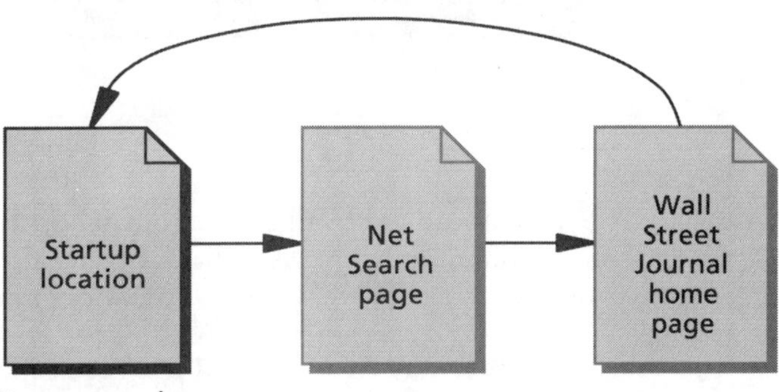

Now you are home

Figure 1.11

Netscape offers another feature to help you revisit Web locations and keep track of where you've been. This feature is called ***history***. As you may have already guessed, for the Back and Forward buttons to work, Netscape must keep track of where you go.

To use the history feature:

1 Choose Go from the menu bar.
Notice that all the locations you have visited during this session are listed as options on the Go menu, as shown in Figure 1.12. The checked location is the one currently displayed on the screen.

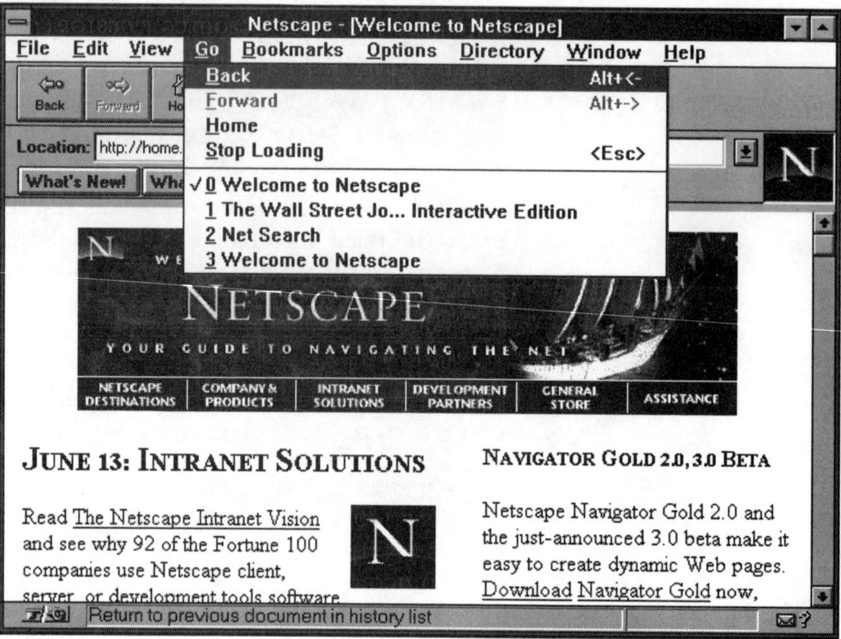

Figure 1.12

2 Choose the Wall Street Journal option, or type the number corresponding to the Wall Street Journal menu option. Netscape takes you directly to the Wall Street Journal home page.

Another way to access and use Netscape's history information is through the History window. In addition to the names of locations you've visited, the History window provides the complete URL for each location.

To use the History window:

1 Choose Window from the menu bar. The Window menu is displayed as shown in Figure 1.13.
Notice that the name of the current location is displayed at the bottom of this menu.

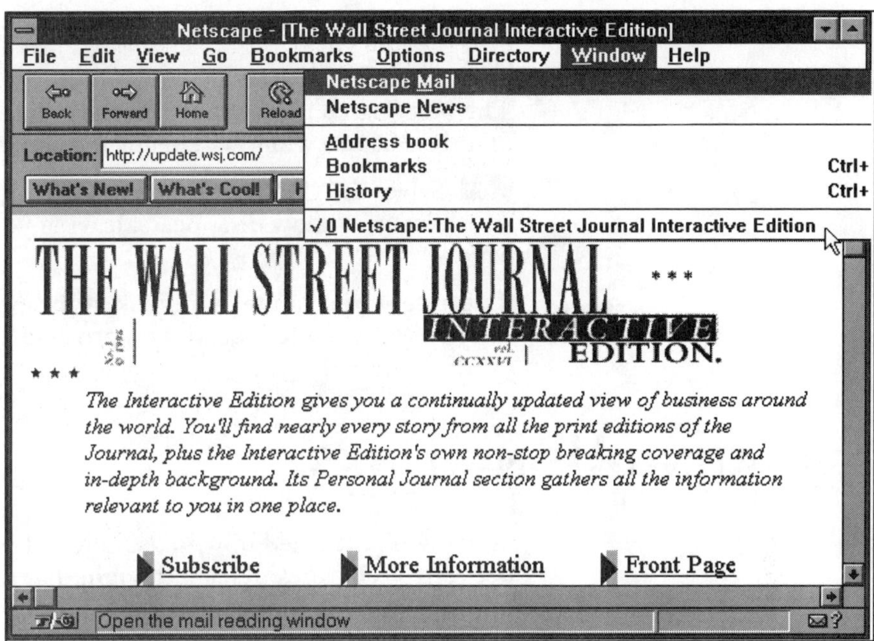

Figure 1.13

2 Choose the History option from the Window menu.
The History window appears as shown in Figure 1.14. Notice that, like the Go menu, all of the locations you have visited during this session are listed in the History window. From here you can easily jump to any previously visited Web location.

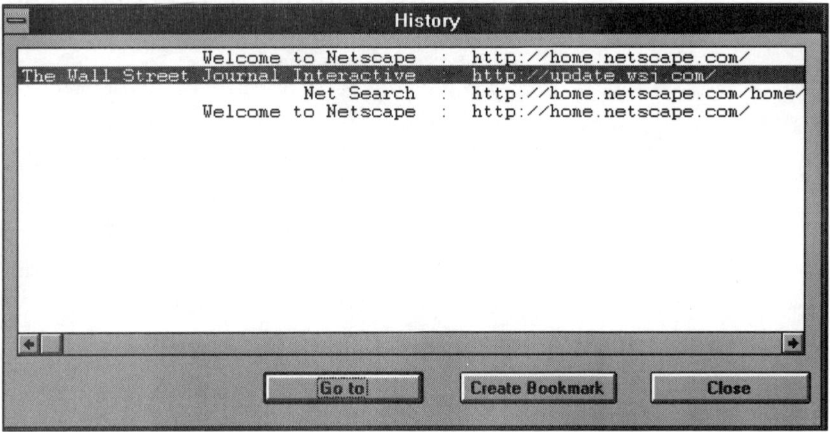

Figure 1.14

Tip You can also access the History window by pressing CTRL + H

3 Select Net Search, then select the Go to button (or simply double-click on Net Search).

The Net Search page appears in the Netscape window. Notice, however, that the History window remains the active window.

4 Select the Close button at the bottom of the History window.
The history window disappears, leaving you looking at the Net Search page.

If necessary, you can take a break at this point. When you come back, just start up Netscape Navigator and proceed.

NAVIGATING USING LINKS

So far you've learned how to use some of Netscape's features for navigating between Web pages. Recall, though, that the single most powerful feature of the World Wide Web is the use of linked documents. In this section you will learn to identify links on Web pages and to use them for navigating the Web.

Finding Links on Web Pages

Most Web pages contain *links* to other Web pages. ***Links*** can be text or pictures appearing on a Web page, and Netscape makes it easy to identify them. Depending on the specific Netscape setup you are using, ***text links*** appear in a different color, or underlined, or both. ***Picture links*** can be identified by moving the cursor around on the screen. When you pass over either a text or picture link, the cursor icon changes from an arrow ( ) to a hand ( ). Finally, when the cursor is on a link, the URL of the linked document appears in the Netscape status bar. Figure 1.15 shows the Net Search page with the cursor positioned over a picture link. Notice that the cursor icon has become a hand and the URL of the linked document appears in the status bar.

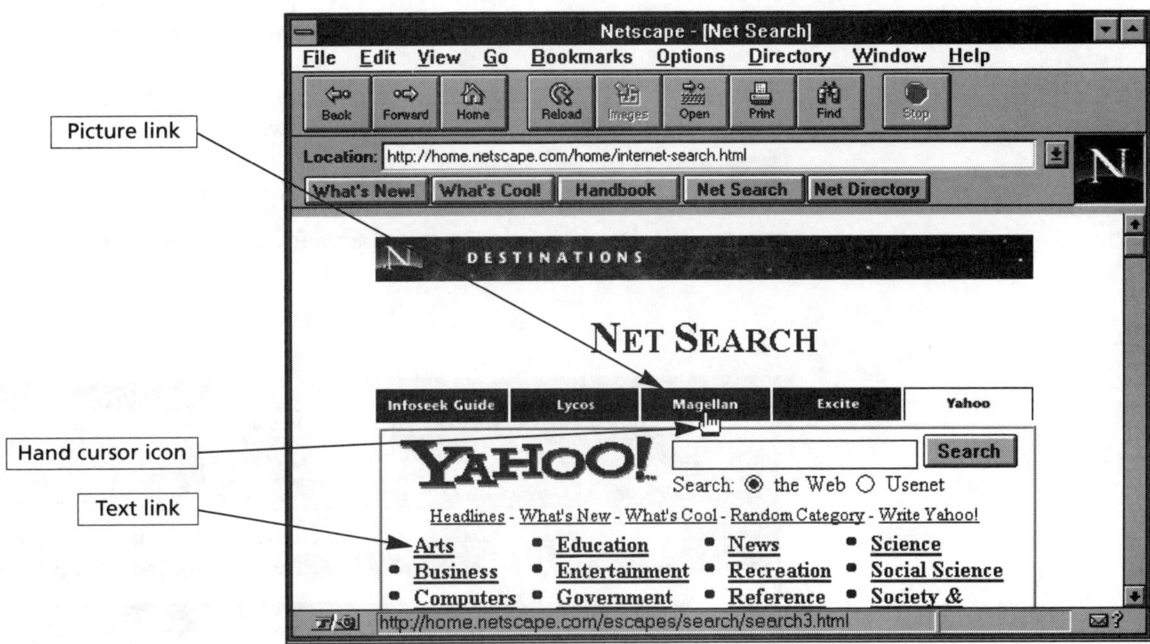

Figure 1.15

To locate links:

1 If you are not already there, go to the Net Search page. You can select the Net Search button located below the Location field in the Netscape window, or use the Go menu or History window.

2 Move the pointer around on the Net Search page. Locate picture and text links by looking for colored or underlined text and watching for the hand icon that appears when you find a link.

3 Use the vertical scroll bar to display more of the Net Search page, and look for more text and picture links.

> ***Don't Panic*** If you click on any of the links you find and are transported away from the Net Search page, remember you can use the Back button to get back to where you were before.

Going Places Using Links

Now that you know how to find links on Web pages, it's time to start using links to get around.

To select a link:

1 Go to the Net Search page, if you're not already there.

2 Position the cursor over the Magellan picture link, as shown in Figure 1.15.
Notice the URL that appears in the status bar. This is the address of the linked document to which you will jump when you select the link.

3 Select the picture link by clicking it.
As shown in Figure 1.16, you are transported to a special Net Search page featuring a direct interface with Magellan, a tool for performing Internet searches.

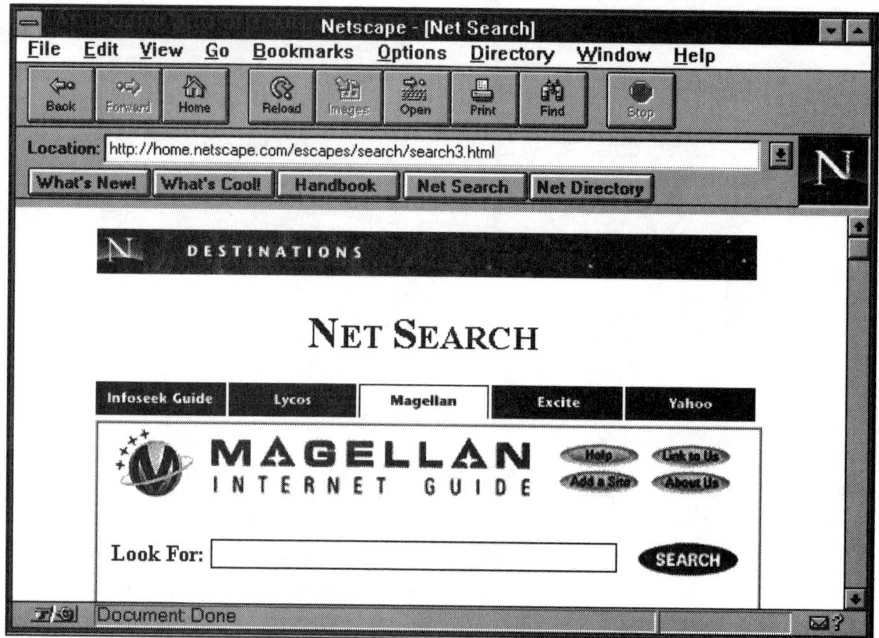

Figure 1.16

Don't Panic Don't forget that Web pages displayed on your screen may not look exactly like the ones shown in this book. Remember, the Web is constantly changing, and it is very likely that many pages used as examples have changed in the short time since this book was printed.

To go further using links:

1 Find the Stellar Sites picture link on the Magellan Net Search page (You may have to scroll down to find the Stellar Sites picture link).

2 Click the Stellar Sites picture link.
Netscape takes you to a new Web site. This time it is the Magellan Stellar Sites page, a selection of nifty Web sites that the people at Magellan think are worth visiting. At this writing, the Stellar Sites page looked like the one shown in Figure 1.17.

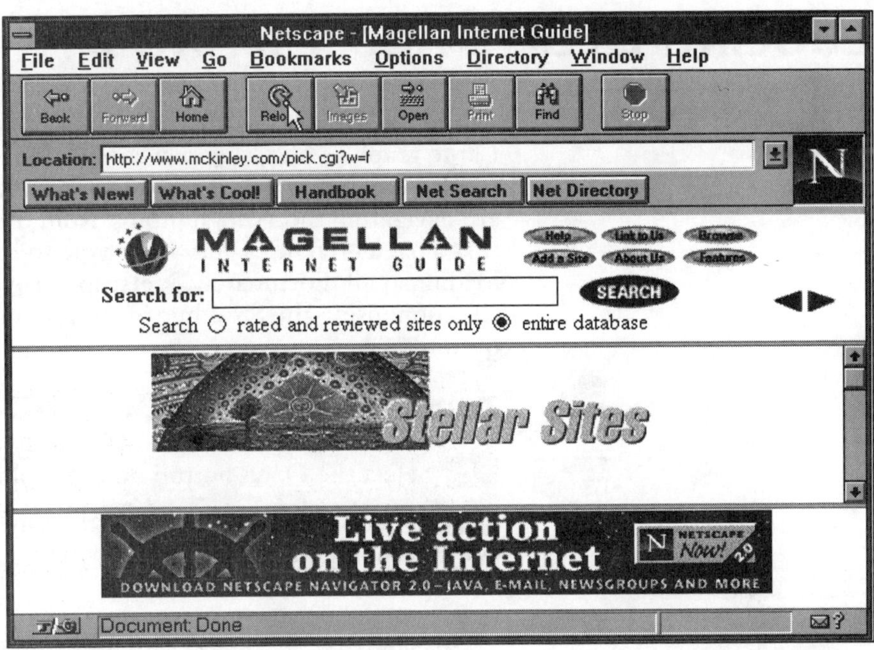

Figure 1.17

3 From here you can scroll down and select specific sites by using text and picture links. This is a fun place from which to explore a bit using links.

4 As you check out some of the cool sites listed on the Magellan Stellar Sites page, don't forget you can use the Back and Forward buttons and history functions to revisit your favorite sites.

5 Select the Home button when you are finished exploring. You return to the startup location.

Identifying Links You've Already Explored

In your exploration of the Magellan Stellar Sites page, you may notice that text links that have been selected change color. This is Netscape's way of telling you what links you've already explored. Because some Web pages (like the Magellan Stellar Sites page) have many text links, this ***followed links*** feature can be very handy in helping you avoid inadvertently visiting the same site more than once.

If you do return to a site you've already visited during the current session, you will notice that the Web page appears on your screen much more quickly than when you first selected the link. This is because Netscape not only keeps track of where you've been, but also it stores, or ***caches***, each page you visit. When you revisit cached sites, they are displayed much more quickly because the Web page is now stored in your computer's memory or on your hard drive, and Netscape does not have to perform the downloading activities it did when you first visited the site.

REDUCING DELAYS AND TIDYING UP

While the Web has many virtues, speed is unfortunately not among them. Large graphics files, sluggish connections, and inaccessible servers can all result in irritating delays while you wait for a Web page to load. When you are navigating the Web, jumping from one site to another, you may find that a page is taking a very long time to load or even seems not to be loading at all. Fortunately, Netscape provides two ways to help improve the situation: using the Stop button and disabling the Auto Load Images option.

To use the Stop button:

1 Select the Open button on the toolbar.

2 Type the following URL in the Open Location field:
`www.autonet.com`

> ***Tip*** Notice that you are leaving off the http:// portion of the URL (the complete URL is http://www.autonet.com). Netscape is actually pretty smart and knows that all documents whose domain names begin with www are indeed Web documents and must be loaded using the Hypertext Transfer Protocol (http). So, you can leave off http:// when opening Web documents whose domain names begin with www.

3 Select Open

Autonet.com is an example of a Web site that makes extensive use of graphics. Such graphics are the main culprit in bogging down the Web. It is when you stumble upon a graphics-intensive site like this one, or a downright unresponsive site, that you may want to use the Stop button.

4 While the page is still loading, select the Stop button.
Notice that the animation in the Netscape activity icon stops, the Stop button becomes unavailable, and the loading process stops. You are now free to open another location without waiting for the Autonet page to finish loading.

> ***Tip*** There are other ways to select the Stop function. You can select Stop Loading from the Go menu, or you can press ESC

Something else you can do to avoid long waits for large graphics to load when visiting Web pages is to disable the Auto Load Images option. This allows Netscape to load Web pages without loading any of the graphics associated with those pages. The results are not often pretty, but you will increase your surfing speed significantly.

To disable the Auto Load Images option:

1 Choose Auto Load Images from the Options menu, as shown in Figure 1.18.

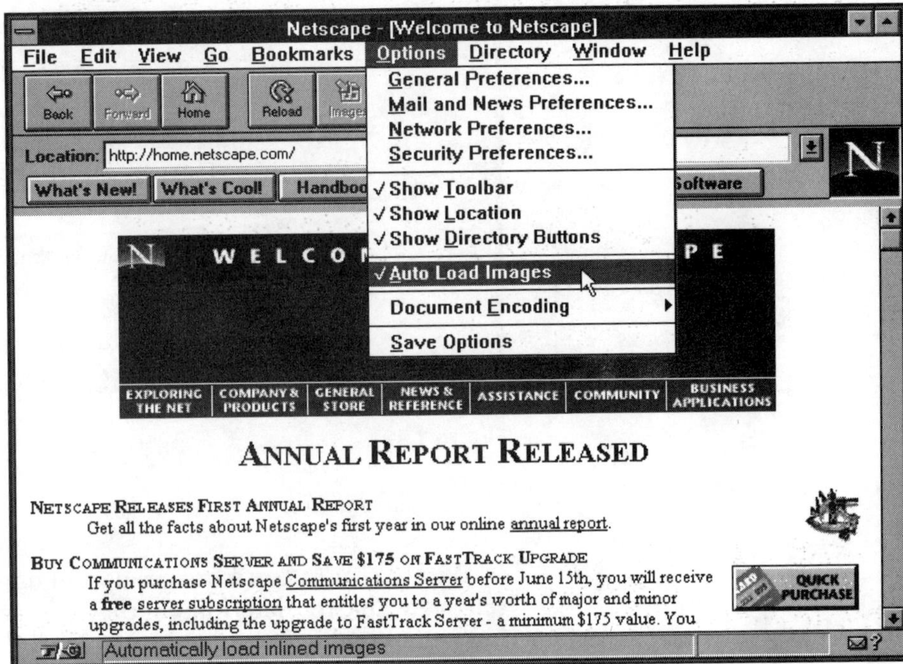

Figure 1.18

2 Select the Open button on the toolbar.

3 Type the following URL in the Open Location field:
`www.collegegrad.com`

4 Select Open.
The College Grad Job Hunter page opens without graphics and looks something like Figure 1.19.

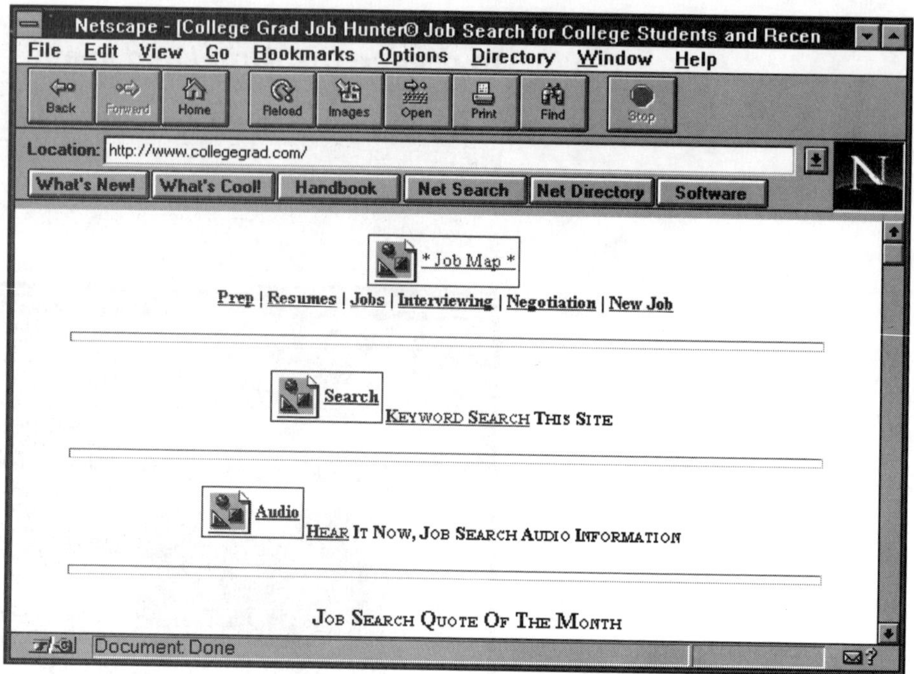

Figure 1.19

With the Auto Load Images option disabled, you can load Web sites relatively quickly, determine if they deserve a longer look, and then load images manually if you decide it's worth the wait.

To load images manually:

1 Select the Images button on the toolbar.
The graphics that did not load automatically with the Web page are now loaded, as shown in Figure 1.20. If you're lucky, this process won't take much time. Depending on Internet traffic, however, the time will vary and will sometimes be more than you are willing to spend, so don't forget the Stop button!

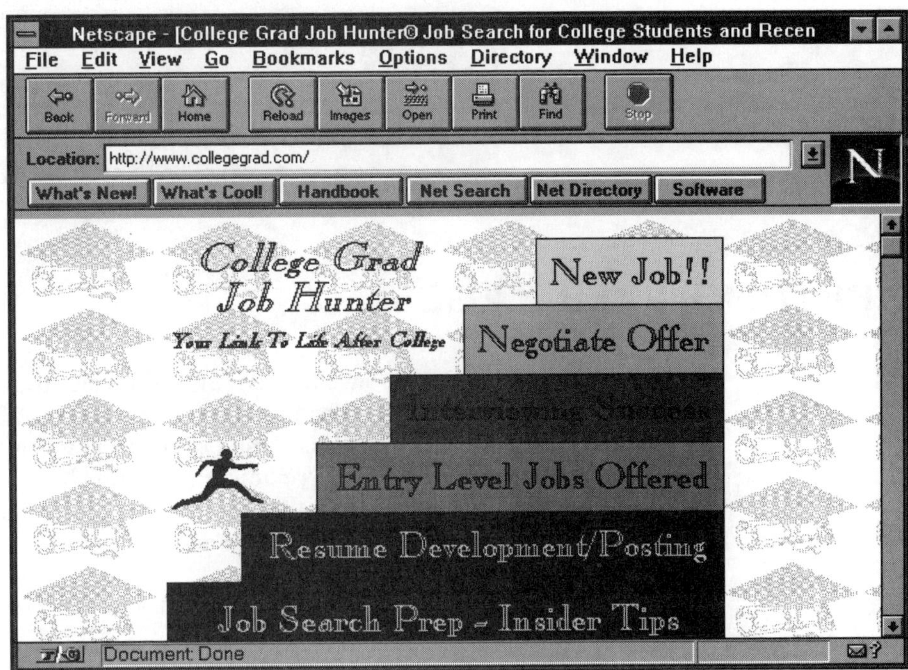

Figure 1.20

> ***Tip*** There are other ways to select the Images function. You can select View/Load Images from the main menu, or you can press CTRL + I

Now let's say you have determined that a page you want to visit is taking too long to load because of its graphics, and you have stopped the loading process (by selecting the Stop button). As you have seen, you can get a relatively quick look at the page by disabling the Auto Load Images option. Now that Auto Load Images is disabled, you can use the Reload button to reload that pesky graphics-intensive page much more quickly. If you absolutely must see all the pretty graphics, you can select the Images button to load images manually.

To reload the currently displayed Web page:

1 Use the Back button or the History window to return to the partially loaded Autonet.com page.

2 Select the Reload button from the toolbar.
Notice that the Autonet page is reloaded (and much more quickly than before) without images.

> ***Tip*** There are other ways to select the Reload function. You can select Reload from the View menu, or you can press CTRL + R

Another Tip There is another situation when the Reload button comes in handy. If you find that the Web page currently displayed is "going to pieces" (the graphics are becoming fragmented or text appears in weird and overlapping positions), use the Reload button to tidy up. Better yet, try the Refresh option on the View menu.

PRINTING WEB PAGES

Once you have landed on a Web site that contains valuable information, you may wish to print that page. Printing Web pages in Netscape is just like printing documents in other Windows applications. Netscape offers standard Print Preview, Print, and Page Setup options.

To use Print Preview:

1 Return to the College Grad Job Hunter page using the Back button or the History window.

2 Choose Print Preview from the File menu.
The Web page is displayed in a print preview window, as shown in Figure 1.21. Notice the buttons along the top of the window. You can use these buttons to print the page, view the next page (remember, Web pages can be very long!), view two pages at once, zoom in for a closer look, zoom out, or close the print preview window.

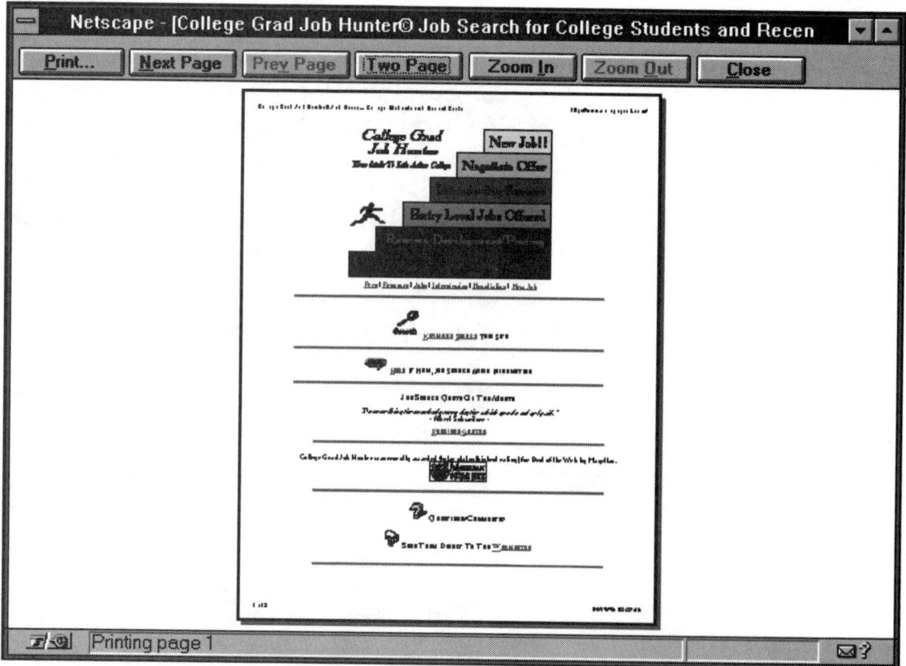

Figure 1.21

If you are unhappy with the way the page is displayed, you can make some adjustments using Page Setup before actually printing the page.

3 Select the Close button.

To use Page Setup:

1 Choose Page Setup from the File menu.
The Page Setup window appears as shown in Figure 1.22.

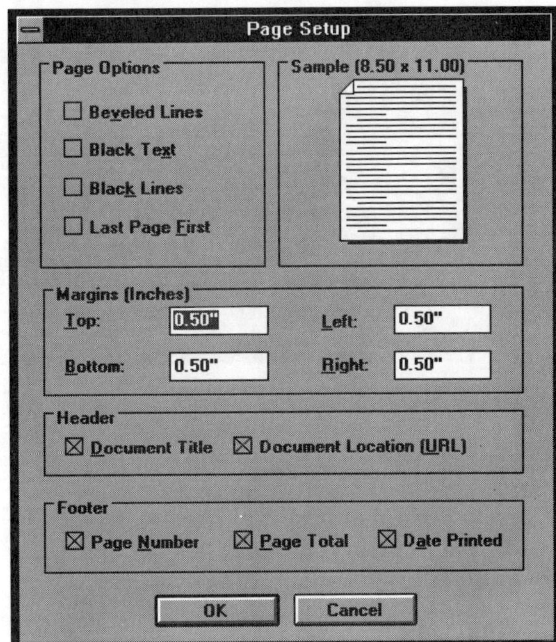

Figure 1.22

The Page Setup options allow you to handle some of the color issues inherent to Web pages by offering black lines and text. In addition, you can opt to print the Web document in reverse order, last page first.

Margins can be set by typing in values. Netscape prints the document title and URL at the top of each page if you select those options. Finally, you can include page numbers and the date in the footer if desired.

2 Select the Page Setup options that appeal to you.

3 Select the OK button.

Now that you have previewed your document and made adjustments using Page Setup, you are ready to print.

To use Print:

1 Choose Print from the File menu.
The Print window appears as shown in Figure 1.23.

> ***Tip*** Another way to use the print function in Netscape is to select the Print button from the toolbar.

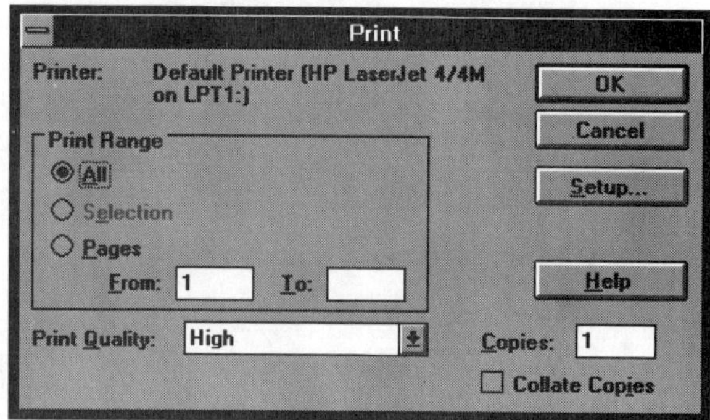

Figure 1.23

The Print window allows you to specify which pages you wish to print, the print quality, the number of copies, and whether or not you wish to have multiple copies collated.

2 Make any changes you wish to the print options, and then select the OK button. The College Grad Job Hunter page is printed on your computer's default printer.

THE NEXT STEP

In this project you have been introduced to the World Wide Web through Netscape. You have acquired important skills for navigating and controlling Web page and image loading. The next step in your exploration of the Web is to learn to keep track of the places you have visited so that you can return later. In the next project you will learn to use bookmarks in Netscape to help you get organized on the Web.

This concludes Project 1. You can either exit Netscape or go on to work the Study Questions, Review Exercises, and Assignments.

Summary and Exercises

Summary

- The location of Web pages on the Internet is designated by the URL (Uniform Resource Locator), a standardized address composed of three parts: protocol, domain name, and file name (including directory path).
- You can jump to Web sites with Netscape using URLs and the Open button or the Location field.
- You can move back and forward between Web sites you have visited during the current session using the Back and Forward buttons.
- You can return to the Netscape startup location using the Home button.
- Netscape's history feature allows you to jump directly to Web sites you have visited during the current session. To do this, select the desired site from the Go menu or from the History window. The Netscape history is only temporary. It lasts only as long as the current session.
- Most Web pages contain links to other Web pages. Text links appear in a different color and are sometimes underlined. When the cursor is over a text or picture link, the cursor icon becomes a hand.
- You can click on a link on a Web page to jump to the Web page referenced by that link.
- Links that you have selected appear in a different color to indicate that you have visited the referenced site.
- You can stop a page from loading if it is taking too long to load.
- The Reload button can be used to refresh the screen or to reload the current Web page with different options selected.
- Disabling Auto Load Images can dramatically increase the speed at which pages are loaded.
- The Images button is used to load images manually when the Auto Load Images option is disabled.
- Web pages are printed in Netscape in much the same way as documents are printed in other Windows applications.
- Netscape offers standard Print Preview, Page Setup, and Print options under the File menu.

Key Terms and Operations

Key Terms

cache
domain name
file name
followed link
history
link
picture link
protocol
text link

Operations

Go back, forward, and home
Jump to Web sites using links
Jump to Web sites using URLs
Use the history feature to revisit Web sites
Use Page Setup and Print
Use Reload, Auto Load Images, and Stop

Study Questions

Multiple Choice

1. The three parts of a URL (Uniform Resource Locator) are
   a. protocol, denominator, and file name.
   b. prototype, domain name, and file folder.
   c. protocol, domain name, and file name.
   d. prototype, denominator, and file folder.

2. Which of the following Netscape toolbar buttons will *not* allow you to navigate from one URL to another?
   a. Back
   b. Reload
   c. Home
   d. Open

3. You know that you have already visited a URL if the link is displayed in a different
   a. size.
   b. shape.
   c. color.
   d. icon.

4. Netscape Navigator belongs to a group of applications know as Web
   a. crawlers.
   b. skimmers.
   c. browsers.
   d. surfers.

5. You know the cursor is on a picture or text link if the cursor is displayed using a(n)
   a. arrow icon.
   b. I-beam icon.
   c. flashing icon.
   d. hand icon.

6. The character used to separate the components of URLs is typically a
   a. /
   b. :
   c. \
   d. None of the above.

7. A link displayed in another color to indicate you have already clicked on it is called a
   a. traveled link.
   b. followed link.
   c. used link.
   d. expired link.

8. The History window displays the _______________ of Web sites you've visited during the current session.
   a. name and phone number
   b. document name and URL
   c. program and address
   d. document name and program

9. The Stop button may be used to
   a. stop an application that has bombed.
   b. exit Netscape.
   c. close your Internet connection.
   d. stop a Web page from loading.

10. The Images button causes Netscape to
    a. load images for the currently displayed Web page.
    b. load images for all cached Web pages.
    c. open the Images window.
    d. load images for all Web pages you visit during the current session.

Short Answer

1. Each page on the Web has a unique ____________ called a ________ that allows all computers connected to the Internet to retrieve and display that page.
2. The Netscape feature that keeps track of Web pages that you have already visited during the current session is called _____________.
3. The ____________ is the name of the computer system where a Web page is located.
4. Web pages are actually just text documents that are created using a special language called _____________________________________.
5. Among the most powerful features of most Web pages are ____________________, which allow you to jump between Web sites.
6. ____________________ allow you to link graphics, sounds, and movies to Web pages.
7. The Web has many virtues, but __________ is not one of them.
8. The Stop button can be used when a Web page fails to load or when the associated ______________ are larger than your patience.
9. The Auto Load Images option allows you to decide in advance whether you want Netscape to ________ images automatically.
10. If the currently displayed Web page begins to look a little weird or messy, the __________ button can be used to clean it up.

For Discussion

1. How is the World Wide Web different from having multiple subject-specific CD ROMs?
2. What kinds of information do *you* think would be important for a corporation to have on the Internet?
3. The Netscape Corporation allows educational institutions to use their software free. Why? What do think is the impact on their company?
4. Why is it important to know how to use the history feature of your Web browser? What are its limitations?

Review Exercises

Starting Your Job Search

1. Examine the Web links provided by Netscape's What's New! and What's Cool! buttons. Look for links to corporations with whom you are familiar.
2. At each corporate home page you locate, try to find their employment opportunities page.

Assignments

More Information About the Internet

Hobbes' Internet timeline is a good starting point for learning more about the history and growth of the Internet. Open the URL http://info.isoc.org/guest/zakon/Internet/History/HIT.html and read the document. Be ready to discuss the growth of the Internet as shown in the figures and graphs provided.

A Netscape Tutorial

Use the Help pull-down menu to access Netscape's Handbook. The handbook page has a Tutorial section that you should read to learn more about the Netscape Web browser. Some of the information may not make much sense now, however, it will by the time that you finish this book.

Project 2: Getting Organized on the Web

Objectives

After completing this project, you should be able to:

- Create bookmarks
- Edit and delete bookmarks
- Arrange bookmarks using folders and separators

Case Study: Organizing the Job Search

So far you've learned how to navigate from one Web site to another, and you've learned that Netscape keeps track of the Web sites you visit. You know that Netscape's history feature allows you to view a list of sites you've visited and to jump directly back to any of those sites. These are convenient features to be sure, but with one important limitation: Netscape will forget everything about your travels through the Web when you exit the program. This is because the list of sites you've visited is only temporary. It lasts only as long as your current session and vanishes when you exit Netscape.

In your job search you have realized that you need to keep track of the Web pages you find containing employment information. You can see that you are going to find many pages you'll want to mark somehow so you can return to them later. You've already lost track of some of the hot job sites you've found. You realize that this issue could become a very important one as you search the Web further for employment sites.

An Internet Solution

In this project you will learn how to mark and organize Web pages you've found to help you in your job search. You will learn to use Netscape ***bookmarks***, which you can use to permanently record Web pages you wish to revisit. You will also learn to organize your bookmarks into groups. Then in the next project you will begin searching the Web in earnest for more pages containing employment information.

WHAT ARE BOOKMARKS?

Bookmarks provide a way for you to make a permanent record of the addresses (URLs) of your favorite Web sites or of Web sites you would like to remember and perhaps visit again sometime in the future. Netscape bookmarks include the name of the site, its URL, the date you "marked" the site, and the last time you visited the site. Unlike the history feature, bookmarks persist from one Netscape session to another and do not disappear unless you manually delete them.

CREATING BOOKMARKS

Before you can begin creating bookmarks, you must first start Netscape. This procedure is covered in the Overview if you need a refresher.

Unlike Netscape's history feature, which automatically records sites you have visited during the current session, bookmarks must be created manually. There are several ways to create a bookmark using Netscape, and they are all relatively simple.

To mark the currently displayed Web page, you should use the Bookmarks menu.

To create bookmarks using the Bookmarks menu:

1 With Netscape running use the Open button or the Location field to go to the College Grad Job Hunter page (http://www.collegegrad.com).

2 Choose Add Bookmark from the Bookmarks menu, as shown in Figure 2.1.
You have just created a bookmark for the College Grad Job Hunter page.

> ***Tip*** You can also create a bookmark by pressing CTRL + D

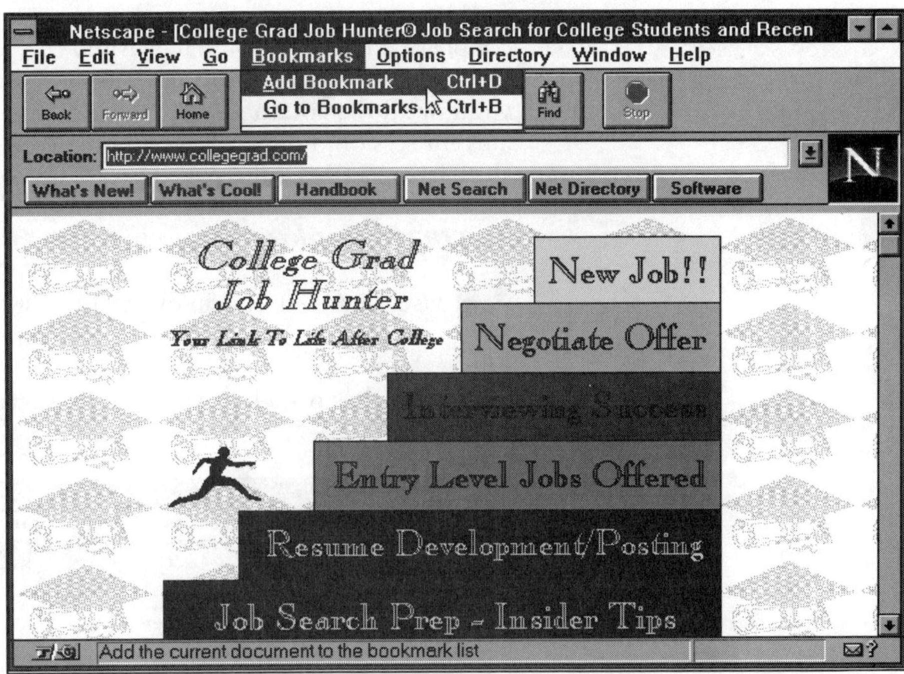

Figure 2.1

3 Choose Bookmarks from the menu bar again.
Notice that "College Grad Job Hunt..." is now displayed in the Bookmarks menu, as shown in Figure 2.2. Each time you create a bookmark, it will be added to this list in the Bookmarks menu. When you want to return to a Web site you have marked, you simply select that site in the Bookmarks menu, and Netscape will take you directly there.

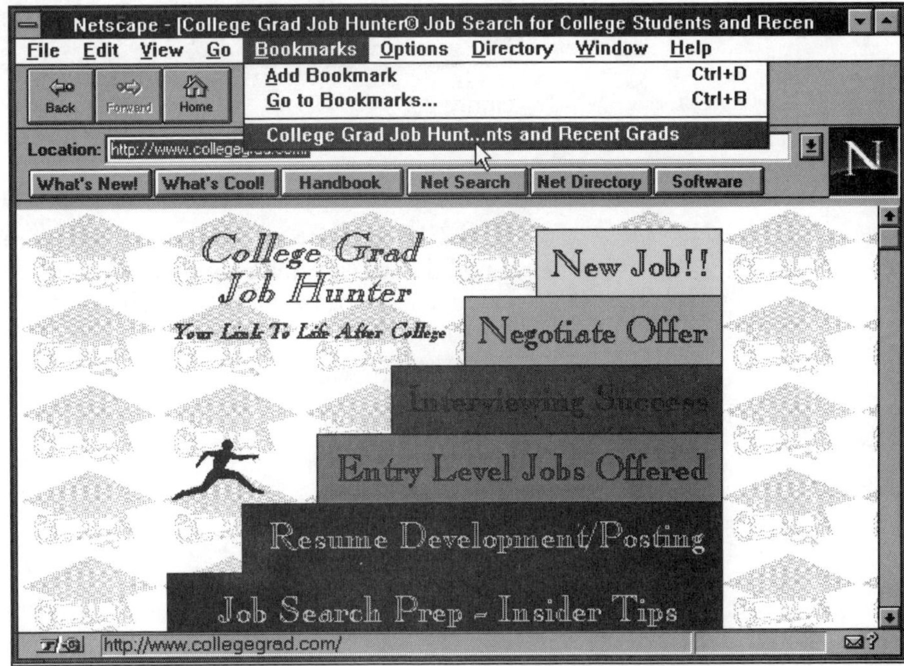

Figure 2.2

If you want to mark a page that is not currently displayed, you have a couple of choices. If you have visited the page you want to mark during the current session, you can use the History window. Remember, the History window allows you to view all of the Web sites you have visited during the current session. It also allows you to create bookmarks for any of those sites, irrespective of the page that is currently displayed.

To create bookmarks using the History window:

1 Use the Open button or the Location field to go to the Career Magazine page (located at http://www.careermag.com), as shown in Figure 2.3.
This is another page that could be of interest for your job search.

Figure 2.3

2 Choose History from the Window menu.
The History window contains all of the Web sites you've visited during the current session. In the list you should find NCS Career Magazine, as shown in Figure 2.4.

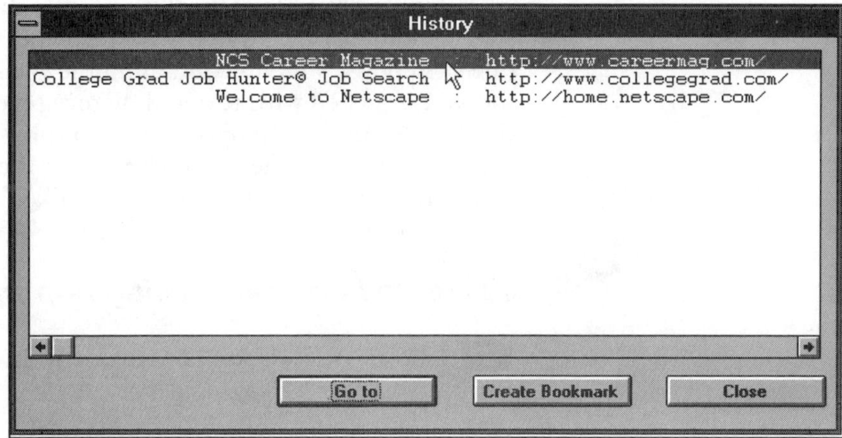

Figure 2.4

3 Select NCS Career Magazine in the History window.

4 Select Create Bookmark at the bottom of the History window to create a bookmark for the NCS Career Magazine page.

5 Select the Close button to close the History window.

6 Select the Home button from the Netscape toolbar to return to the Netscape startup location.

7 Choose NCS Career Magazine from the Bookmarks menu, as shown in Figure 2.5.
Netscape loads the NCS Career Magazine page.

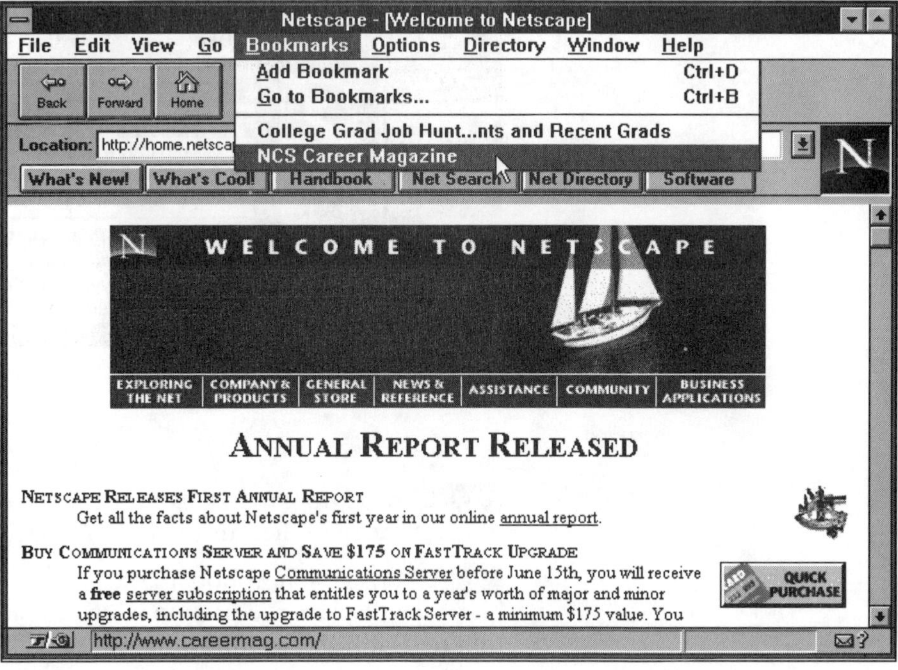

Figure 2.5

Netscape provides context-sensitive pop-up menus that contain shortcuts to many commonly performed functions. You have already seen one such pop-up menu containing the Back and Forward options. Pop-up menus associated with text and picture links contain a number of other options. Among these options is creating a bookmark for the link. So Netscape's pop-up menus offer another method for creating bookmarks for pages not currently displayed. But unlike the History window method, you can use pop-up menus to mark pages you have not yet visited.

To create bookmarks using pop-up menus:

1 Choose NCS Career Magazine from the Bookmarks menu to go to the NCS Career Magazine page.

2 Position the cursor over the Job Openings picture link on the NCS Career Magazine page, and click the right mouse button.
A Netscape pop-up menu for this link appears.

3 Choose Add Bookmark for this Link from the pop-up menu, as shown in Figure 2.6. A bookmark for the Job Openings link is created.

Figure 2.6

4 Choose Bookmarks from the menu bar.
Notice that the URL for the link has been added to the menu.

5 Choose the new bookmark.
Netscape displays the page to which the link points: Career Magazine Jobline Database, as shown in Figure 2.7.

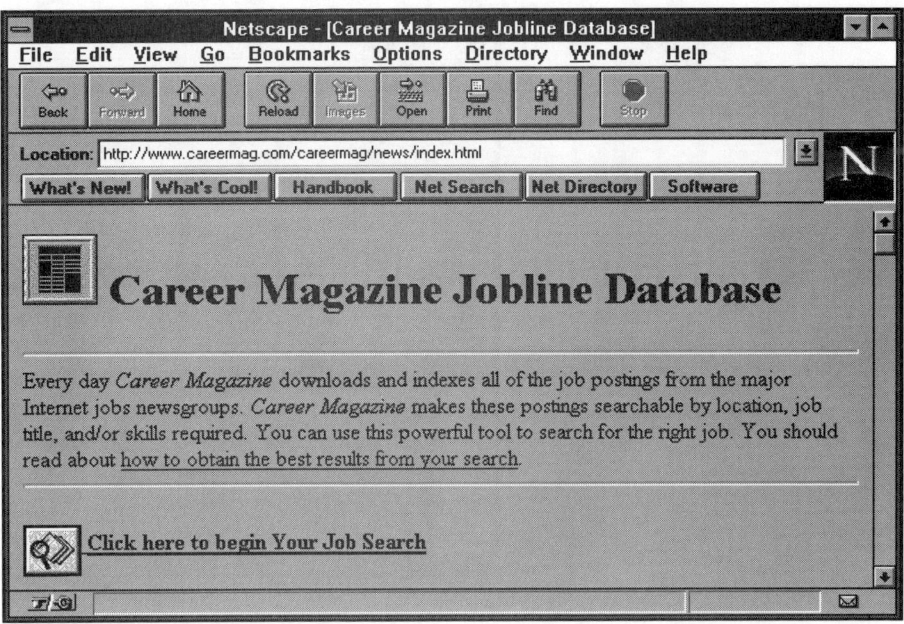

Figure 2.7

EDITING BOOKMARKS

As you create bookmarks, you may sometimes find that the information gathered and displayed by Netscape is not very descriptive. You have probably already noticed a good example of this: The name Netscape assigned to the bookmark for the Career Magazine Jobline Database page is the URL for that page, which is not a very descriptive name. To remedy situations like this, you can edit the bookmark.

To edit bookmark properties:

1 Choose Go to Bookmarks from the Bookmarks menu.
The Bookmarks window appears as shown in Figure 2.8. All of your bookmarks are displayed in this window.

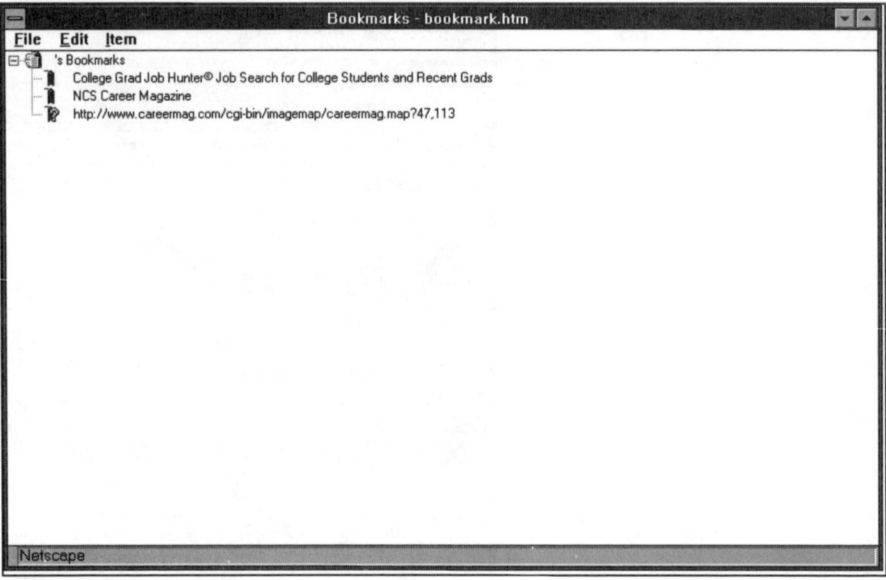

Figure 2.8

> ***Tip*** You can also access the Bookmarks window by pressing CTRL + B

2 Select the last bookmark in the list (the one using its URL for a name).

3 Choose Properties from the Items menu, as shown in Figure 2.9. The Bookmark Properties window appears as shown in Figure 2.10.

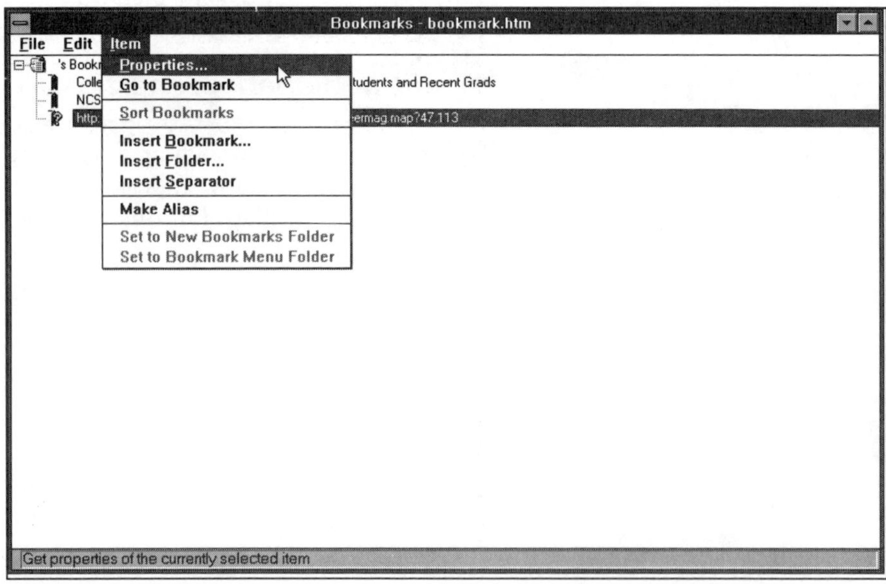

Figure 2.9

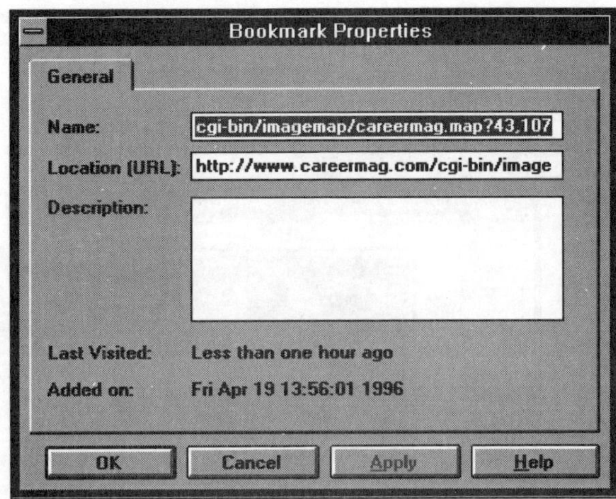

Figure 2.10

The Bookmark Properties window contains fields for the name, location, and description of the bookmark, each of which you can modify at any time. In addition, the Bookmark Properties window gives the amount of time that has elapsed since you last visited the site and the date on which the bookmark was created. Notice that the name field contains the address of the page rather than a descriptive name.

4 Type **`Career Magazine Jobline Database`** in the Name field.

5 Select the OK button.

The Bookmark Properties window disappears. Notice that the name of the bookmark has been changed in the Bookmarks window and also in the Bookmarks menu, as shown in Figures 2.11 and 2.12.

Figure 2.11

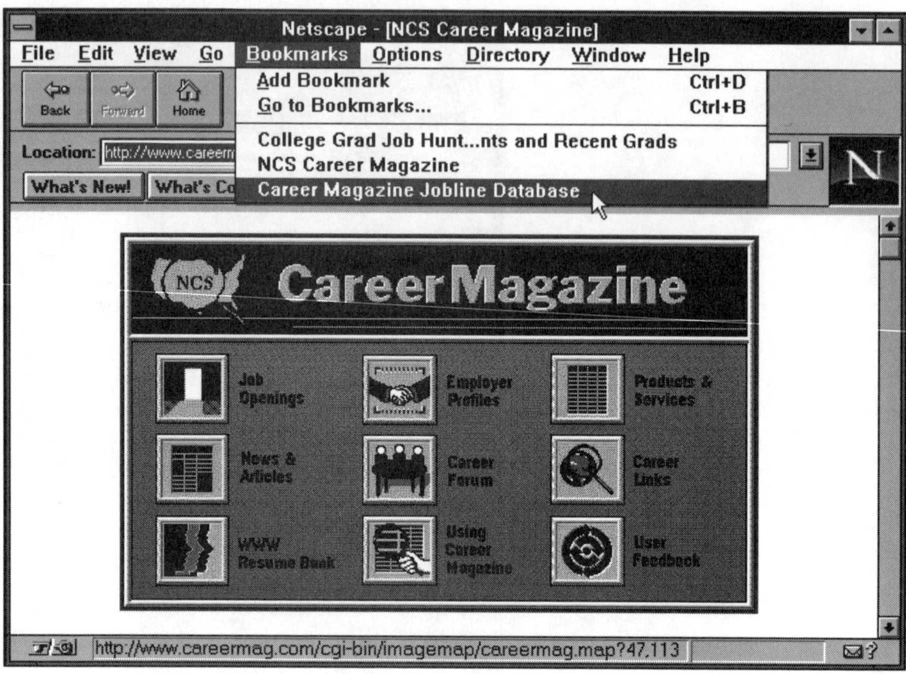

Figure 2.12

DELETING BOOKMARKS

Because the World Wide Web is always changing, so must your list of bookmarks. Pages will change and even disappear over time. Or, if a particular marked Web page persists long enough, your interests may change, and you may wish to remove it from your list of bookmarks. For these reasons, it is important to be able to delete bookmarks.

To delete a bookmark:

1 Choose Go to Bookmarks from the Bookmarks menu.

2 Select the Career Magazine Jobline Database bookmark.

3 Choose Delete from the Bookmarks window Edit menu, as shown in Figure 2.13.
The bookmark disappears from the Bookmarks window and also from the Bookmarks menu.

> ***Tip*** You can also delete a bookmark from the bookmarks window by selecting it and pressing DEL

Figure 2.13

4 Choose Undo from the Bookmarks window Edit menu to undelete the bookmark.
Notice that the Career Magazine Jobline Database bookmark is restored in both the Bookmarks window and menu.

If necessary, you can take a break at this point. When you come back, just start up Netscape Navigator and proceed.

ORGANIZING BOOKMARKS

As you have seen, bookmarks you create are displayed in both the Bookmarks menu and the Bookmarks window. As you become an active Web surfer, you will soon find yourself accumulating large numbers of bookmarks, and you may wish to organize them into categories to make them easier to find. Netscape provides *folders* and *separators* for just this kind of organizing. ***Folders*** are used to group bookmarks into categories, and ***separators*** are used to divide the Bookmarks menu into sections.

To create a bookmark folder:

1 Choose Go to Bookmarks from the Bookmarks menu.

2 Choose Insert Folder from the Bookmarks window Item menu, as shown in Figure 2.14.
The Bookmark Properties window appears.

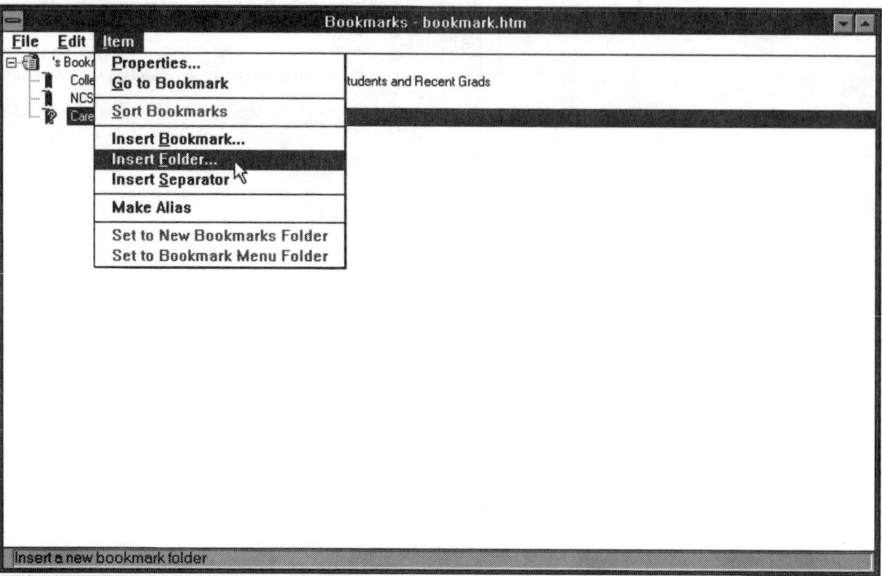

Figure 2.14

3 Type **`Employment`** in the Name field, as shown in Figure 2.15.

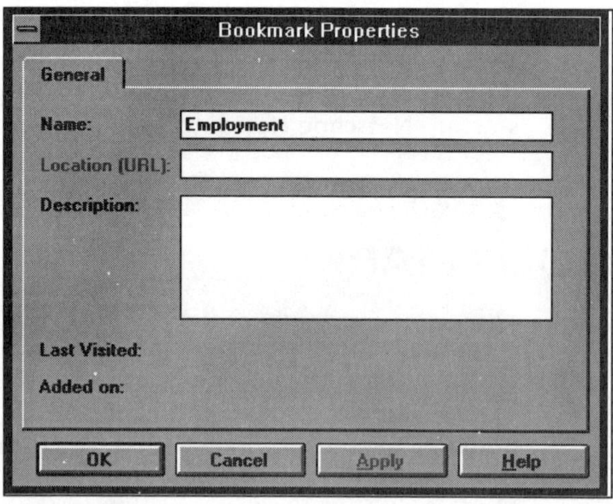

Figure 2.15

4 Select the OK button.

As shown in Figure 2.16, a folder called Employment has been added to the Bookmarks window. This new bookmarks folder does not contain any bookmarks yet, and because it is empty, it does not appear in the Bookmarks menu. The next step is to move a bookmark into the folder.

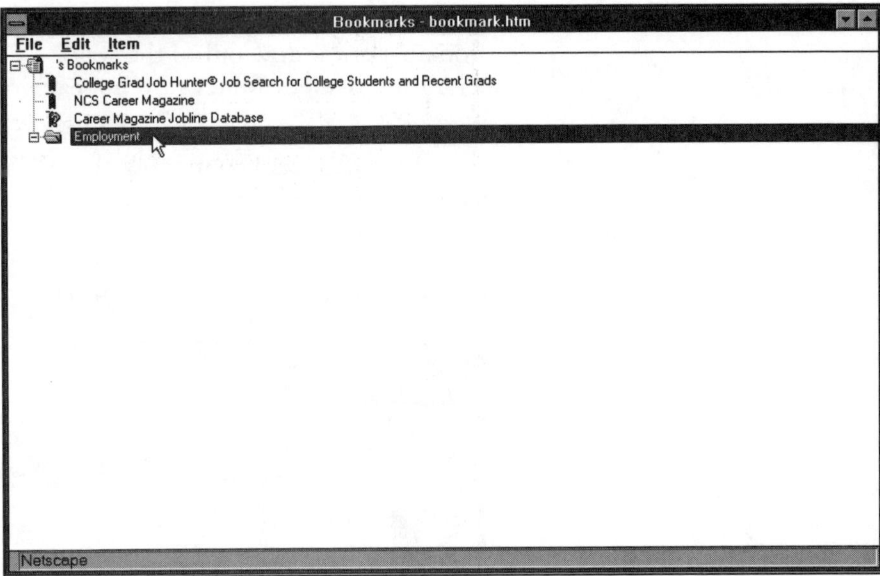

Figure 2.16

To move bookmarks into a folder:

1 Select NCS Career Magazine bookmark in the Bookmarks window, and drag it to the Employment folder, as shown in Figure 2.17. Notice that the NCS Career Magazine bookmark is indented beneath the Employment folder. This means that it is now inside the folder.

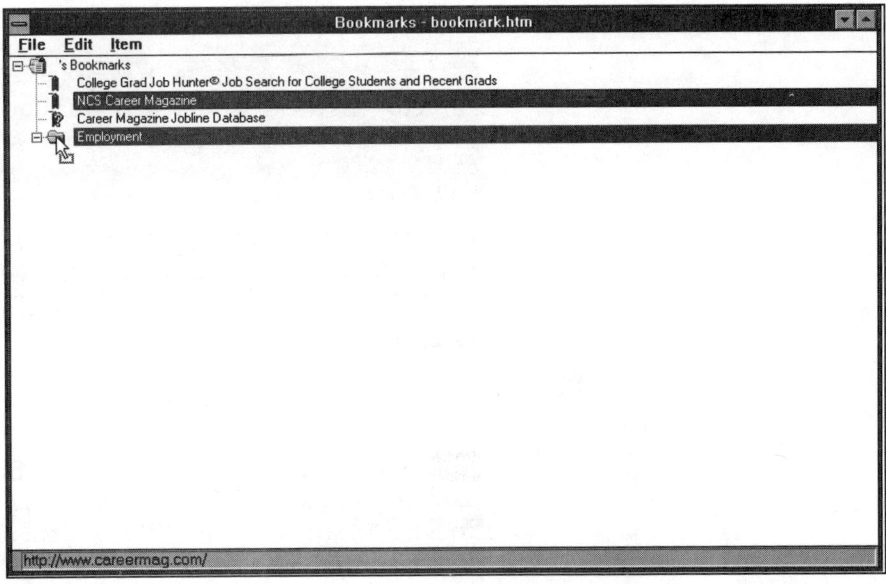

Figure 2.17

2 Choose Bookmarks from the menu bar (if necessary, move the Bookmarks window out of the way).
The Employment folder now appears in the Bookmarks menu.

3 Select the Employment folder.
A submenu appears containing the NCS Career Magazine bookmark, as shown in Figure 2.18.

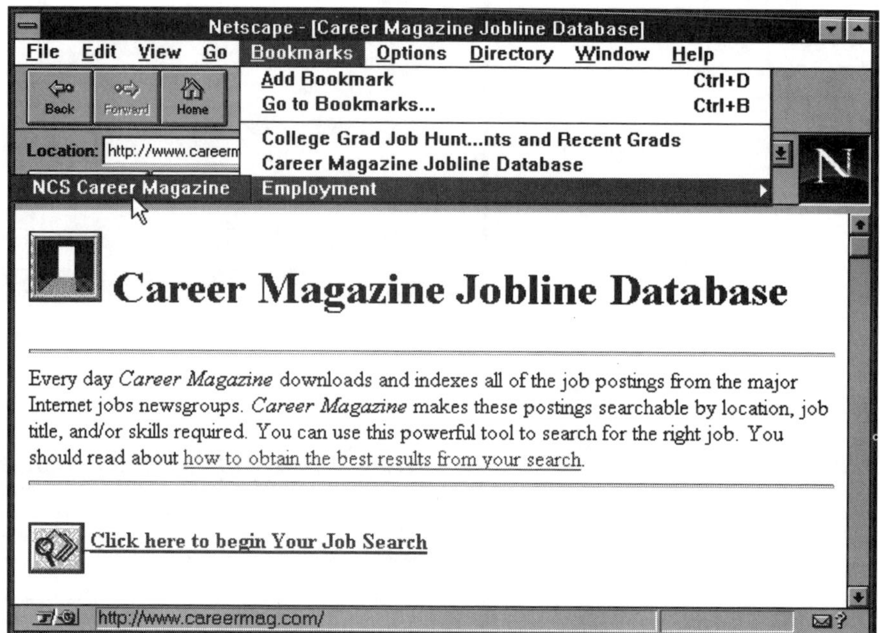

Figure 2.18

> ***Don't Panic*** if the Web pages displayed on your screen do not look exactly like the ones shown in this book. Remember, the Web is constantly changing, and it is very likely that many pages used as examples have changed in the short time since this book was printed.

In the next project you will add more bookmarks to the Employment folder. At that time you may also wish to create additional folders to help you further organize the information you locate on the Web for your job search.

To create a separator:

1 If it's not already open, open the Bookmarks window.

2 Select Career Magazine Jobline Database in the Bookmarks window.

3 Choose Insert Separator from the Bookmarks window Item menu, as shown in Figure 2.19.
A separator entry appears above the Employment folder, as shown in Figure 2.20.

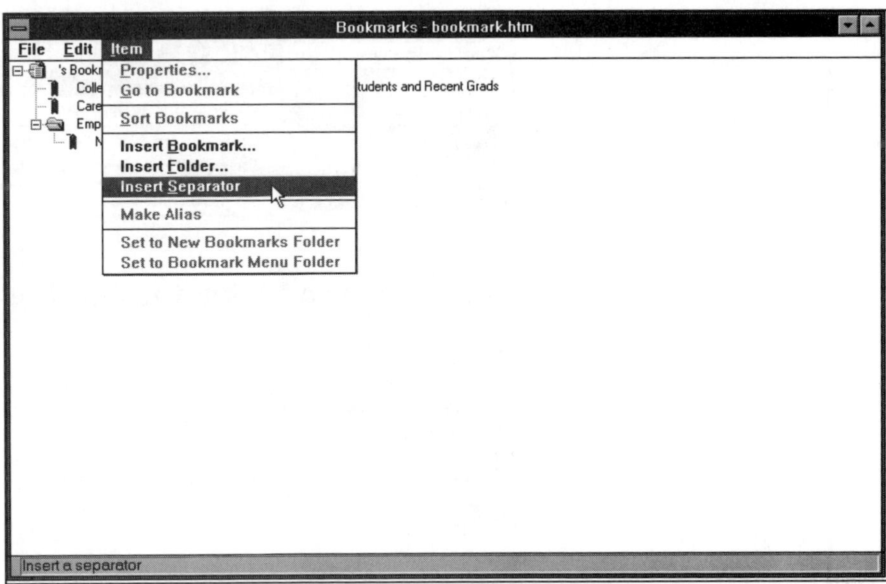

Figure 2.19

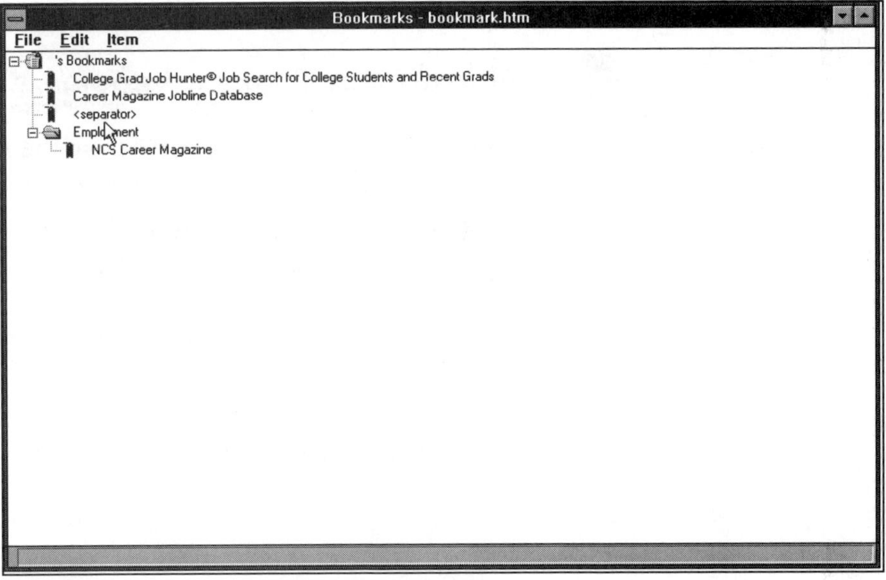

Figure 2.20

4 Choose the Bookmarks menu (move the Bookmarks window out of the way if necessary).
A line appears below the Employment folder, as shown in Figure 2.21.

Once you have created a number of bookmarks, folders, and separators, you may wish to rearrange their display order. You can move bookmarks out of a folder or into a different folder, or you can move a folder into another folder. You can do any of these things by dragging the item to a new location in the Bookmarks window.

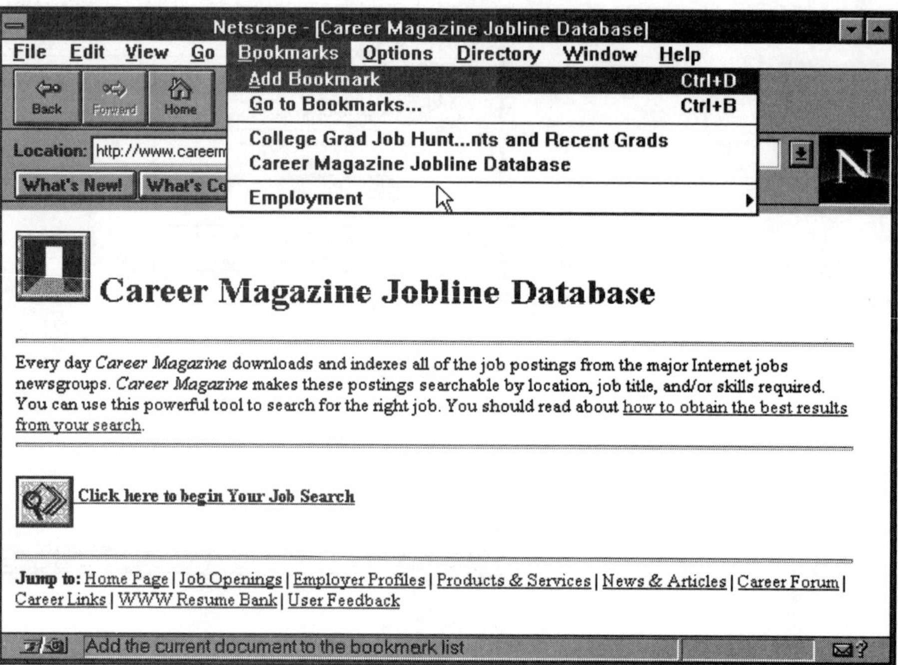

Figure 2.21

To rearrange bookmarks, folders, and separators:

1 Choose Go to Bookmarks from the Bookmarks menu.
The bookmarks window is displayed.

2 Select the Employment folder.

3 Drag the Employment folder to the top of the list of bookmarks and drop it.
Notice that the folder stays in its new location, as shown in Figure 2.22.

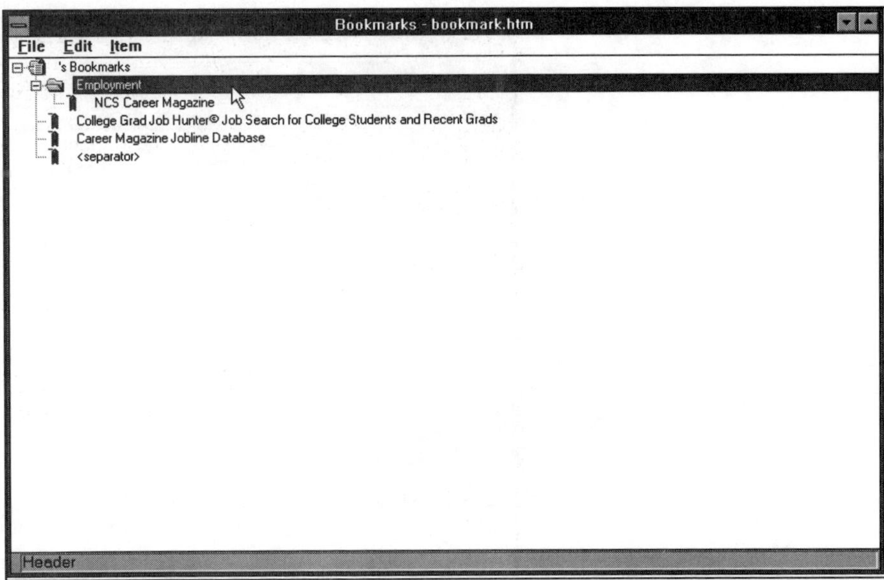

Figure 2.22

4 Select the separator (<separator>).

5 Drag the the separator to a new location and drop it.

Any rearranging you do in the Bookmarks window is reflected in the Bookmarks menu as well. The Employment folder is now the last item displayed in the Bookmarks menu.

6 Practice moving items around and rearranging items in the Bookmarks window. Try moving the NCS Career Magazine bookmark out of the Employment folder, and then put it back into the folder.

To delete folders and separators:

1 If it is not already displayed, go to the Bookmarks window.

2 Select the separator (<separator>).

3 Choose Delete from the Bookmarks window Edit menu, or simply type DEL
The separator disappears both from the Bookmarks window and the Bookmarks menu.

You can delete folders in the same way: You select a folder in the Bookmarks window, and then choose Delete from the Edit menu (or type DEL). Use caution, however, when deleting folders. The folder *and all its contents* disappear when deleted. If you inadvertently delete a folder containing bookmarks you wanted to keep, you can recover them by choosing Undo from the Edit menu, as shown in Figure 2.23. You can then drag any bookmarks you want to keep out of the folder before deleting it.

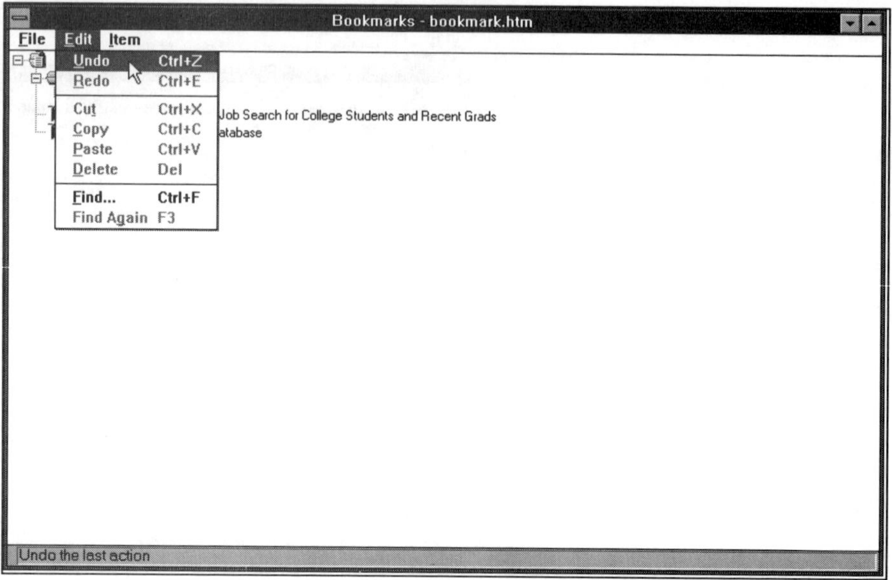

Figure 2.23

THE NEXT STEP

In this project you have acquired important skills for organizing your travels on the Web. You still have seen only a tiny glimpse of the vast amounts of information now available at your fingertips. The next step in your exploration of the Web is to learn to search for specific information. There is a wide variety of tools available on the Web designed specifically for locating Web pages for you. The Netscape Net Search and Net Directory pages provide links to a number of such tools. In the next project you will be formally introduced to search engines and directories, and you will become a fully qualified Web surfer.

This concludes Project 2. You can either exit Netscape or go on to work the Study Questions, Review Exercises, and Assignments.

SUMMARY AND EXERCISES

Summary

- Bookmarks permanently record the addresses of Web sites you visit often.
- To create a bookmark for the currently displayed page, select Add Bookmark from the Bookmarks menu.
- To create a bookmark for any Web site you have visited during the current session, open the History window, select the desired Web site from the list, and select Create Bookmark.

- To create a bookmark for a Web page referenced by a link, position the cursor over the link, click the right mouse button, and choose Add Bookmark for this Link from the pop-up menu.
- Bookmarks you have created are listed in the Bookmarks menu and in the Bookmarks window.
- You can edit the name, address, and description of a bookmark by selecting the bookmark in the Bookmarks window and using the Properties option on the Bookmarks window Item menu.
- You can delete a bookmark by selecting the bookmark in the Bookmarks window and choosing Delete from the Bookmarks window Edit menu.
- You can create folders and separators to organize your bookmarks using the Insert Folder and Insert Separator options on the Bookmarks window Item menu.
- You can rearrange bookmarks, folders, and separators by dragging them in the Bookmarks window.
- You can delete bookmarks, folders, and separators by selecting them in the Bookmarks window and choosing Delete from the Bookmarks window Edit menu.

Key Terms and Operations

Key Terms	Operations
bookmark	Create, delete, and edit bookmarks
folder	Arrange bookmarks
separator	Create folders and separators

Study Questions

Multiple Choice

1. Bookmarks differ from the history feature in that bookmarks
   a. must be created by the user.
   b. do not disappear at the end of each Netscape session.
   c. mark only those sites the user wishes to remember or revisit.
   d. All of the above.

2. When a folder in the bookmarks window is deleted, all bookmarks contained in that folder are
   a. moved up to the root level.
   b. deleted.
   c. saved in the bookmarks.ini file.
   d. None of the above.

3. A ______________ can be used to divide the bookmarks menu.
   a. divider　　c. separator
   b. line　　d. segmenter

4. Bookmarks may be created using the
   a. Bookmarks menu.
   b. pop-up menus.
   c. History window.
   d. All of the above.

5. The properties of a bookmark that can be edited include the
   a. name, URL, and location.
   b. URL, type, and date.
   c. name, URL, and description.
   d. URL, type, and frequency.

6. A pop-up menu can be accessed for any object on a Web page by using the
   a. SHIFT key.
   b. OPTION key.
   c. right mouse button.
   d. None of the above.

7. A pop-up menu can be used to
   a. navigate and create a bookmark.
   b. exit Netscape.
   c. print a Web page.
   d. All of the above.

8. Before you can delete a bookmark, you must __________ it in the Bookmarks window.
   a. identify
   b. select
   c. double-click
   d. save

9. To create a folder in the Bookmarks window, choose
   a. Add Folder from the Edit menu.
   b. New Folder from the Item menu.
   c. New Folder from the Edit menu.
   d. Insert Folder from the Item menu.

10. Bookmarks can be moved into a new folder by __________ them.
    a. moving
    b. selecting
    c. dragging
    d. editing

Short Answer

1. A ____________ will allow you to mark a Web page that you have never visited.

2. Creating a ____________ allows you to display related bookmarks in a submenu in the Bookmarks menu.

3. You can use a ____________ to create a line between groups of bookmarks displayed in the Bookmarks menu.

4. ___________ and ____________ are used to organize bookmarks.

5. Bookmarks, folders, and separators can be rearranged in the Bookmarks window by _____________ them to a new location.

6. A bookmark can be deleted only from the Bookmarks ___________.

7. Before a bookmark, folder, or separator may be deleted, it must be ____________.

8. Bookmarks contained in a folder in the Bookmarks window are displayed in a ______________ in the Bookmarks window.

9. A bookmark may be deleted using Delete in the Bookmarks window Edit menu or by typing _________.

10. Bookmarks are displayed in the ________________ menu.

For Discussion

1. How is creating bookmarks different from the history feature?
2. Why would you want to create folders to organize your bookmarks?
3. In what situations would you be most likely to want to rename a bookmark?

Review Exercises

Organize Your Job Search

1. Place all three of your employment-related bookmarks in the Employment folder.
2. Go to the Career Magazine Jobline Database page. Locate and select the Career Links text link. Bookmark employment Web pages you find.
3. Place the new bookmarks you have created in the Employment bookmarks folder.

Assignments

Folders Within Folders

Create two or three new bookmarks folders. Give these folders names that identify them as subcategories of Employment (for example, Job Searches, Corporations, Resume Banks). Place these new folders inside the Employment folder. Group your employment-related bookmarks into these new folders.

Separators Within Folders

Separate each folder contained in the Employment folder with a separator.

Project 3: Searching the Web

Objectives

After completing this project, you should be able to:

- Understand the difference between search engines and directories
- Find search engines and directories on the Web
- Use search engines and directories
- Interpret search results
- Find specific text on a Web page
- Use multiple browsers

Case Study: Searching for Jobs

You are finishing your undergraduate degree and preparing to enter the job market following graduation. In the last two projects you were inspired to learn how to get around on the World Wide Web (the Web) by the prospect of finding valuable employment information there. You now know how to surf the Web using Netscape Navigator, and you are ready to begin searching for employment information. But how do you *find* Web sites related to jobs or jobs in your specific field?

An Internet Solution

You already know that the Web is a vast virtual landscape. There are Web pages out there on just about any topic. In fact, there are well over a million Web pages currently in existence with hundreds more appearing each day. So with all that information out there, how do you sift through it to find information on something specific?

To search the Web for employment information, you must learn something about some Web tools called *search engines* and *directories*. In this project you will become an expert at using these powerful tools to search for any information on the Web.

WHAT ARE SEARCH ENGINES AND DIRECTORIES?

Search engines and ***directories*** are actually Web pages. These Web pages, however, have been designed for the express purpose of helping you find what you're looking for on the Web. Traditionally, the difference between a search engine and a directory has been its strategy for getting you to where you want to go; Search engines use a bottom-up strategy while directories use a top-down approach.

Search engines rely on you to provide the ***search parameters***. Rather than beginning with the broadest possible description of the information you want, you begin with a specific word or phrase. In this sense, you are starting your search at the most detailed level, or at the bottom. Hence, the term bottom-up search strategy. For example, you type a name, keyword, or concept for which to search using an interface like the one shown in Figure 3.1. While search engines work in a number of ways, searching document headers, document titles, the text of documents, or even other indexes or directories, they all rely on you to enter search parameters.

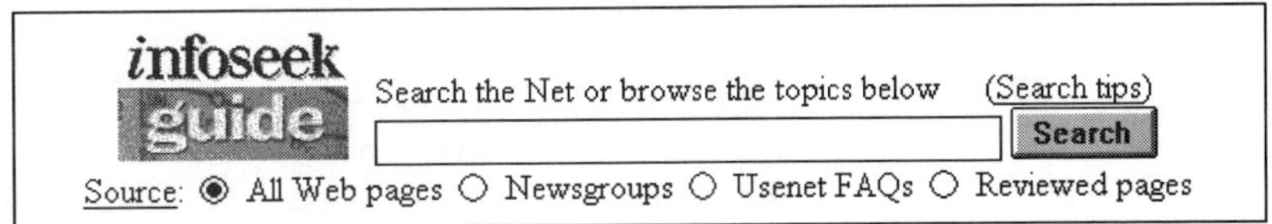

Figure 3.1

Directories, on the other hand, provide you with a number of ***topics*** from which to choose, as shown in Figure 3.2. The top-down ***search strategy*** of directories involves selecting a top-level category, like business, and working your way through subsequent menus of subtopics until you arrive at a list of Web sites matching your specific requirements. There is a great variety of directories available on the Web. Some directories are limited to a particular topic or field. Some cover the entire Internet.

• Arts	• Entertainment	• Money & Investing	• Regional
• Business	• Health & Medicine	• News & Reference	• Science
• Computing	• Hobbies	• Personal Home Pages	• Shopping
• Education	• Life & Style	• Politics & Law	• Sports

Figure 3.2

Like most things on the Web, the concepts of search engines and directories are in flux. Currently, most directories contain search engines, and many search engines have been augmented to include directories. Thus the traditional distinction between search engines and directories has become a bit fuzzy. In fact, Netscape is using nearly identical Web pages to display popular search engine and directory services, since most Internet search services offer both.

USING SEARCH ENGINES

In the last project you visited Web pages maintained by Netscape called Net Search and Net Directory. With these Web pages, Netscape makes it easy for you to access a host of good Web searching services. In this project you will visit the Net Search and Net Directory pages again. But this time you will dig in and do some exploring using the Internet search services linked to those pages.

Before you can begin using Internet search services, you must first start Netscape. This procedure is covered in the Overview if you need a refresher.

A Closer Look at Net Search

Net Search and Net Directory are both Web pages maintained by Netscape that provide access to a number of popular search services offered on the Internet. Net Search is a great place to start in getting your feet wet with search engines.

To access Net Search:

1 With Netscape running, select the Net Search button located below the Location field in the Netscape window.
The Net Search page appears similar to Figure 3.3. Notice that a number of search services are listed on tabs. At the time of this writing, these services included Infoseek Guide, Lycos, Magellan, Excite, and Yahoo!.

> ***Tip*** Another way to access the Net Search page is by choosing Internet Search from the Directory menu.

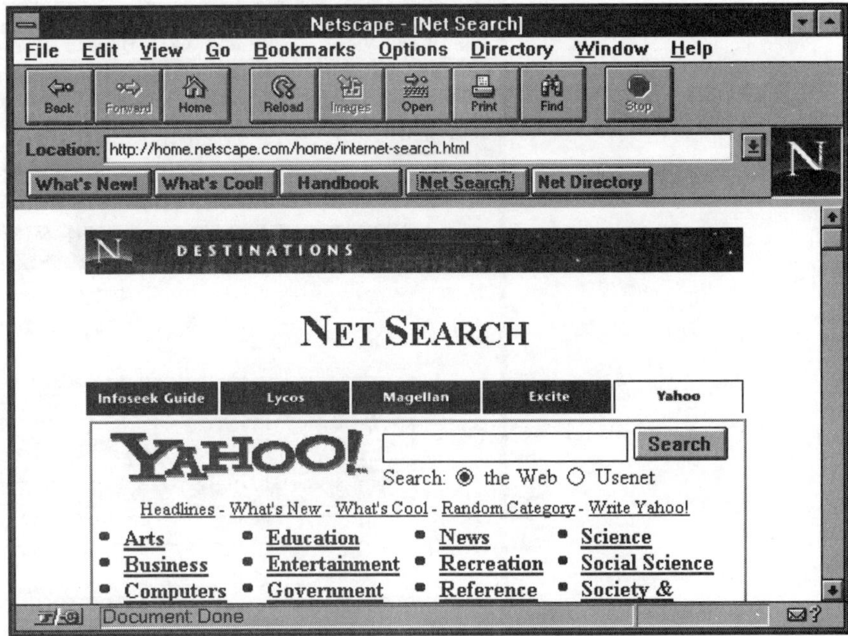

Figure 3.3

2 Using the vertical scroll bar, scroll down to find descriptions of all the search services linked to the Net Search page.

3 Read the descriptions of each search engine listed. When you have finished, scroll back to the top of the Net Search page.

4 Select the Infoseek Guide tab on the Net Search page.
A new Net Search page is loaded. This page contains a search interface linked directly to the Infoseek Guide service, as shown in Figure 3.4.

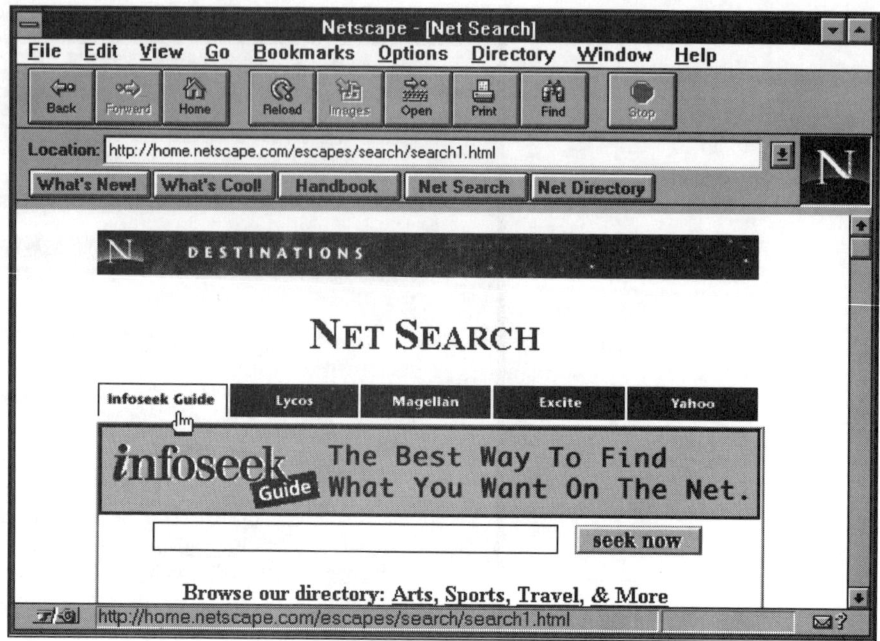

Figure 3.4

Jumping to the Infoseek Guide Search Engine

You can perform a search directly from the Net Search page using any of the search engines listed as tabs. Alternatively, you can jump directly to the home page of any of these search services using the links provided by Netscape.

To get to Infoseek Guide's search engine:

1 Select the Infoseek Guide logo on the currently displayed Net Search page (notice that it is a picture link).
Netscape takes you to the Infoseek Guide home page, as shown in Figure 3.5.

Figure 3.5

2 Scroll down to view the entire page.
Notice that, in addition to a search criteria field, Infoseek Guide also offers a directory. Infoseek Guide qualifies as both a search engine and a directory because it offers both a field for search parameters and a list of topics.

Using Infoseek Guide's Search Engine

You won't be learning to use all of the search engines linked to the Net Search page in this project. You will instead focus on learning to use just one of the search services, Infoseek Guide. Most search engines are functionally very similar, though, so once you've learned to use one, learning others will be a snap.

Infoseek Guide has provided some Basic Search Tips on its home page. These tips will help the uninitiated become familiar with the syntax used by Infoseek Guide for search parameters. Search Tips also offers a more detailed tutorial on how to perform different types of searches using the Infoseek Guide search engine. A link to this document is provided on the Infoseek Guide page.

Using search parameters in Infoseek Guide:

1 Locate the Search tips text link in the Basic Search Tips section of the Infoseek Guide page.

2 Click on the Search tips text link.
The Infoseek Guide Search Tips page appears as shown in Figure 3.6. Read through the search tips, using the vertical scroll bar as needed to view all of the text.

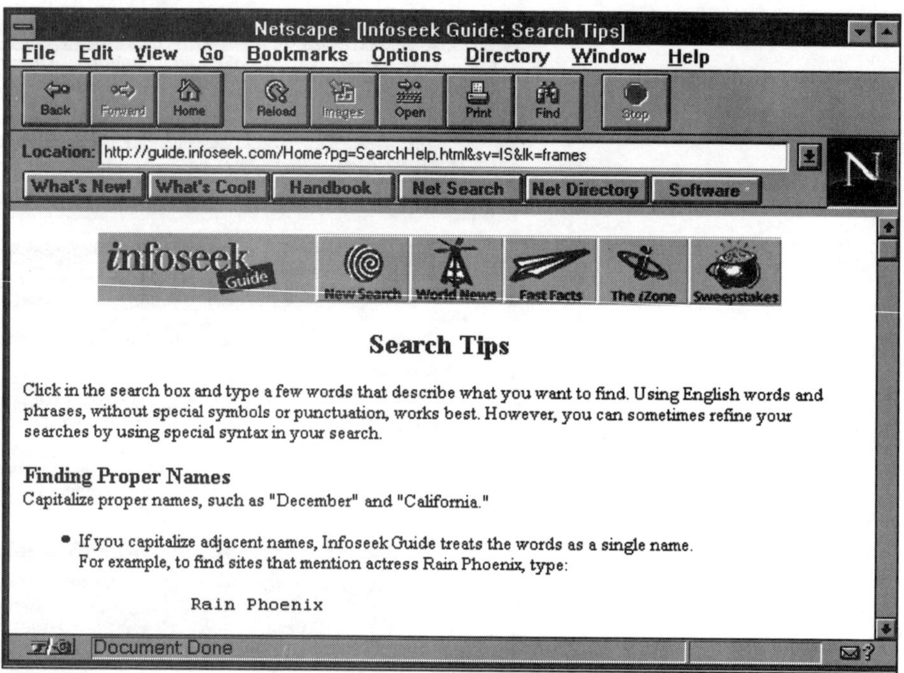

Figure 3.6

3 When you have finished going over the Infoseek Guide search tips, use the Back button to return to the Net Search page displaying the Infoseek Guide search interface.

You are now ready to enter search parameters in the Infoseek Guide search field. Recall that your original purpose in exploring the Web was to search for job opportunities in your field.

To search the Internet using Infoseek Guide:

1 Type `employment` in the Search for field on the Net Search page.

2 Select the Seek Now button, as shown in Figure 3.7.

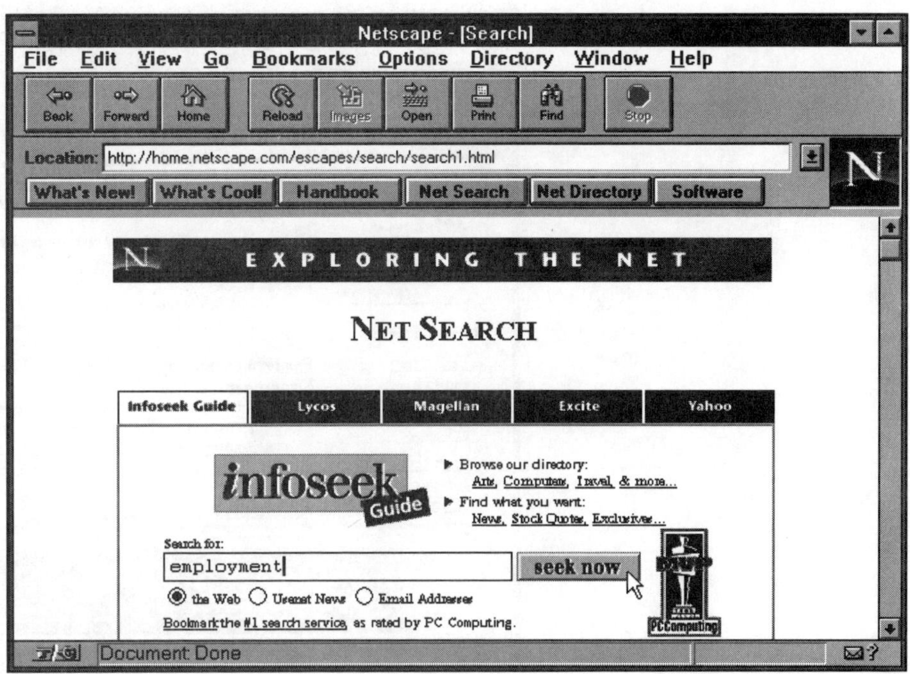

Figure 3.7

Infoseek Guide searches for the word *employment* among Web pages currently indexed in its database. Generally, the header, description, and body of documents are searched, although different search engines perform searches differently. After a brief delay, Infoseek Guide returns a search results page.

3 Scroll down a bit to begin to view the names and descriptions of documents matching your search parameter, as shown in Figure 3.8.

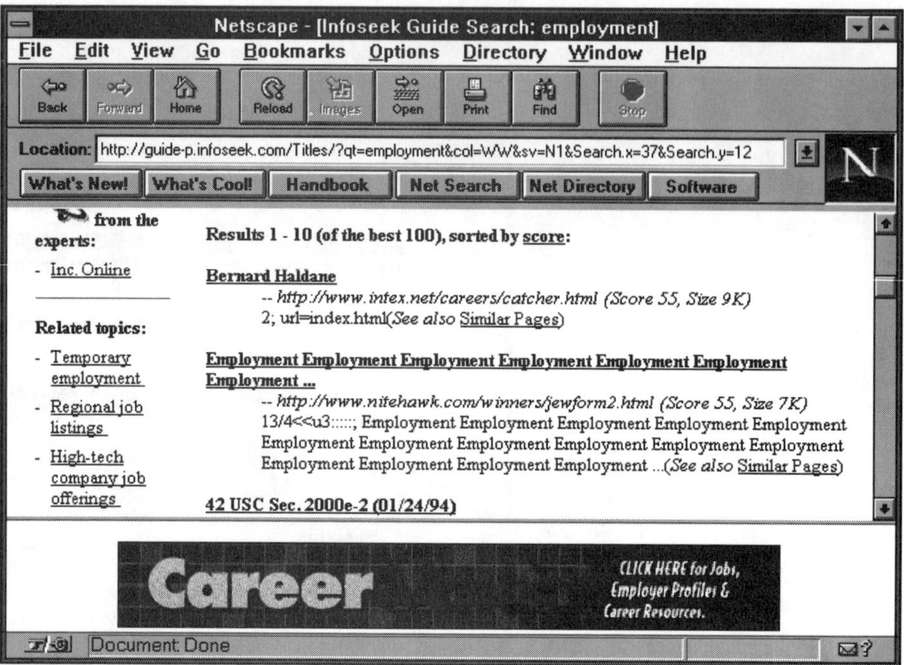

Figure 3.8

Searches often result in hundreds of "hits," that is, Internet documents matching your search parameters. Most search services handle this situation in the same way: They return a maximum of 100 documents and display those documents 10 at a time.

Because *employment* is a fairly common word, your search probably resulted in a list of 100 documents and your results page displays the first 10 documents on that list. Near the bottom of the results page is a text link that allows you to view the next 10 documents of the 100 returned.

To navigate through Infoseek Guide search results:

1 Scroll to the bottom of your results page.
As shown in Figure 3.9, a text link appears near the bottom of the page called Next 10 Results (11 - 20).

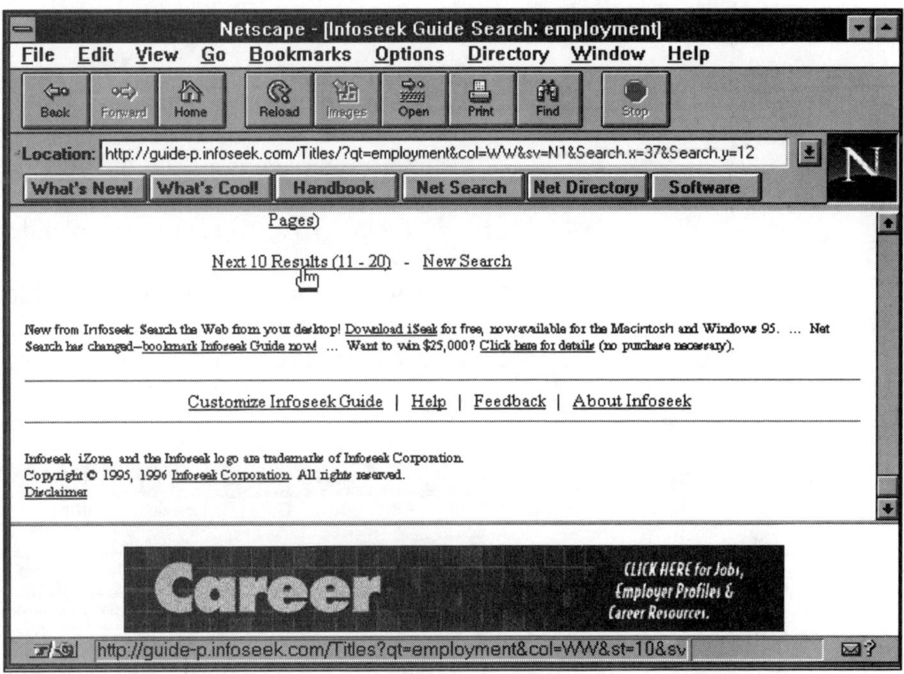

Figure 3.9

2 Click the Next 10 Results (11 - 20) link.
A new results page is loaded, displaying found documents 11 to 20. Notice that the text link at the bottom of the results page now reads Next 10 Results (21 - 30). An additional link reads Previous 10 Results. You will use text links like these to navigate through the results generated by most search engines.

> ***Note*** In some search services like Infoseek Guide, you can also use the Back and Forward buttons to navigate through your search results. Some search services, however simply update the same page with incremental search results. In such cases you cannot use the Back and Forward buttons to navigate through search results.

3 Continue navigating through the search results list using the Previous and Next text links.

4 Visit any employment related Web sites listed by clicking the titles.

5 When you have finished exploring, return to the first page of your Infoseek Guide search results (displaying documents 1 to 10) using the Back button or the history feature.

Interpreting Search Results

Generally, the descriptions of Web pages returned by search engines and directories are excerpts of material provided by Web page owners. While most document descriptions (as shown in Figure 3.10) give you a good idea of what a Web page is all about, these descriptions are sometimes quite cryptic and make little sense. Similarly, the document names (also pointed out in Figure 3.10) will leave you wondering how they wound up in your search results.

As shown in Figure 3.10, Infoseek Guide search results include several pieces of information designed to help you interpret and determine the quality of search results.

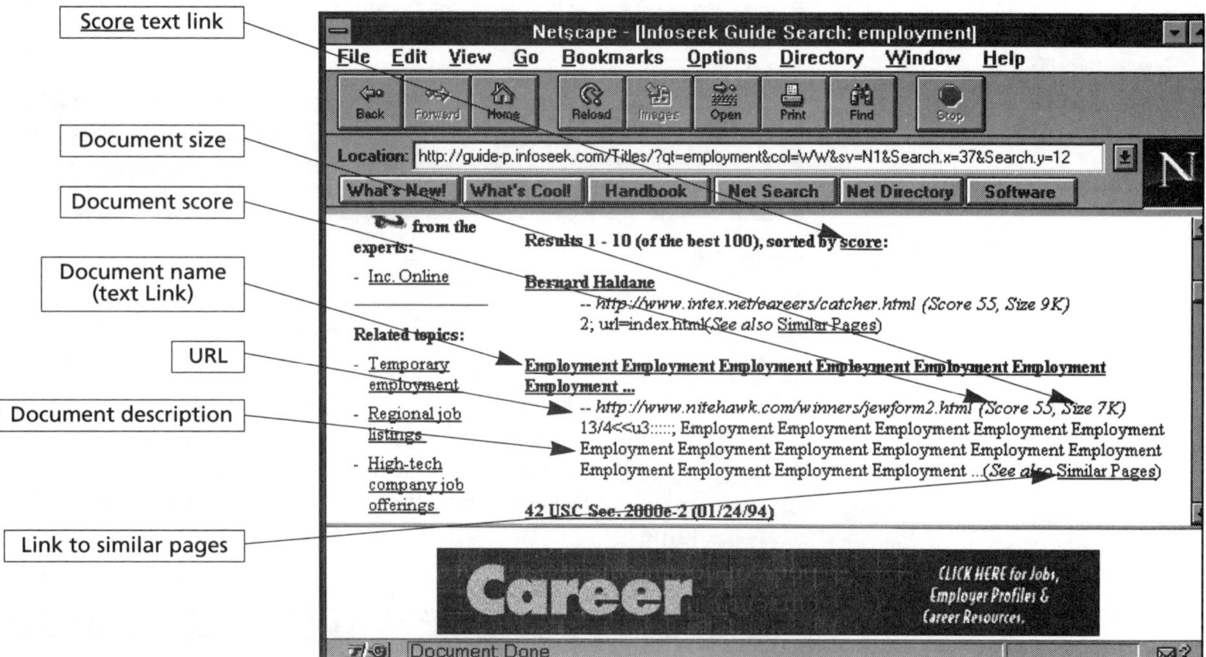

Figure 3.10

To understand document scores in search results:

1 Look at the scores of the first 10 documents listed in your search results.
The scores are probably relatively low (in the 50s) since the search parameter you entered was very general.

2 Locate the score text link near the top of the current search results page, as shown in Figure 3.10.

3 Click the score text link to get more information about Infoseek Guide scores.

Netscape takes you to the Infoseek Guide Scoring of Search Results page. Read through this page. It provides information on what the scores assigned to your search results mean. As you read this page, consider ways you might improve your search and raise the scores of your best results.

4 Return again to the Net Search page using the Back button or the history feature.

Improving the Quality of Search Results

The quality of your search results is a function of the quality and specificity of your search parameters, any filtering or reviewing performed by the managers of the search service, and the search strategy used by the search tool. Some search tools look only at the titles of documents, others search the text of all text links in the document, still others search the entire text of documents in their database. Often search results contain a lot of irrelevant information. For example, in the case of a full text search, a search parameter like *cat* (referring to a household feline) would return documents containing the word *cat*. However, it would also return documents containing the words *caterpillar*, *catch*, *education*, *vacation*, and so on. These results are not particularly helpful.

You already looked over Infoseek Guide's search parameter syntax on the Search Tips page. The guidelines provided there are an important resource for posing specific queries that will weed out most of the sites not applicable to your search. For example, to improve the results of your *cat* search, you might use a phrase enclosed in quotes to indicate the words must appear next to each other: "house cat". You might try using a more specific word such as *feline*. You could use a plus sign (+) to indicate that a word must appear in the results, as in *feline +pet*. You might even try eliminating some irrelevant results by using a minus sign to specify words that should not appear in the results, as in *cat -hobie*.

There are a few basic things to consider when performing searches. Read any help screens provided by the search engine, and familiarize yourself with the search parameter syntax used by the search tool.

- Be as specific as possible.
- Try to avoid words that are very general or common.
- Don't use plural forms.
- Remember that no matter how complex and sophisticated your search parameters, you can always expect a few surprises in your search results.

So, capitalize on the good hits—similar documents on the subject are often linked together. Finally, use bookmarks freely to avoid losing those really good hits!

Visiting Other Search Engines

There are other search engines available on the Net Search page, including Excite, Lycos, Magellan, and Yahoo!. Netscape is continuously updating its Net Search page to include links to Internet search tools that they feel are particularly useful, so the Net Search page you see may include tools not shown in Figure 3.11.

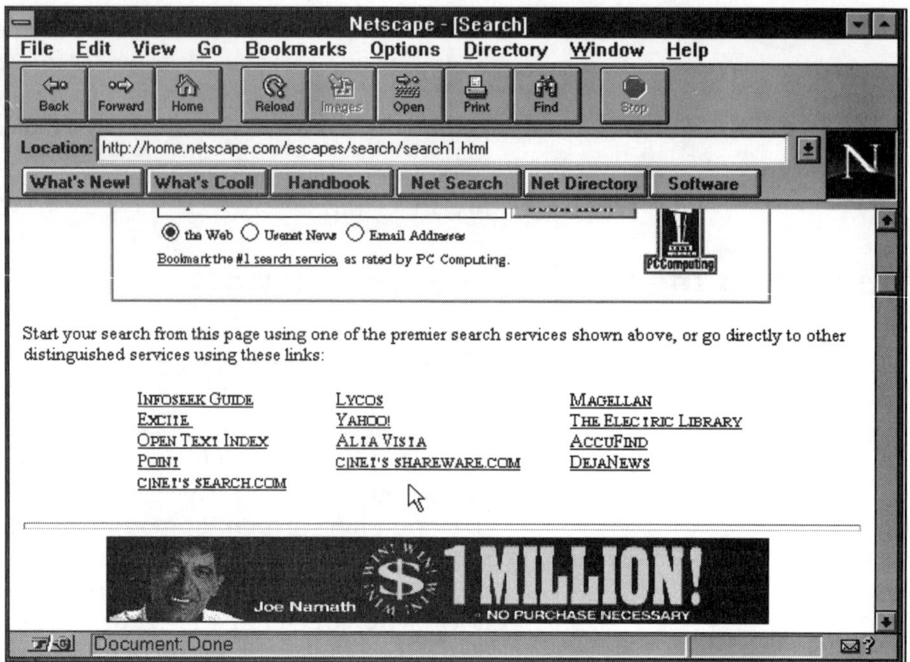

Figure 3.11

To access other search engines:

1 Scroll down the Net Search page until you come to a list of search services like the one shown in Figure 3.11.

2 Scroll down further and locate the description of Yahoo!, as shown in Figure 3.12.

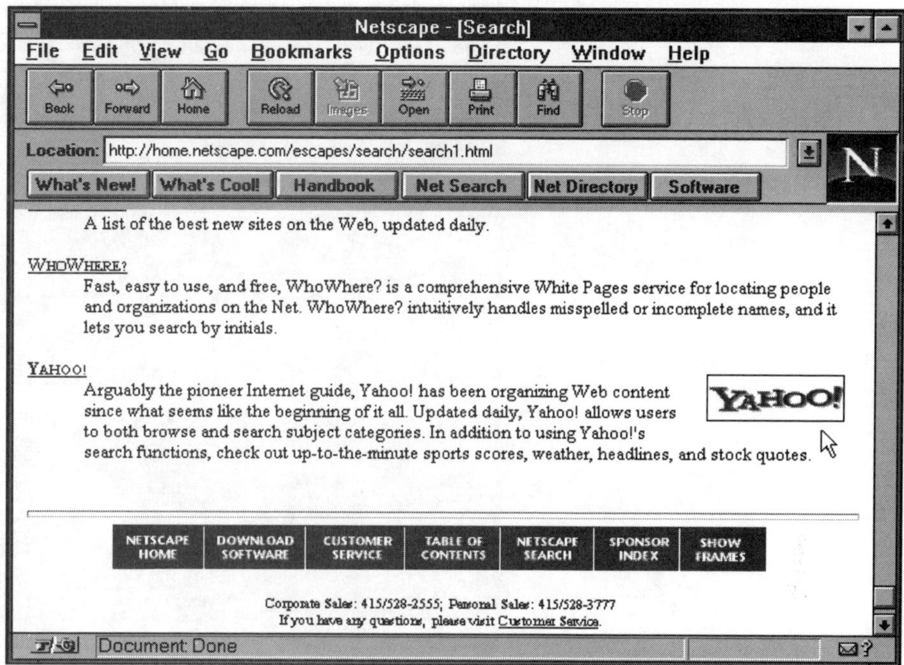

Figure 3.12

3 Read the description of Yahoo!.

4 Click the Yahoo! text or picture link.

Netscape takes you to the Yahoo! search service, as shown in Figure 3.13. Notice the similarities between Yahoo! and Infoseek Guide. Both provide a field for entering search parameters and also a list of topics from which to choose.

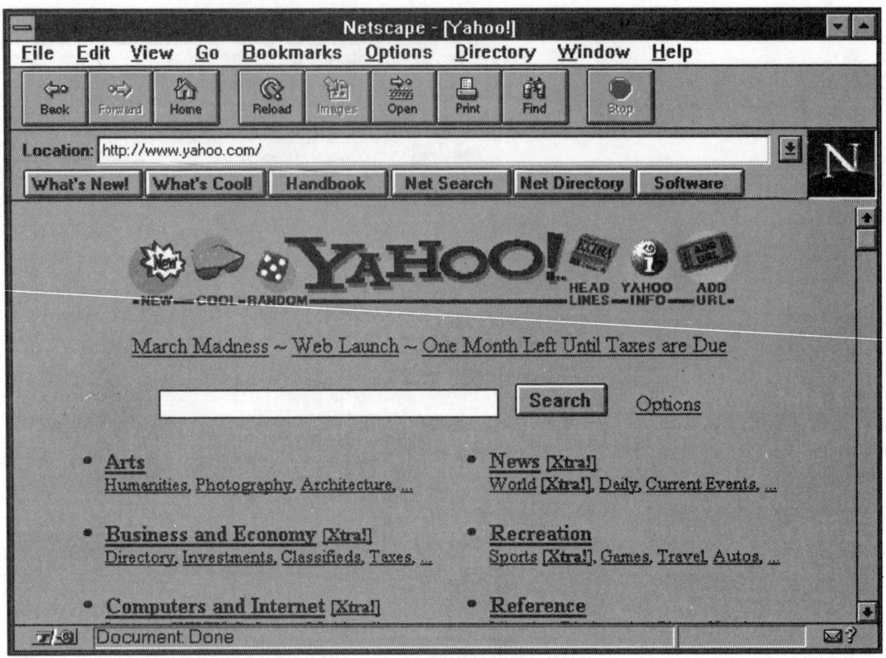

Figure 3.13

Remember The Web is constantly changing. The Web pages you see on your screen will very likely look different than those shown in this book.

If necessary, you can take a break at this point. When you come back, just start up Netscape Navigator and proceed.

USING DIRECTORIES

You have seen most of the popular search engines available on the Web, and learned to use one tool linked to the Net Search page, Infoseek Guide, to perform key word searches. Now you will learn to use an Internet directory that is linked to the Net Search page.

Using the Net Directory Page

Net Directory is a Web page maintained by Netscape that provides the same access to popular search services available on the Net Search page. In fact, the Net Search and Net Directory pages are nearly identical, and both are titled Net Search. This is because most search services now offer both a search engine and a directory. Net Directory is a good starting point from which to learn about directories.

To access Net Directory:

Net Directory

1 Select the Net Directory button located below the Location field in the Netscape window.

The Net Directory page appears similar to the page shown in Figure 3.14. Excite is the default search service. At the time of this writing, Netscape was rotating default status among all of the search services listed on the tabs. So the default search service displayed on your screen may not be Excite.

> ***Tip*** Another way to access the Net Directory page is by selecting Internet Directory from the Directory menu.

Like Infoseek Guide, Excite provides both directory and search engine tools. Excite's search engine functions much like that provided by Infoseek Guide. Here we will focus on Excite's directory.

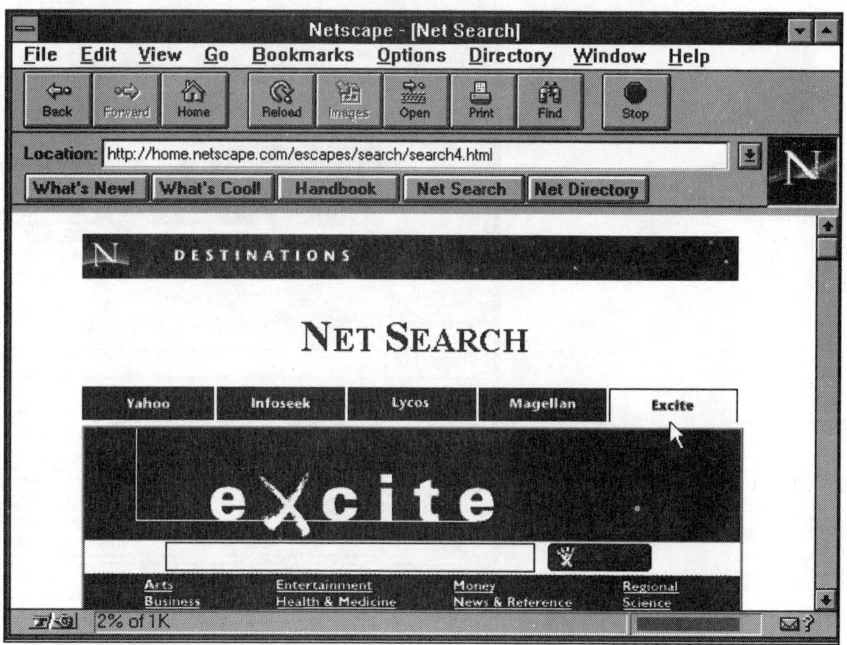

Figure 3.14

2 If it is not already selected, select the Excite tab on the Net Directory page to display the search interface to Excite.

Jumping to Excite's Directory

You can perform a search directly from the Net Directory page using any of the search services listed as tabs. Alternatively, you may jump directly to the home page of any of these search services using the links provided by Netscape.

To get to Excite's directory:

1 Select the Excite logo picture link on the currently displayed Excite Net Directory page.
Netscape takes you to the Excite home page, something like the one shown in Figure 3.15.

At the time this book was written, Excite's home page appeared as shown in Figure 3.15. But chances are the home page you see is not the same. (Can you guess why?) Functionally, however, Excite will not have changed much.

The Excite search engine is currently displayed, but Excite also offers a directory (see the pointer in Figure 3.15). Like Infoseek Guide, Excite qualifies as both a search engine and a directory because it offers both a field for search parameters and a list of topics.

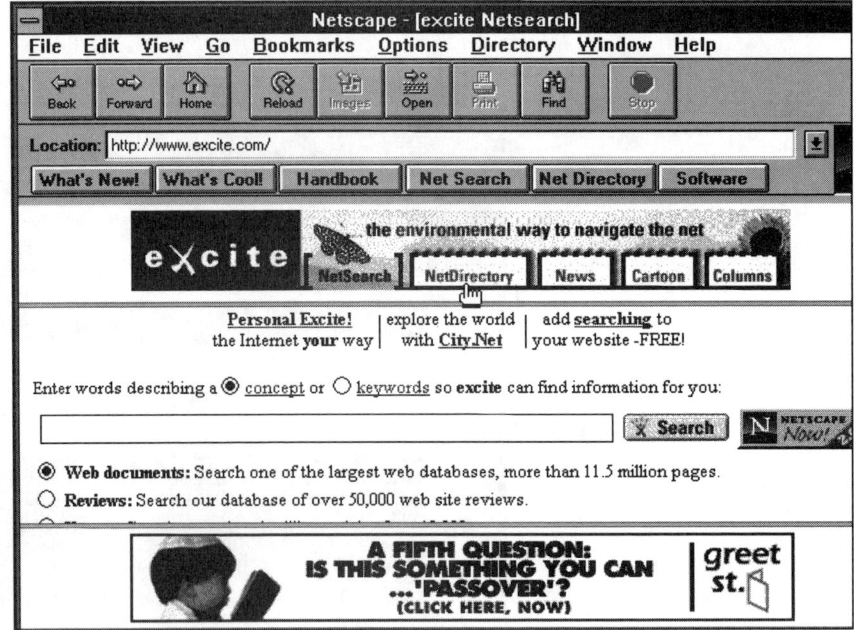

Figure 3.15

2 Select the NetDirectory tab, as shown in Figure 3.15.
Excite's directory page is loaded and displayed.

3 Scroll down to view the list of directory topics displayed on the Excite NetDirectory page, as shown in Figure 3.16.

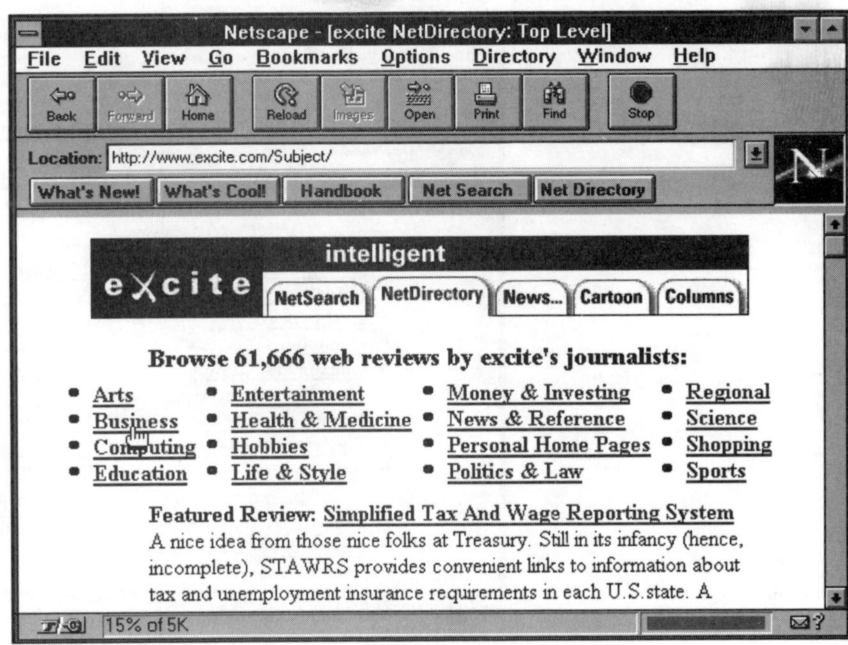

Figure 3.16

Using the Excite Directory

As was the case with search engines, you won't be learning to use all of the directories linked to the Net Directory page in this project. You will instead focus on learning to use just one of the directories, Excite. You will find that most other directories are functionally similar, and learning to use others will be a snap.

To begin an Excite directory search:

1 Select the Excite Business topic, as shown in Figure 3.16.
An Excite directory page listing the available topics under the Business topic is loaded and displayed.

2 Use the vertical scroll bar to view Excite's Business subtopics, as shown in Figure 3.17.

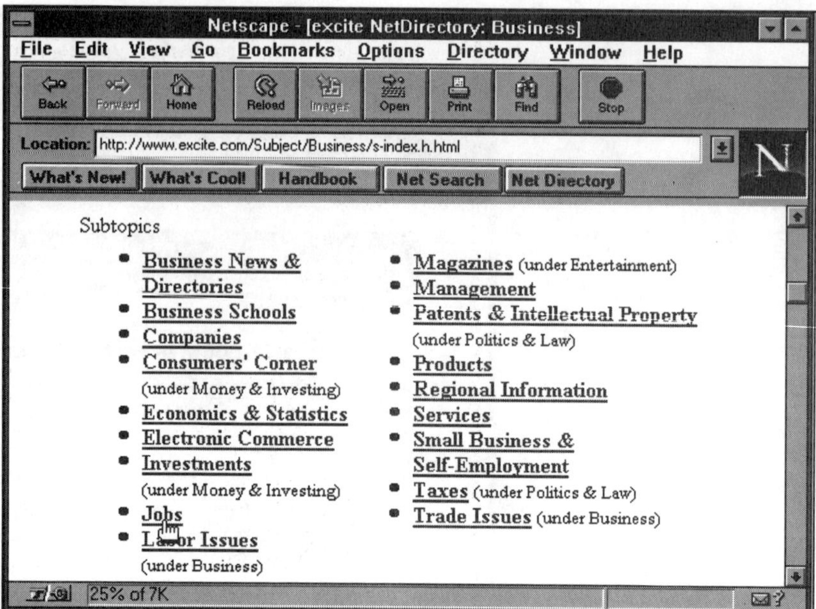

Figure 3.17

You are now ready to continue your Excite directory search by selecting a subtopic of Business. Recall that your original purpose in exploring the Web was to search for job opportunities in your field.

3 Select Jobs from Business subtopics listed.
Excite displays a Jobs subtopics page.

4 Scroll down to view all of the Jobs subtopics listed, as shown in Figure 3.18.

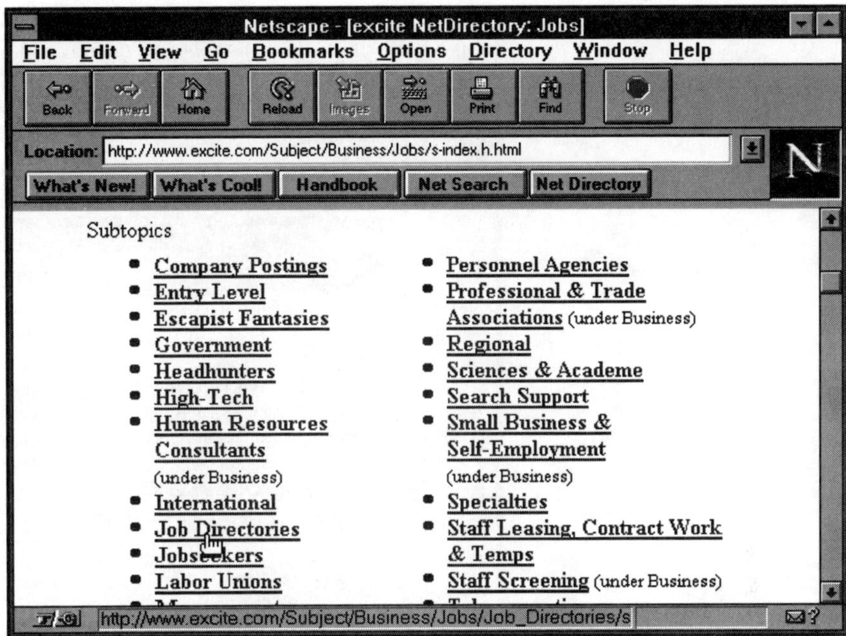

Figure 3.18

5 Select Job Directories from Jobs subtopics listed, as shown in Figure 3.18.
Excite displays a list of reviewed Job Directories Web sites. From this list you can select links to any one of the Web sites listed.

To navigate through Excite directory search results:

1 Scroll down to view all of the Web site reviews. Use the descriptions provided for each site to help you decide if it is worth a visit.

2 If it is displayed as shown in Figure 3.19, select The Job Web from the Excite list of reviewed Job Directories sites. If The Job Web is not in the list, select another site that sounds like it might be helpful in your job search.

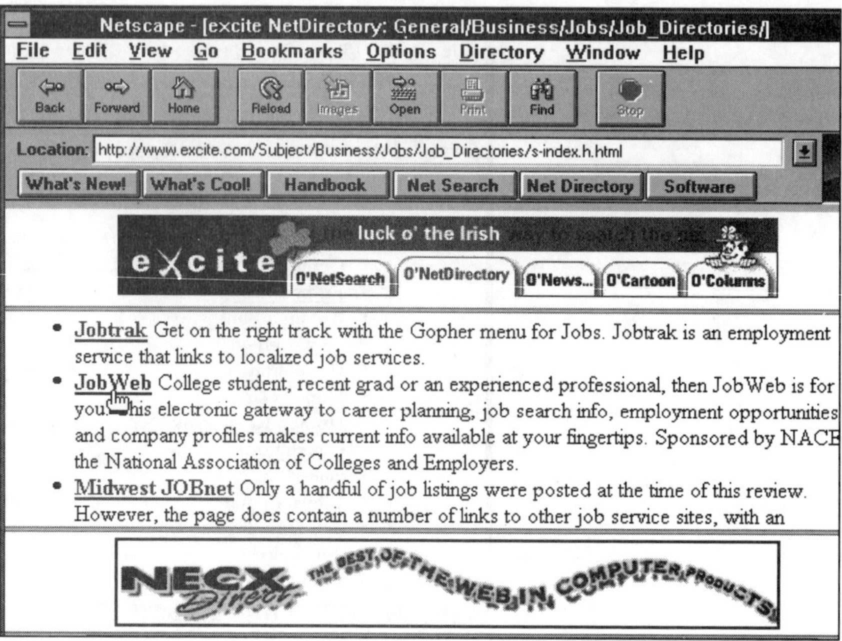

Figure 3.19

If you were able to select the link to The Job Web, Netscape delivers you to The Job Web home page shown in Figure 3.20.

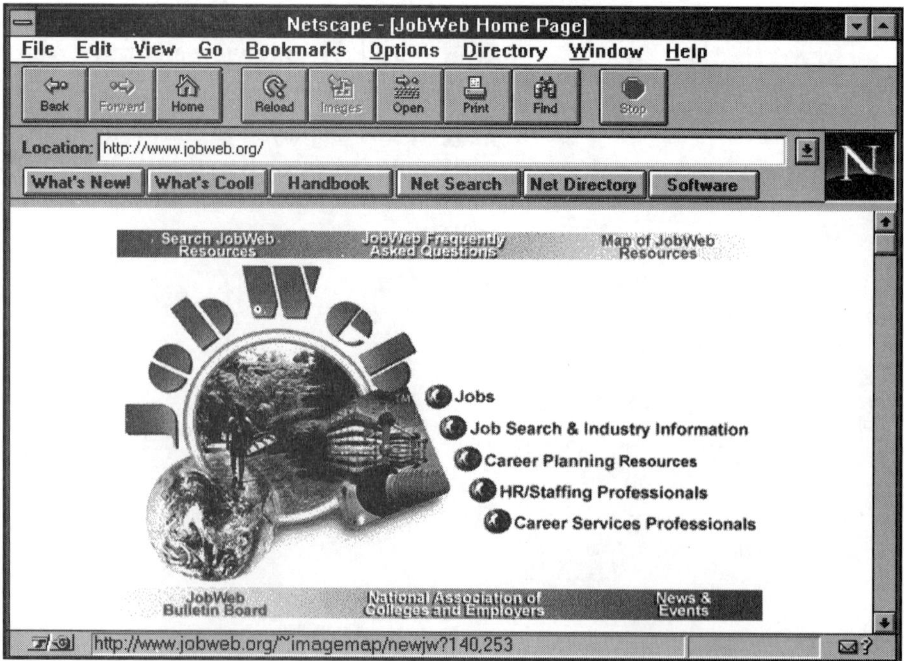

Figure 3.20

3 Explore the The Job Web site by clicking on links displayed on its home page.

> ***Tip*** Remember to use the Back and Forward buttons and the history feature to help you explore the JobWeb site , to explore other employment sites listed in your search results, and to explore other topics within the Excite Jobs category.

4 When you have finished exploring The Job Web site, or any other jobs-related sites you have visited using the Excite directory search results, select the Net Directory button or use the history feature to return to the Net Directory page.

Visiting Other Directories

Other search engines are available on the Net Directory page, including A2Z, Point, Magellan, and Open Text Index. Netscape is continuously updating its Net Directory page to include links to Internet search tools they feel are particularly useful, so the Net Directory page you see may include other tools, too.

To access other directories:

1 Scroll down the Net Directory page until you come to the list of Internet search services accompanied by descriptions and picture links to each.

2 Scroll down further and locate the description of Magellan, as shown in Figure 3.21.

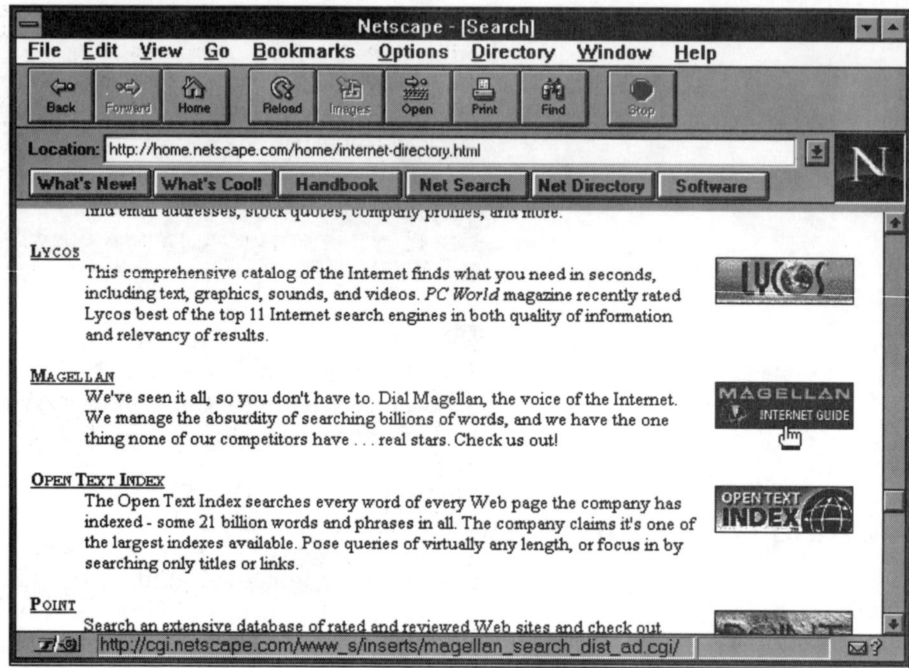

Figure 3.21

3 Read the description of Magellan, then click the Magellan text or picture link.

Netscape takes you to the Magellan search service, as shown in Figure 3.22. (Recall that Magellan was also one of the tabs available at the top of the Net Directory page.)

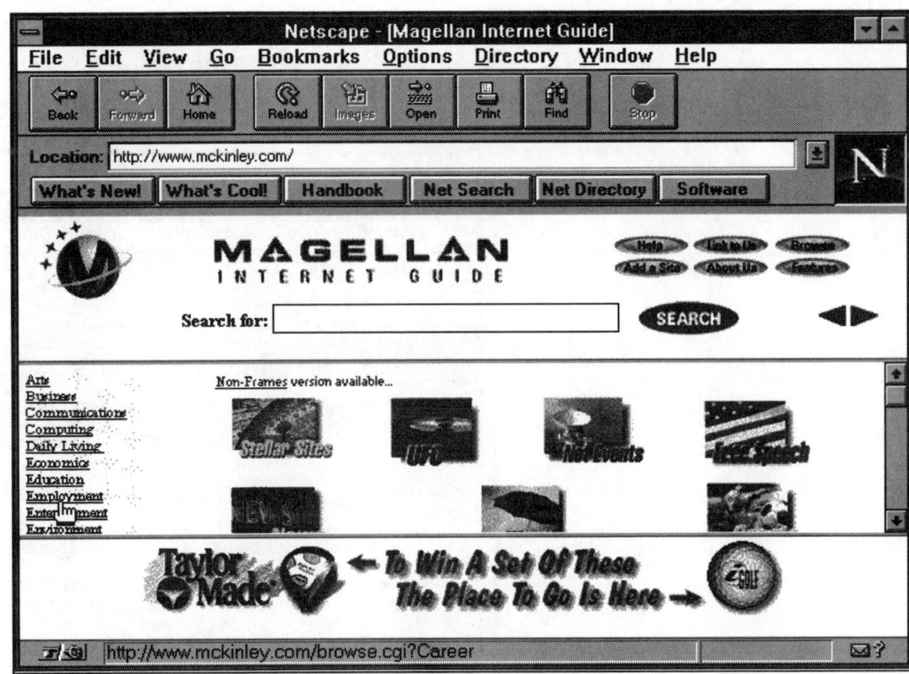

Figure 3.22

Like Excite and Infoseek Guide, Magellan provides both a search field and a directory of topics.

4 Scroll through the list of Magellan directory topics.
Notice that Magellan offers an Employment topic.

If necessary, you can take a break at this point. When you come back, just start up Netscape Navigator and proceed.

SEARCHING FOR TEXT ON A WEB PAGE

In addition to searching for Internet documents on specific topics, you will frequently need to search for specific text in a document you are viewing. As you know, Web pages can be very long documents, the equivalent of many printed pages. What if you want to find a particular word or phrase within such a document? The Find button on the Netscape toolbar is available for just that purpose—finding text on a Web page.

To use the Find button:

1 Go to the Netscape Handbook.

> ***Tip*** You can either use the Handbook button or select the Handbook option from the Help menu.

2 In the Tutorial section of the Netscape Navigator Handbook page, select the Learn Netscape text link, as shown in Figure 3.23.

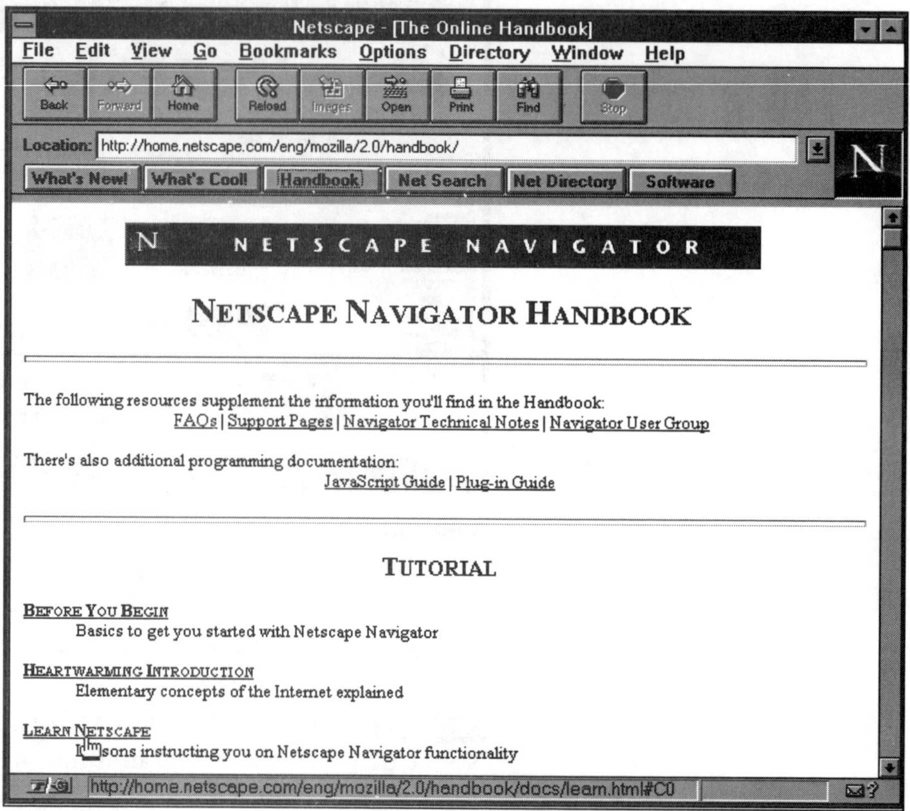

Figure 3.23

3 Scroll through the Handbook: Learn Netscape page that is displayed. Notice that this is one of those Web pages that is very long and contains a great deal of text. At the top of the page is a table of contents made of text links that, when selected, will take you to different points within the document.

Let's look for some reference to the Find button in this table of contents. At the time of this writing, there was no specific reference to the Find button in the table of contents. Chances are, however, that the Find button is discussed in this section. It's just a matter of finding it! This is where the Find button comes in.

4 Select the Find button on the toolbar.
As shown in Figure 3.24, the Find dialog appears. Notice that this dialog box allows you to determine whether Netscape will find only text that matches the case (uppercase and lowercase letters) of the text you enter. It also allows you to determine the direction in which Netscape will search the document: going down from the top or going up from the bottom.

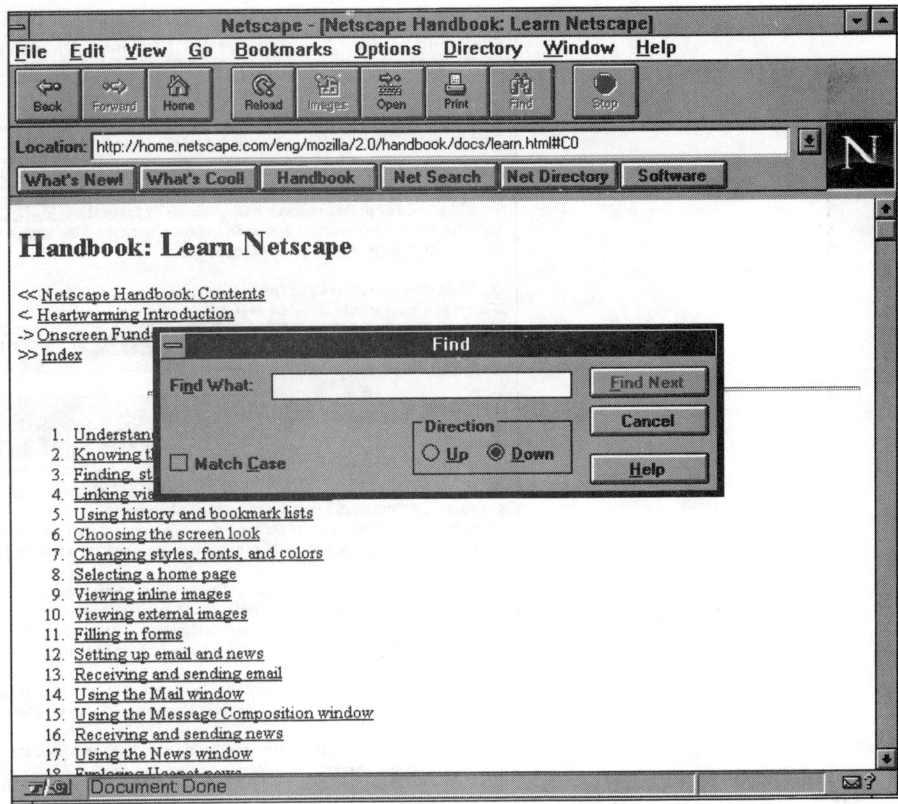

Figure 3.24

> ***Tip*** There are other ways to access the Find dialog box. You can choose Find from the Edit menu, or you can press CTRL + F

5 Type **`Find button`** in the Find What field.

6 Select the Find Next button.

As shown in Figure 3.25, Netscape locates and selects the first occurrence of the text you entered. Notice that you have located a tutorial on using the Find button.

> ***Tip*** You may need to move the Find dialog out of the way to see the found text. Do this by using the mouse to drag the Find dialog box by its title bar.

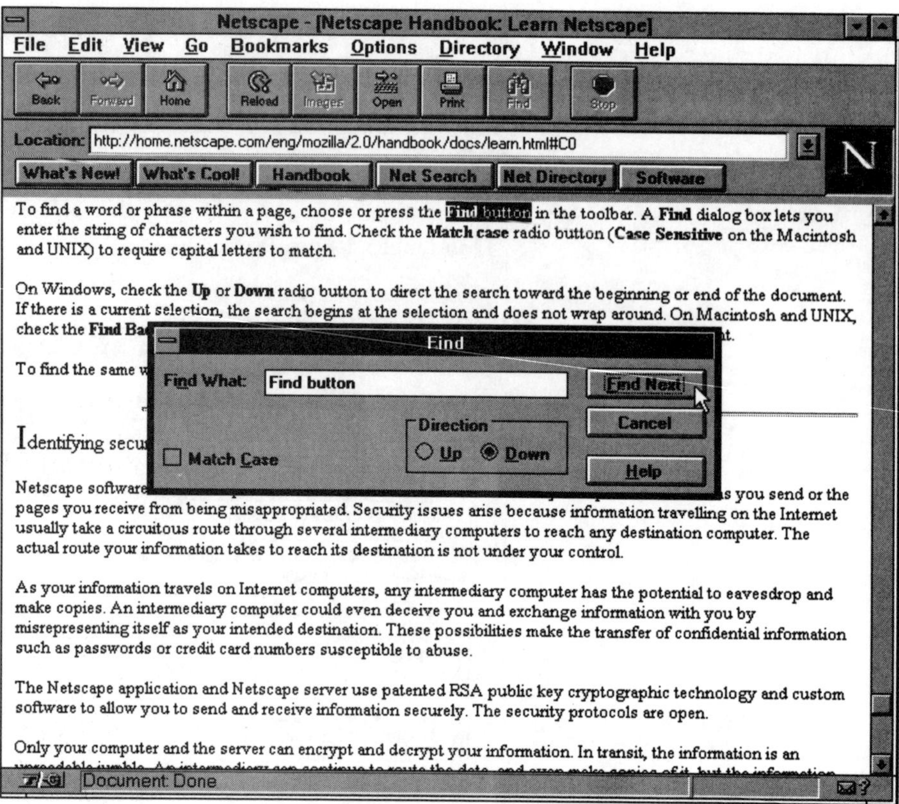

Figure 3.25

7 Select the Find Next button again to see if any other occurrences of *Find button* are in this document.

> ***Tip*** You can still use the Find Next function even when the Find dialog is not displayed. Simply press F3.

When Netscape has located all occurrences of the given text, it displays the Search String Not Found dialog box shown in Figure 3.26.

Figure 3.26

8 Select the OK button in the Search String Not Found dialog box.

9 Select the Cancel button on the Find dialog box to exit the Find function.

VISITING MULTIPLE LOCATIONS AT ONCE

Often when you are searching for information on the Web, you will want to follow a link but keep the original page up at the same time. Or you may be loading a graphics-intensive page (which is taking forever) and you'd like to make yourself useful while you wait. These are times when Netscape's New Web Browser function comes in handy. New Web Browser actually allows you to open more than one Netscape window at once and to display different Web pages in each one.

To open a New Web Browser:

1 Choose New Web Browser from the File menu, as shown in Figure 3.27.

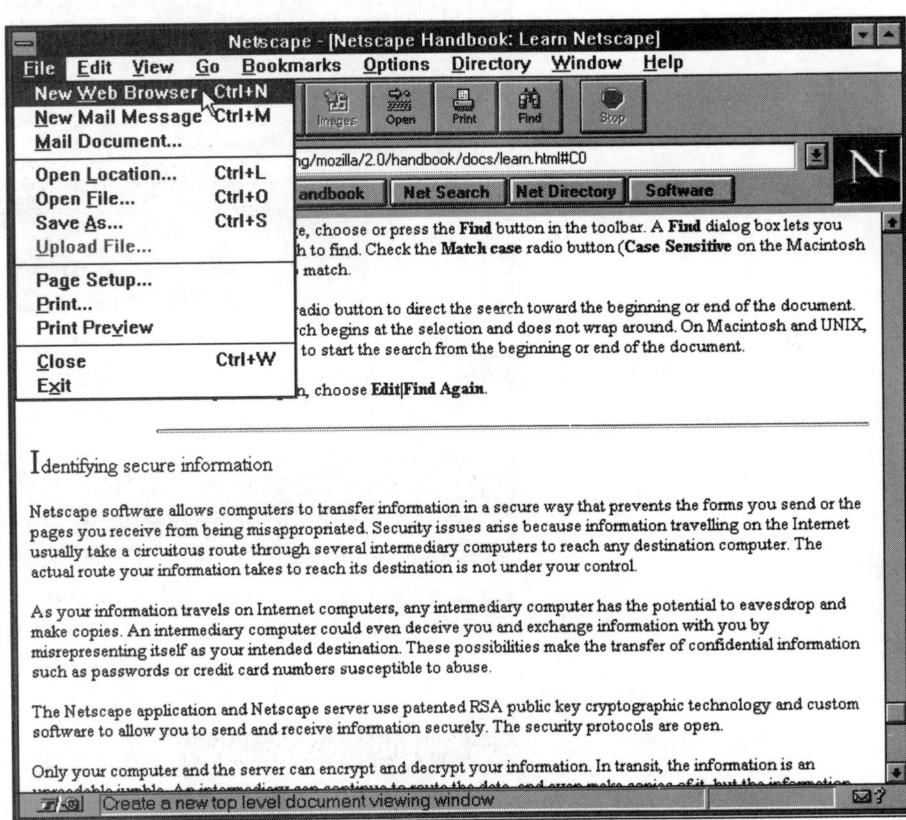

Figure 3.27

A new Netscape window opens, and the default startup page is loaded. Now both the Handbook: Learn Netscape and the Netscape startup pages are displayed in different windows.

> ***Tip*** You can also open a new Web browser by pressing CTRL + N

The number of Web browser windows that you can use at one time is limited by your Windows configuration, the type of communication line you are using, and the horsepower of the computer you are using. Generally speaking, four or five Web browser windows running at once will bog down both your communication link and your computer. A more reasonable number is two or three Web browser windows running at once.

To switch between Web browsers:

1 Choose Window from the menu bar on either of the open browser windows.

Notice that the names of both currently displayed Web pages are now listed at the bottom of the Window menu, as shown in Figure 3.28. The checked item is the name of the Web page in the currently active window.

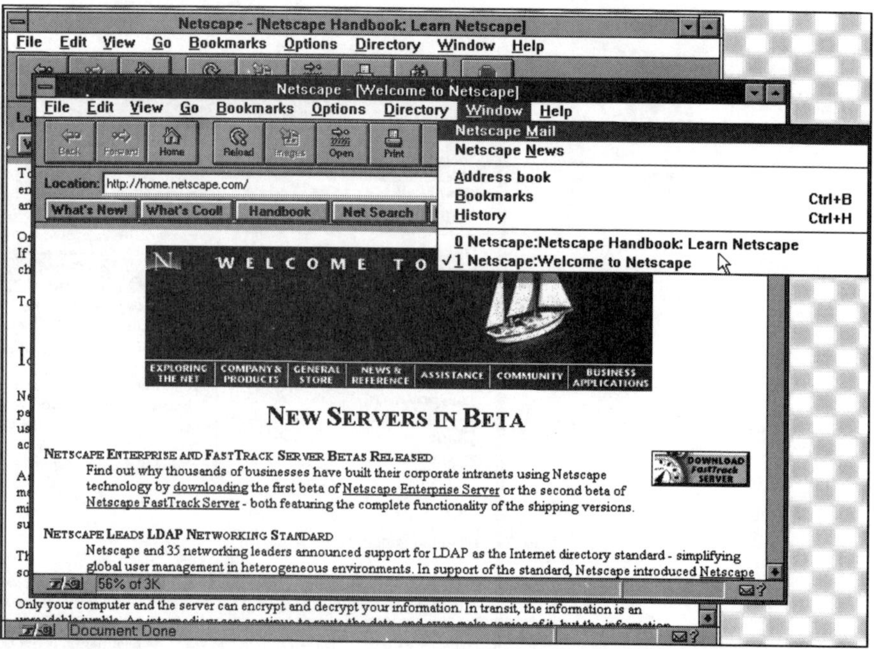

Figure 3.28

2 Choose the Learn Netscape option.

The Web browser window displaying the Netscape Handbook: Learn Netscape page is brought to the front and made the active window.

> ***Tip*** Another way to switch between open Web browsers is to press CTRL + TAB

With multiple browsers open, you are free to navigate in each one simultaneously. While one browser is loading a Web page, you can be reading a document displayed in another window, or even loading other Web pages. When a computer application allows you to do several things at once like this, it is called ***multitasking***.

To close Web browser windows:

1 Choose Close from the File menu on either of the open Web browser windows, as shown in Figure 3.29.
The currently active Web browser window closes. Notice that Netscape is still running in the remaining Web browser window. It is important to note that if you close the last remaining Web browser window, the effect is the same as exiting Netscape.

> ***Tip*** There are two other methods for closing Web browser windows. You can press CTRL + W or ALT + F4, or you can double-click the control-menu box in the upper-left corner of the window.

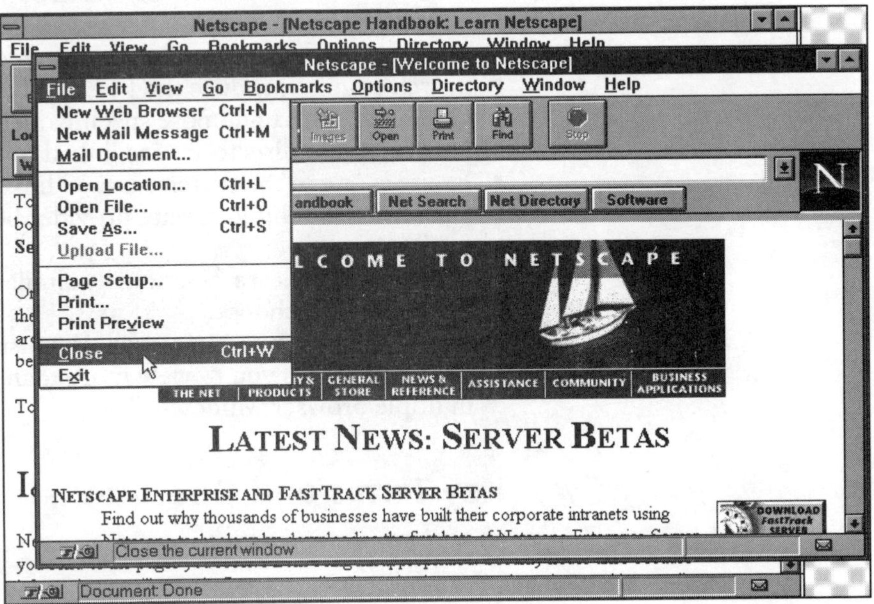

Figure 3.29

THE NEXT STEP

So far you have learned to get around on the Web using Netscape. You have learned to speed up your travels and how to use bookmarks to keep track of places you've been. In this project you have learned to search for specific information on the Web using two different types of tools—search engines and directories—and the Find function. You've even learned how to view more than one Web page at a time using multiple Web browsers. Now its time to look at some other Internet tools that Netscape offers. In the next project you will learn to use Netscape to send and even receive electronic mail.

This concludes Project 3. You can either exit Netscape or go on to work the Study Questions, Review Exercises, and Assignments.

SUMMARY AND EXERCISES

Summary

- Search engines and directories are special Web pages designed to help you find information on the Web.
- Directories use a top-down search strategy, starting with topics.
- Search engines use a bottom-up strategy starting with key word(s).
- Many popular search engines are linked to Netscape's Net Search page.
- Most search engines are functionally similar and easy to use.
- Infoseek Guide is one of the search services linked to the Net Search page.
- Infoseek Guide contains both a search engine and a directory.
- Search engines produce the best results when you learn to use the search parameter syntax and pose specific queries.
- Many popular directories are linked to Netscape's Net Directory page.
- Excite is one of the search services linked to the Net Directory page.
- Like Infoseek Guide, Excite provides both a directory and a search engine.
- Most directories are functionally similar, providing nested lists of topics from which to choose.
- You can find text within a Web page using the Find function.
- Netscape allows you to view more than one Web page at a time using multiple browser windows.

Key Terms and Operations

Key Terms

directory
multitasking
search engine
search parameter
search strategy
topic

Operations

Search by key word(s)
Search by topic
Use search parameter syntax
Navigate through search results
Interpret search results
Find text
Open New Web Browser

Study Questions

Multiple Choice

1. Search engines and directories are
   a. used to help locate specific information on the Web.
   b. Web pages.
   c. sometimes both included in Internet search tools.
   d. All of the above.

2. Search engines work best when
   a. very general, common words are used for search parameters.
   b. search parameters are posed in plural form.
   c. you wish to perform a search based on a key word or phrase.
   d. All of the above.

3. Infoseek Guide has its own ________________ that helps users improve the quality of search results.
   a. search parameter syntax
   b. autosearch strategy language
   c. query domain language
   d. context-sensitive query form

4. The Find function in Netscape allows you to locate
   a. Web pages on specific topics.
   b. all of the Web pages you have viewed during the current session.
   c. specific words or phrases within a Web document.
   d. None of the above.

5. ____________ is a popular search service available on the Web.
   a. WebSpan
   b. CyberScape
   c. Yahoo!
   d. Columbus

6. Directories are used to perform ____________ searches.
   a. categorical
   b. key word
   c. proper name
   d. phrase

7. Loading multiple Web documents simultaneously using multiple browser windows is called
   a. supercomputing.
   b. multileveling.
   c. multitasking.
   d. lots of fun.

8. When searching the Web, remember that __________ documents are often linked together.
   a. unrelated
   b. similar
   c. incompatible
   d. special

9. When search parameters are carefully composed,
   a. search results will include only documents of interest.
   b. all irrelevant information will be eliminated from search results.
   c. search results may still include unwanted information.
   d. None of the above.

10. Different search engines may search the
   a. document header.
   b. entire text of the document.
   c. document's text links.
   d. All of the above.

Short Answer

1. A ________________ uses key words provided by the user to perform its searches.

2. Search services allow you to find _____________ information on the Internet.

3. You may view more than one Web page at a time using the _____________________ function.

4. A ___________________ is sometimes used to indicate the confidence a search service has that the document is of interest.

5. You may locate specific text on a Web page using the ________ function.

6. _______________ are designed to perform categorical searches.

7. Search results pages generally provide __________ to the documents listed.

8. __________ was a pioneer of Internet search services and is still among the premier search services available on the Web.

9. When performing searches on the Web, it is often helpful to use _____________ to avoid losing documents of interest.

10. Most search services provide a brief _____________ of each document in the search results list.

For Discussion

1. Describe some situations when it makes more sense to use a directory to perform an Internet search? When is it better to use a search engine?

2. How do you think search services work? Why do different search tools often produce different results based on the same search parameters?

3. Search services such as Infoseek Guide, Yahoo!, and Excite are business ventures. Where do you think their revenues come from?

4. How might Web site owners help their Web pages get high scores and/or be among the first documents listed in search results? (Web site developers use a number of tricks to accomplish this!)

Review Exercises

Mark Your Place

1. Using Magellan, find The Job Web site again.

2. Place a bookmark on The Job Web.

3. Move the new bookmark into an appropriate folder in using the Bookmarks window.

Continue Your Job Search

1. Use Magellan to locate five more employment-related Web sites you feel will be useful in your job search.

2. Bookmark each site.
3. Place those bookmarks in appropriate folders using the Bookmarks window.

Assignments

Using Other Search Services

Try performing searches for employment-related Web sites using other search services linked to the Net Search and Net Directory pages. Use both search engines and directories. Bookmark sites you feel may be useful in your job search. Organize those bookmarks using folders and separators.

Exploring Search.com

Go to www.search.com. What kind of a Web page is this? Is it a search service like Magellan, or is it more like Netscape's Net Search page? Why do you suppose Search.com is rapidly becoming a very popular point at which to begin an Internet search? Try accessing Excite, Magellan, Yahoo!, and Infoseek Guide from this Web site.

Using Search Engines to Find Search Engines

In this project you visited the search services linked to Netscape's Net Search and Net Directory pages. There are other search services emerging all the time. How do you suppose you find them? You guessed it! Use the search engine of your choice to look for other search engines and information about search engines.

Project 4: Using Netscape for E-mail

Objectives

After completing this project, you should be able to:

- Understand basic electronic mail concepts and terms
- Configure Netscape for e-mail
- Use Netscape to send and receive e-mail
- Use e-mail links on Web pages
- Save and delete e-mail messages
- Create an address book

Case Study: Contacting Prospective Employers

You are finishing your undergraduate degree and are preparing to enter the job market following graduation. In the previous projects you found that the Web offers a tremendous number of resources for finding a good job. In fact, you have now located and bookmarked a number of employment directories and have found some companies you would like to contact.

Now you must consider your options for communicating with these companies. You have heard a lot about e-mail and wonder if that would be an option for requesting an application packet from some of the human resource departments you have to contact. You know you have an e-mail address (although you may not know what it is), since you have a computer account at your school. But how do you go about sending e-mail? Can you use Netscape to do it?

An Internet Solution

Until recently, Netscape only allowed you to send e-mail. However, its most recent incarnation has a full featured e-mail interface that rivals some of the best (and easiest to use) e-mail front-ends around. So the next step is to learn how to use Netscape to compose, send, receive, and manages e-mail for your job search.

WHAT IS E-MAIL?

Electronic mail, or ***e-mail***, is one of the most popular and heavily used services provided by the Internet. E-mail is simply the word we use for sending messages from one computer to another. E-mail can be set up as a local service within an office on a local area network, or it can be set up with access to the Internet. With an e-mail address and access to the Internet, you can send messages anywhere in the world. One of the greatest advantages of e-mail is that in most cases those messages arrive at their destination just moments after they are sent. E-mail is one of the most powerful reasons that mail transported by the U.S. Postal Service has popularly become known as "snail mail." The speed and economy of e-mail is hard to beat.

Understanding E-mail Addresses

As shown in Figure 4.1, every e-mail address must follow a standard format: It is composed of two parts, a *user name* and a *domain name*, separated by an @ sign.

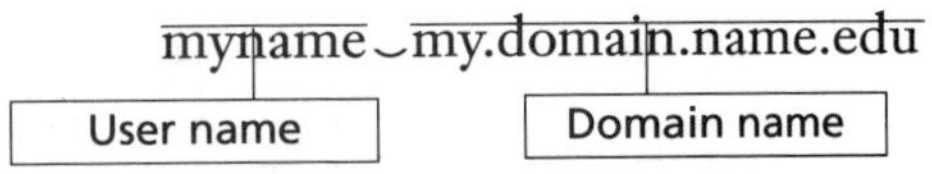

myname@my.domain.name.edu

User name

Domain name

Figure 4.1

Remember the discussion of domain names back in Project 1? Well, here it is again: The ***domain name*** identifies the computer system that handles your e-mail. This is the computer that will recognize your user name. Your ***user name*** identifies you and is unique within the computer system. Remember that domain names are used to identify every computer on the Internet. Each part of the domain name is separated by a dot (.) and tells you something about the location of the computer. In the example in Figure 4.1, edu indicates that the computer is part of an educational institution (as opposed to com or org, which are used to designate other types of organizations); name represents the name of the organization; and my.domain indicates the name of the computer at that organization where your e-mail service is located. The domain name may be as short as asu.edu or aol.com. It can also be long and complex, like ensmtp1.eas.asu.edu or sba1102.sba.pdx.edu.

Parts of an E-mail Message

As shown in Figure 4.2, e-mail messages typically have three parts: a *header*, a *body*, and a *signature*. Your e-mail messages will look somewhat different depending on the e-mail software you use. We will focus here on how Netscape displays e-mail.

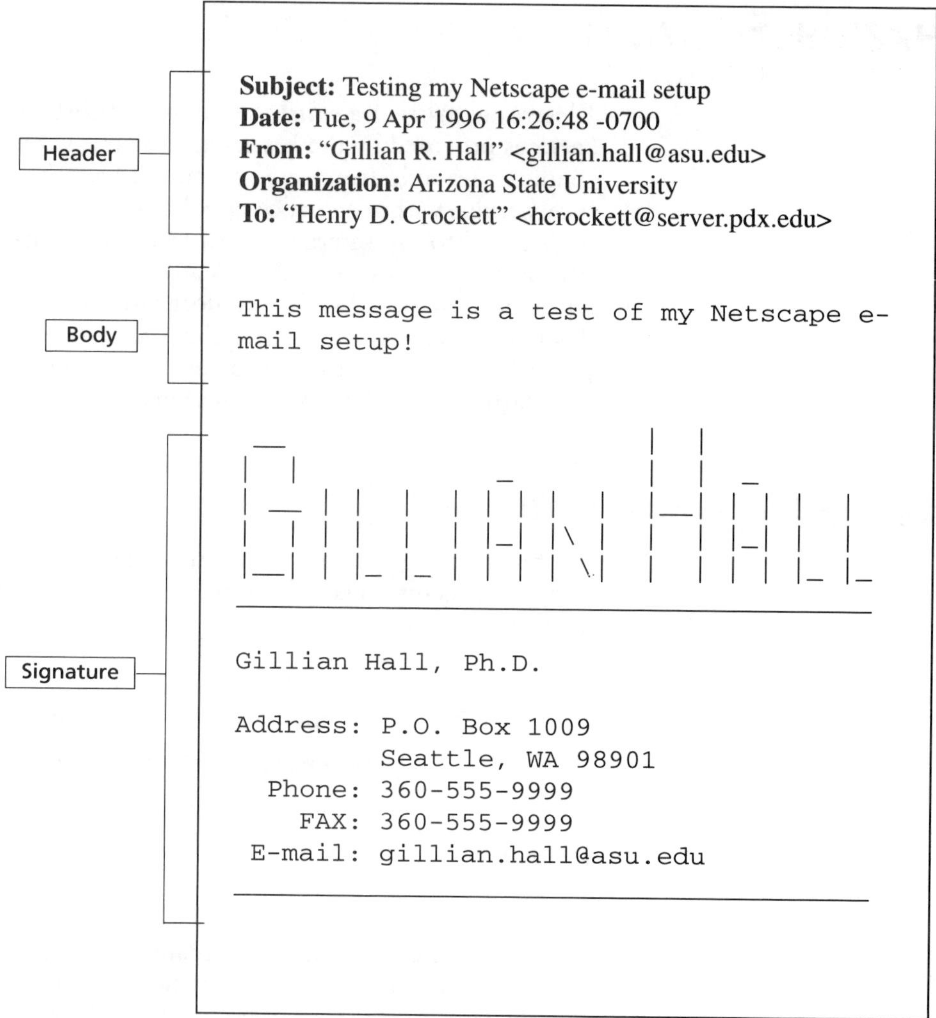

Figure 4.2

The ***header*** displays the subject and date of the e-mail message. It also displays information (including the e-mail address) about both the sender and recipient of the message. The ***body*** of the e-mail message is where the actual message is displayed. In the example shown in Figure 4.2, the message is quite short; however, e-mail messages can be as long as you like. Finally, the ***signature*** is an optional part of the message that you can configure Netscape to place at the end of every e-mail message you send. The signature contains information about you, like your name, address, and phone number. As you can see from the example in Figure 4.2, you can get somewhat creative here.

DIFFERENT E-MAIL APPLICATIONS

There are a number of applications available for using e-mail. All of these provide an interface for sending, receiving, storing, and deleting e-mail messages. Some even provide features for organizing, sorting, replying to, and forwarding e-mail messages. Most provide some sort of address book in which you can store frequently used e-mail addresses, and many allow you to address a message to more than one person. Because there are so many similarities between e-mail applications, once you have learned to use one such application, learning others will be surprisingly easy.

While Netscape provides a fairly complete list of e-mail features, many people prefer to use other applications such as Eudora, Pegasus, and Pine for accessing e-mail services. In this project, you will be using Netscape for e-mail, but it is important to be aware that there are other popular e-mail applications available. In fact, it is likely that your school provides an e-mail application other than Netscape.

If you are interested in learning to use another e-mail application, try searching for it by name using a search engine or directory. For example, a complete tutorial on using the Eudora e-mail package is located at the following address: http://www.netspot.unisa.edu.au/eudora/contents.html You can even download a copy of the Eudora application from the Internet!

There is a tremendouse amount of information and support available on the Internet for users of all e-mail applications. If your school uses something other than Netscape, you can be a rebel and use Netscape anyway, or you can learn more about the application preferred by your school by locating information about that application on the Web!

CONFIGURING NETSCAPE FOR E-MAIL

To use Netscape to send and receive e-mail, you must first configure it. You will need some information about your e-mail services, like your e-mail address and the address(es) of the computer(s) that provide your e-mail services. Most colleges and universities provide computer account services for their students, so we are assuming here that you have a computer account at your school. Your instructor will be able to help you with this and with the other information you will need to configure Netscape for e-mail. To complete this project, you must have a computer account at your school with a user name, password, and e-mail address.

Remember in the Overview of this book that we promised to cover more of the menu items under the Options menu? In this project you will explore the Mail and News Preferences option, but first you must start Netscape. This procedure is covered in the Overview if you need a refresher.

To access e-mail preferences:

1 Choose Mail and News Preferences from the Options menu, as shown in Figure 4.3.

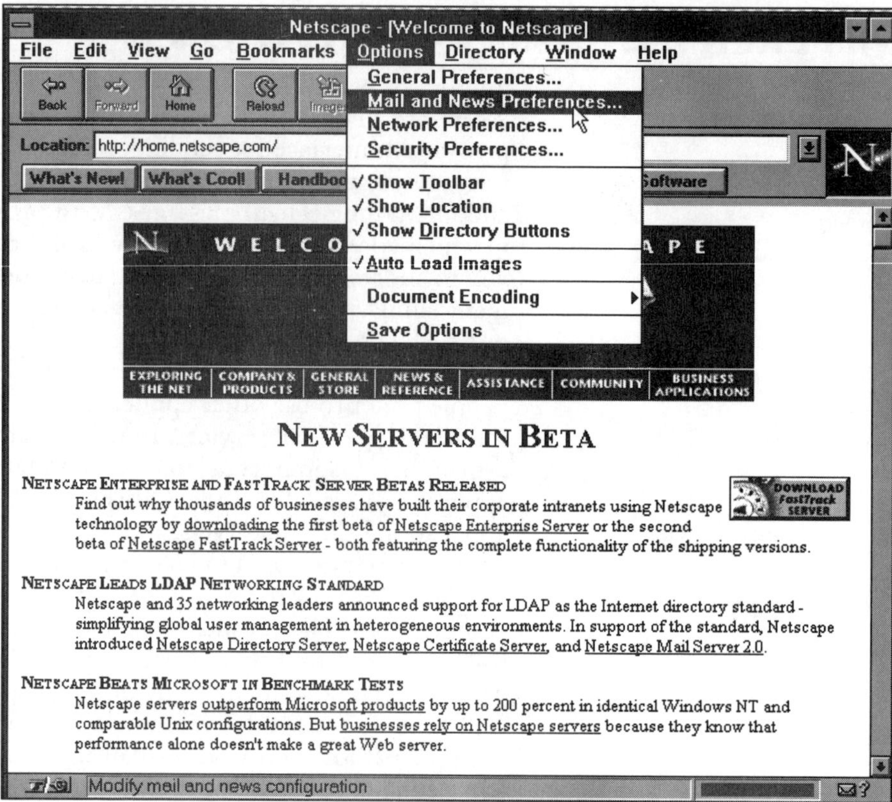

Figure 4.3

The Preferences dialog box is displayed as shown in Figure 4.4. You will use this dialog box to configure Netscape for e-mail.

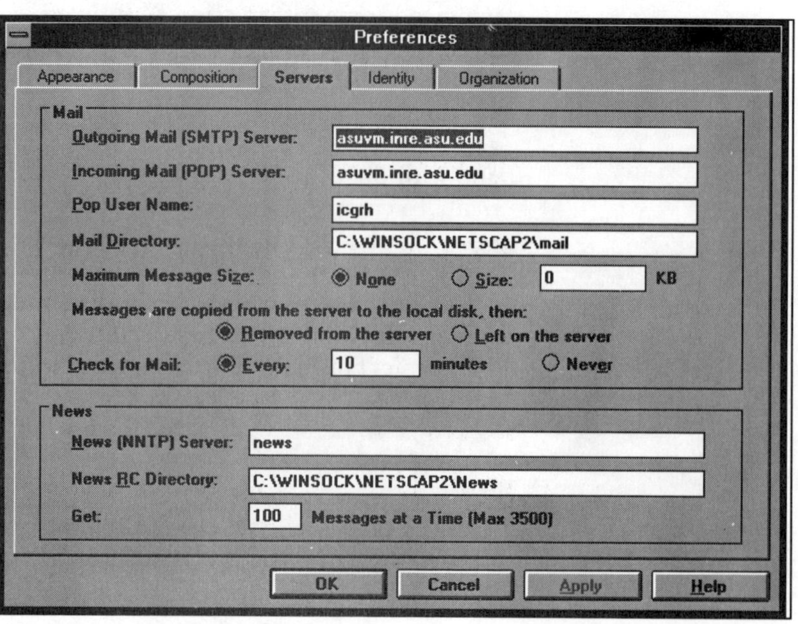

Figure 4.4

Notice the tabs at the top of the dialog box labeled Appearance, Composition, Servers, Identity, and Organization. The information required for using Netscape for e-mail is listed under the Servers tab in the Preferences dialog box. You can explore the rest of the e-mail preferences on your own using the Handbook to understand all the options.

To configure e-mail Servers preferences:

1 Select the Servers tab in the Preferences dialog box, as shown in Figure 4.4.

The Servers screen allows you to specify your e-mail servers, your user name, and a number of other preferences. As you continue through the following numbered steps, we will describe the fields in the Mail section of the Servers screen.

Outgoing Mail (SMTP) Server: To send e-mail, Netscape has to connect to the appropriate ***SMTP*** (Simple Mail Transport Protocol) ***server***. To make this connection, Netscape needs the domain name of your SMTP server. There may already be a default in this field, like ***mail***. Your instructor will tell you if the default is correct for your outgoing mail server.

2 Enter the domain name of your SMTP server in the Outgoing Mail (SMTP) Server field.

Incoming Mail (POP) Server: To receive mail, Netscape must connect to the appropriate ***POP*** (Post Office Protocol) ***server*** . This means that Netscape must have the domain name of your POP server. This is usually the same as your SMTP server, but be sure to check with your instructor.

3 Enter the domain name of your POP server in the Incoming Mail (POP) Server field.

Alert! The information shown in Figure 4.4 is only an example. You must enter your own server addresses, user name, and so on. The ones shown here won't do you any good at all!

POP User Name: This is your user name, the part of your e-mail address before the @ sign. For example, if your e-mail address is sarahm@asuvm.inre.asu.edu, then your POP User Name is sarahm.

4 Enter your user name in the POP User Name field.

Mail Directory: This field should contain the name of the folder (or subdirectory) where Netscape will keep your e-mail files. Netscape may display a default here. Your instructor will help you to determine if the default is appropriate or if you should designate a folder in your computer account at school.

5 With your instructor's help, determine and enter the path and name of your mail directory in the Mail Directory field.

Maximum Message Size: This allows you to limit the size of messages you can receive. This may be useful later on if you subscribe to newsgroups that sometimes send long messages and take up too much disk space. For now just stick with the default, None.

Messages are copied from the server to the local disk, then: This option allows you to determine if messages you have received through Netscape will be left on your mail server or removed from it. Some servers do not support the *Left on server* option. Stick with the default here unless you have some pressing reason to make another selection.

Check for Mail: This option allows you to configure Netscape to check your POP server every so often for new mail messages. The selection you make here will work only while Netscape is running (with your own e-mail preferences configured). Normally, you would either select Never or Every 10 minutes or so. For this project you won't have Netscape check for e-mail.

6 Select the Never option in the Check for Mail section.

7 Select the OK button.

ACCESSING THE NETSCAPE MAIL WINDOW

Now that you have Netscape configured for e-mail, you are ready to open the Netscape Mail Window. You will use this window to compose, send, view, and generally manage your e-mail.

To open the Netscape Mail window:

1 Choose Netscape Mail from the Window menu, as shown in Figure 4.5.

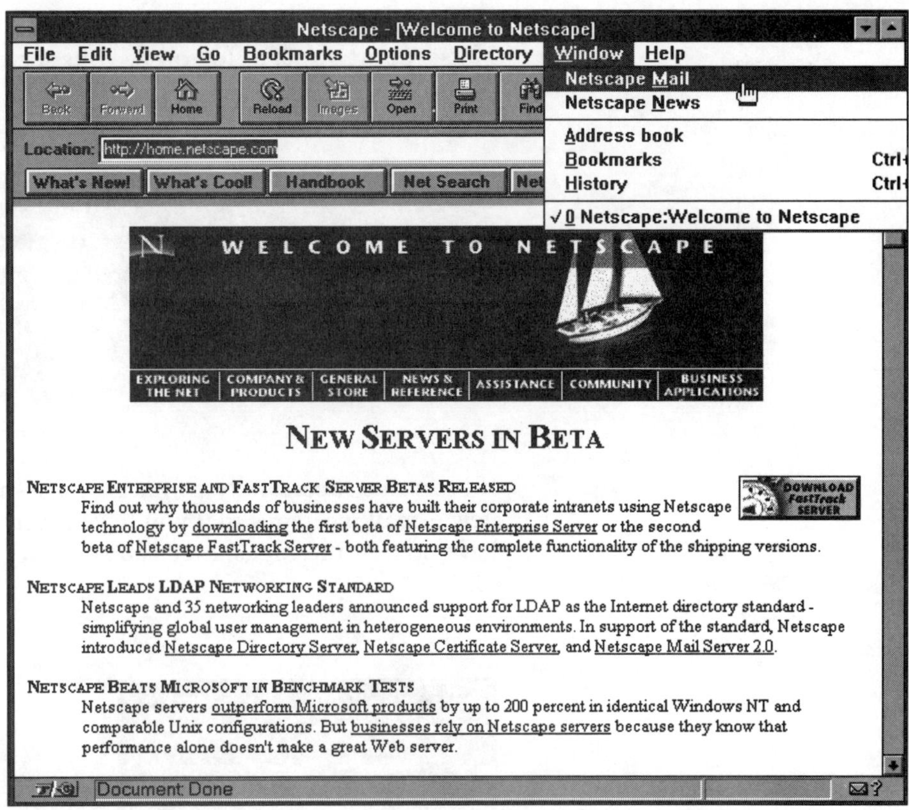

Figure 4.5

Netscape asks for your ***password***, as shown in Figure 4.6. This is the password for the computer account you were given at school. If you don't know your password, your instructor will help you to find out what it is.

Password Entry Dialog

Password for POP3 user
icgrh@asuvm.inre.asu.edu:

OK
Cancel

Figure 4.6

> ***Tip*** Your password is very important and very confidential. It allows you and only you to view your e-mail. Anyone can find out your server information and your user name, but only you and your system administrator know your password, so don't tell anyone what it is!

2 Enter your password in the field provided on the Password Entry dialog box.

3 Select the OK button.
Netscape attempts to log on to your server using your user name and password.

> ***Don't Panic*** If there is something wrong with your Servers configuration, you will get an error message regarding Netscape's ability to communicate with your servers. If this happens, go back to the Servers screen in the Mail and News Preferences dialog box, and get your instructor to help you track down the problem. It is probably just a typo, so don't worry.

If Netscape successfully contacts your e-mail server, it will download any new e-mail messages that you have received and display them. When you have no new messages, Netscape displays the dialog box shown in Figure 4.7.

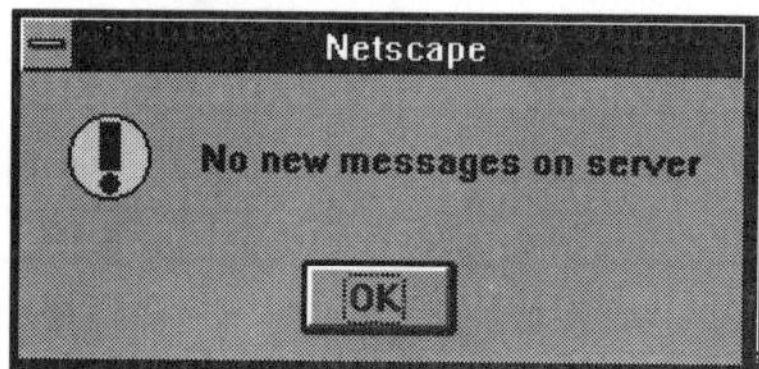

Figure 4.7

4 If a dialog box like the one shown in Figure 4.7 appears, select OK.
The Netscape Mail window appears as shown in Figure 4.8.

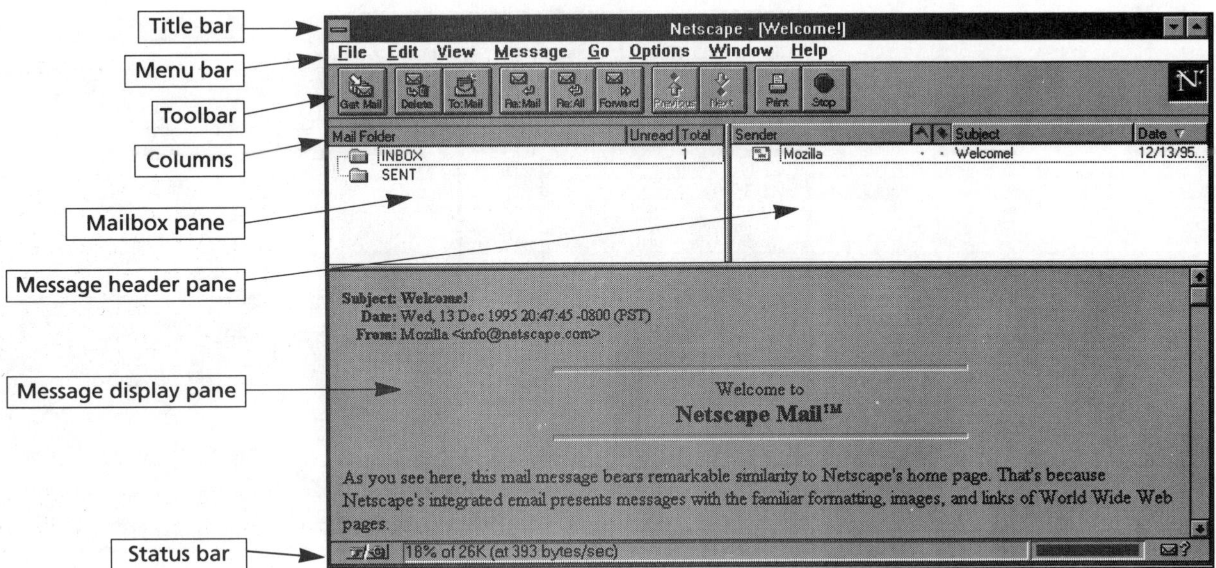

Figure 4.8

If you've gotten this far, then Netscape is properly configured for e-mail. This was the hard part of this project, and you've gotten through it. You are now ready to send and receive e-mail.

THE MAIL WINDOW

The Netscape Mail window is much like the main Netscape window in that it has a title bar, menu bar, tool bar, and status bar. As shown in Figure 4.8, the Mail window is divided into three ***panes***: the ***mailbox pane***, ***message header pane***, and the ***message display pane***. The mailbox and message header panes are divided into ***columns***. Columns in the mailbox pane state the names of mail folders, the number of unread messages in each folder, and the total number of messages in each folder. Columns in the message header pane state the sender name, subject, date, flagged status, and read status of each message.

By resizing the panes and resizing and reorganizing columns in the Mail window, you can customize the look of the window to suit your needs.

To resize Mail window panes:

1 Position the mouse over the divider between the mailbox and message header panes.
The mouse pointer changes shape (↔).

2 Drag the divider to the right, as shown in Figure 4.9.

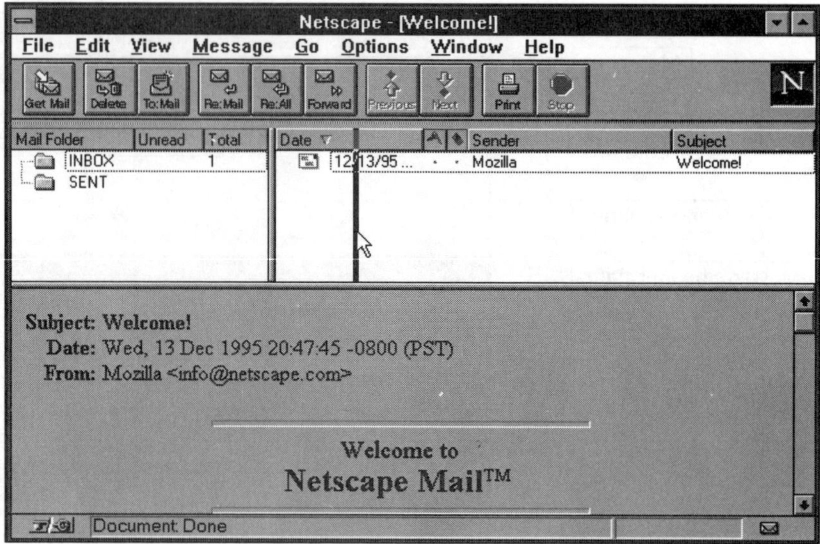

Figure 4.9

3 Drop the divider by releasing the mouse button.
Notice that you have resized both the mailbox and message header panes.

4 Repeat steps 1 through 3 to resize the message display pane using the divider separating the upper two panes from the message display pane. This time you must drag the divider up and down rather than left and right.

To resize columns in Mail window panes:

1 Position the mouse over the divider between the mailbox and message header panes.

2 When the mouse pointer changes shape (+||+), drag the divider left or right.

3 Drop the divider.
Just like resizing a window pane, you have resized a window pane column.

To rearrange columns in Mail window panes:

1 Position the mouse over the Date column header.

2 Drag to a location directly on the Sender column header.

3 Drop the column header.
The Date column appears in front of the Sender column, as shown in Figure 4.10.

> ***Tip*** If the column header does not move as described, try again. The key is to drop the column header with the mouse pointer positioned on the header of the column *in front* of which you want the column you're moving to appear.

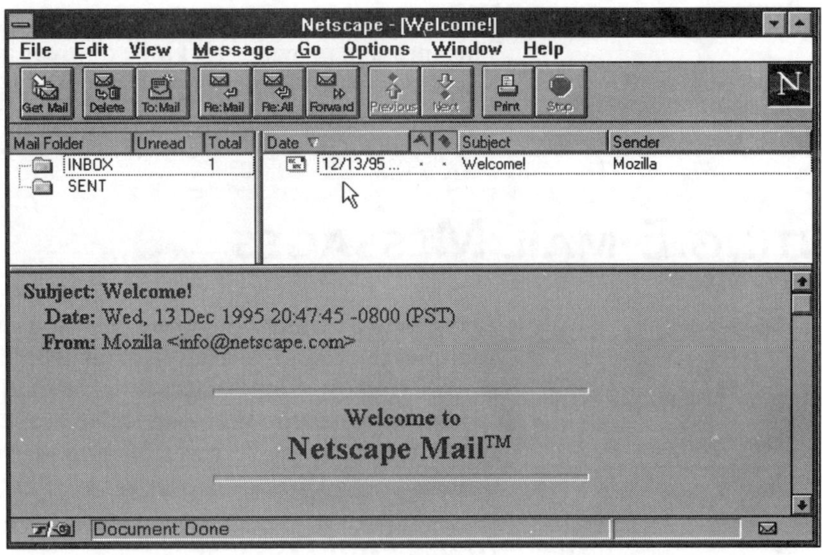

Figure 4.10

4 Repeat the steps to move the Date column back to its original position in the message header pane.

To display mail folder contents:

1 Select the Sent folder in the mailbox pane of the Mail window.
The contents of the Sent folder are displayed in the message header pane. Since you have not yet sent any messages, no messages are displayed.

2 Select the Inbox folder.
The contents of the Inbox folder are displayed in the message header pane.

VIEWING E-MAIL MESSAGES

When you open the Inbox folder, an e-mail message is displayed in the message header pane of the Mail window. As indicated in the Sender column, the message is from someone called Mozilla. This mysterious message did not come to you through your mail server. It is a special delivery from Netscape and is their way of welcoming you to the wonderful world of e-mail using Netscape.

To view your first e-mail message:

1 If the e-mail message from Mozilla is not displayed in the message display pane, click on the message icon under the Sender column header in the message header pane.
The message is displayed in the message display pane, as shown in Figure 4.10.

2 Use the vertical scroll bar to view the entire message.
This message provides all kinds of great information about using Netscape's e-mail functions. If you read it carefully, you'll have a jump start on the rest of this project.

PRINTING E-MAIL MESSAGES

There may be times when you wish to print an e-mail message. For example, the message from Mozilla would be worth printing for its information on using Netscape for e-mail.

Just as it does for Web pages, Netscape offers the standard Windows application printing features for e-mail: Print Preview, Page Setup, and Print.

To use Print Preview

1 In the Mail window message header pane, select the message from Mozilla.

2 Choose Print Preview from the File menu, as shown in Figure 4.11.

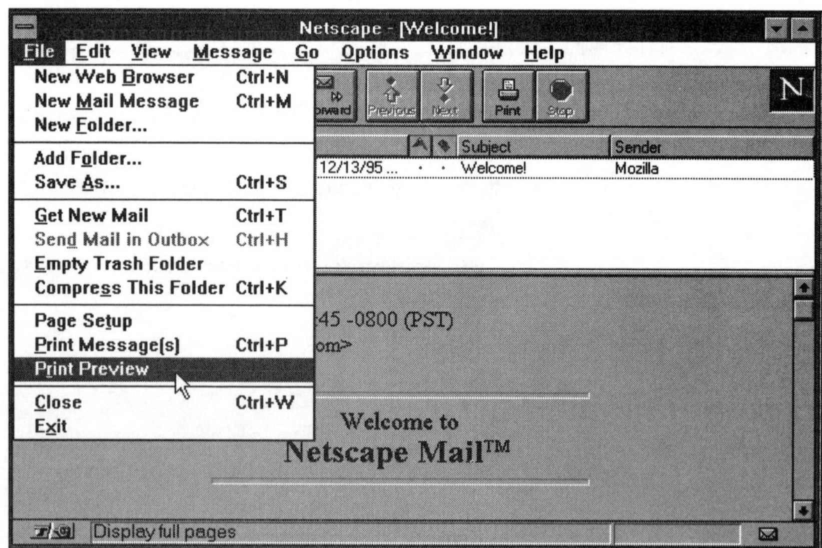

Figure 4.11

The selected message is displayed in the print preview window, as shown in Figure 4.12. The buttons along the top of the window allow you to print the message, view the next page, zoom in for a closer look, zoom out, or close the print preview window.

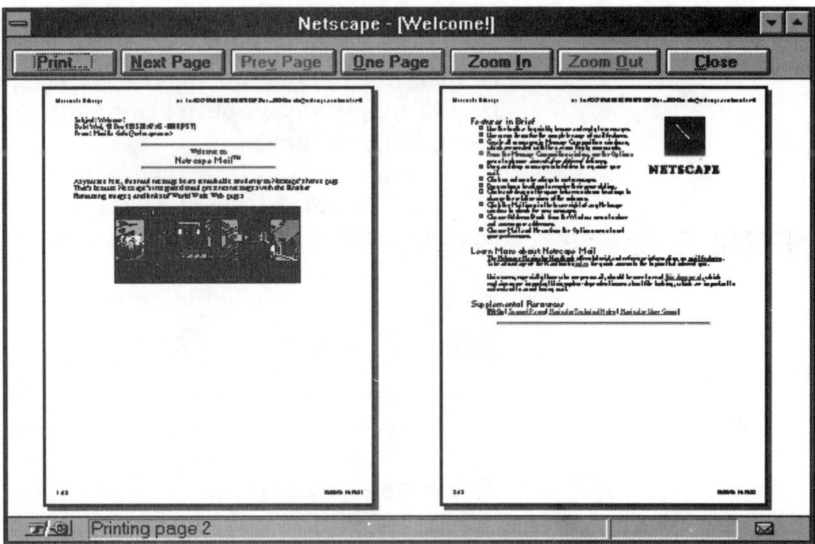

Figure 4.12

3 Select the Close button.

To use Page Setup:

1 If it is not already selected, select the message from Mozilla in the message header pane of the Mail window.

2 Choose Page Setup from the File menu.
The Page Setup window appears, as shown in Figure 4.13.

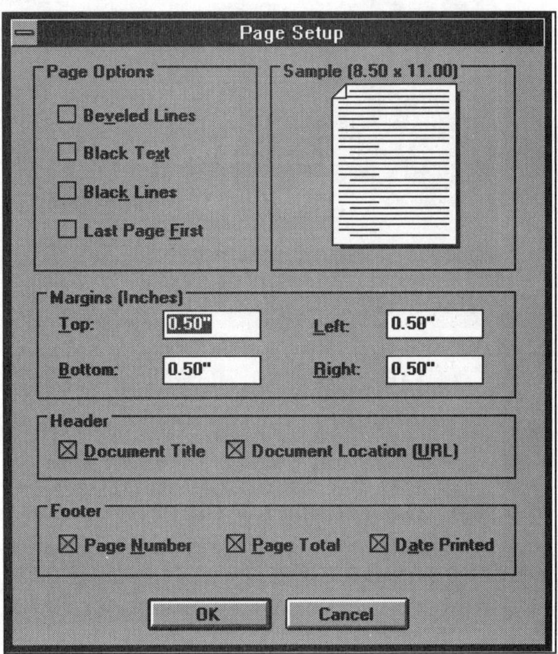

Figure 4.13

The Page Setup options allow you to handle some of the color issues inherent to Web pages (in Netscape, e-mail is displayed as a standardized HTML document—in effect, a Web page) by offering black lines and text. In addition, you can opt to print multipage e-mail messages in reverse order, last page first.

You can set margins by typing in values. Netscape prints the document title and URL at the top of each page if you select those options. Finally, you can include page numbers and the date in the footer if desired.

3 Select the Page Setup options that appeal to you.

4 Select the OK button.

Now that you have previewed your e-mail message and made adjustments using Page Setup, you are ready to print.

To print a Message:

1 If it is not already selected, select the message from Mozilla in the message header pane of the Mail window.

2 Choose Print Message(s) from the File menu.
The Print window appears as shown in Figure 4.14.

> ***Tip*** There are other ways to select the Print Message(s) function. You can select the Print button from the Mail window tool bar, or you can press CTRL + P

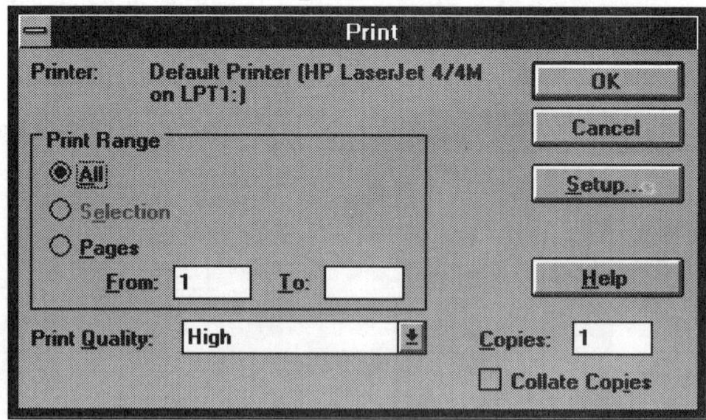

Figure 4.14

The Print window allows you to specify which pages you wish to print, the print quality, the number of copies, and whether or not you wish to have multiple copies collated.

3 Make changes to the print options as you wish, and then select the OK button.
The e-mail message from Mozilla is printed on your computer's default printer.

If necessary, you can take a break at this point. If you are working at school, make a note of the Servers settings in the Mail and News Preferences dialog box before you exit Netscape. When you come back, start up Netscape Navigator, re-enter your Servers configuration if necessary, and proceed.

IDENTIFYING YOURSELF IN E-MAIL MESSAGES

Remember the signature portion of an e-mail message discussed at the beginning of this project? It is the part of the message at the very end that identifies you (refer to the example in Figure 4.2). The signature allows you to end all your e-mail messages with a professional (or frivolous!) closing that provides recipients with easy-to-read information about you.

Netscape allows you to specify some information about yourself that will be used in the header of all the messages you send. But it also allows you to specify a ***signature file*** that you have created using a word processor or text editor.

To configure your e-mail header identity:

1 If it is not already displayed, open the Mail window by choosing Mail from the Window menu.

2 Choose Mail and News Preferences from the Options menu.

3 Select the Identity tab on the Mail and News Preferences dialog box.

4 Complete the fields on the Identity screen with your own information, as shown in Figure 4.15.

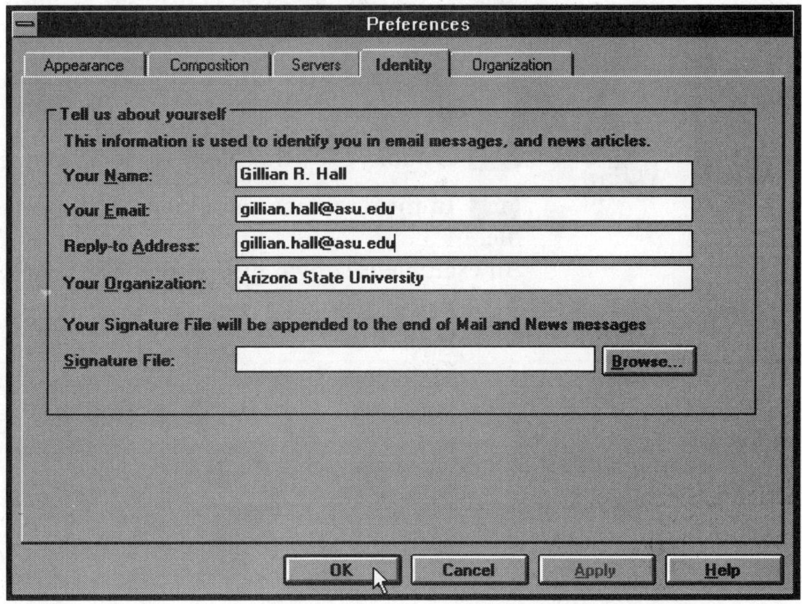

Figure 4.15

5 Select the OK button.

6 Choose Save Options from the Mail window Options menu.
Messages you send will now contain the identity information you specified in the message header, as shown in Figure 4.16.

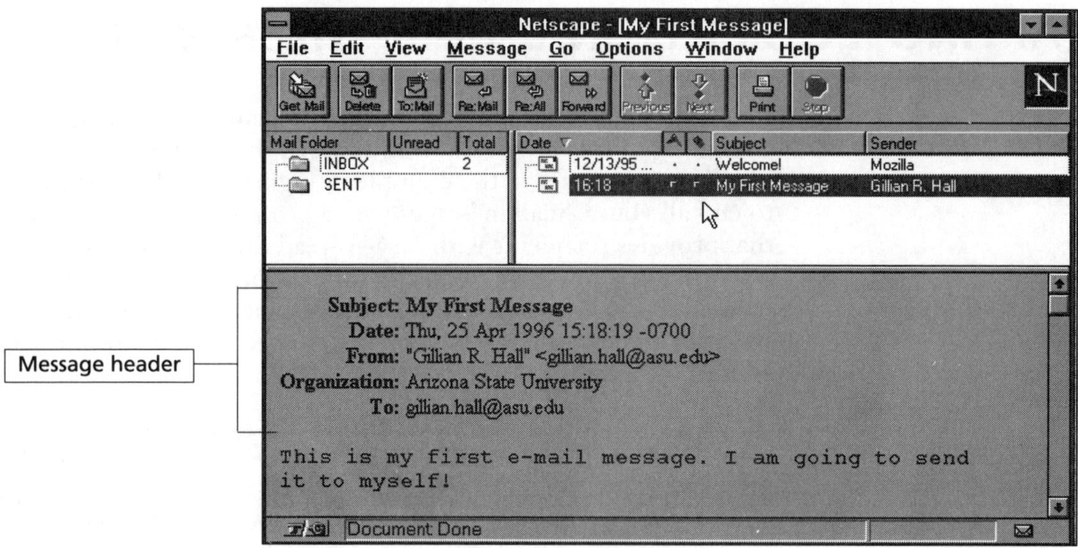

Figure 4.16

To create a signature file:

1 Press (ALT) + (ESC) until the Windows Program Manager window is displayed.

2 Open the Accessories application group (ask your instructor if you cannot find it).

3 Double-click the Notepad icon to open the Notepad application.

4 In the document window that appears, compose your own signature file.
An example is shown in Figure 4.17. Your signature file can be as simple or fancy as you like.

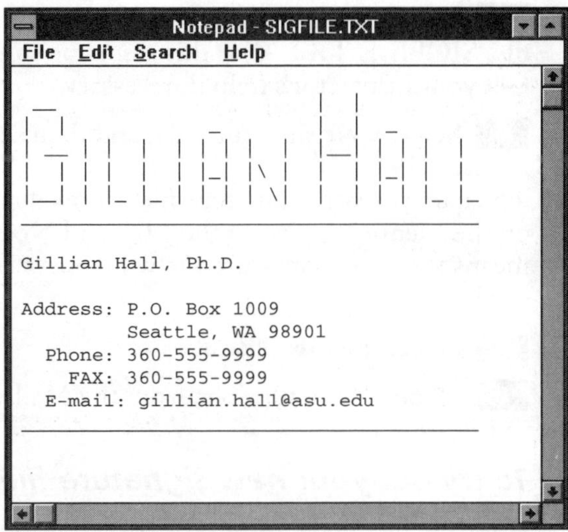

Figure 4.17

5 When you are finished, select Save As from the Notepad file menu. Save your file as SIGFILE.TXT. Ask your instructor whether you should save it on a floppy disk, to your computer account, or to the hard drive on the computer you are using.

6 Select Exit from the Notepad file menu to exit the Notepad application.

To select your signature file:

1 Press ALT + ESC until the Netscape Mail window is displayed.

2 Choose Mail and News Preferences from the Mail window Options menu.

3 Select the Identity tab on the Mail and News Preferences dialog box that appears.

4 Select the Browse button.
The Signature file dialog box appears as shown in Figure 4.18.

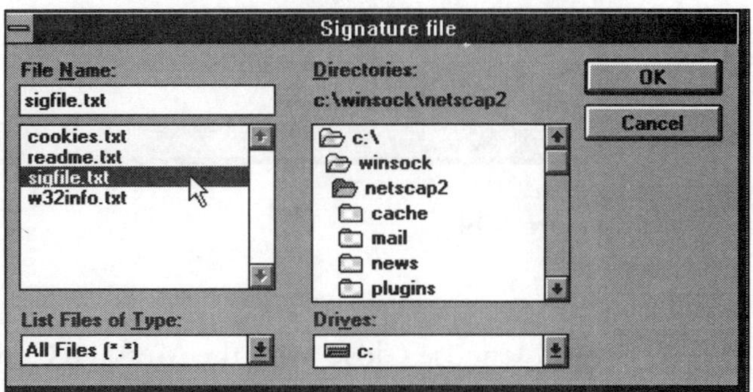

Figure 4.18

5 Look through the Drives and Directories list to locate your signature file, SIGFILE.TXT. (For this step, you must know where you put the file. Get your instructor's help if necessary.)

6 Select your signature file, and then select the OK button, as shown in Figure 4.19.
The name of your signature file is now displayed in the Signature File field on the Identity screen of the Mail and News Preferences dialog box. This means that your signature file will appear at the end of all messages you send.

7 Select the OK button.

8 Choose Save Options from the Mail window Options menu.

To try out your new signature file:

1 Select the To: Mail button on the toolbar.
The Message Composition window displays your signature file at the end of the message, as shown in Figure 4.19. All you need to do is type the body of your message and send it.

Figure 4.19

2 Choose Close from the Message Composition window File menu to cancel the new message.

SENDING AND RECEIVING E-MAIL

Now comes the fun part. You are ready to compose and send your first e-mail message using Netscape.

To compose an e-mail message:

1 Open the Mail window.

2 Select the To: Mail button from the toolbar.
The Message Composition window appears as shown in Figure 4.20.

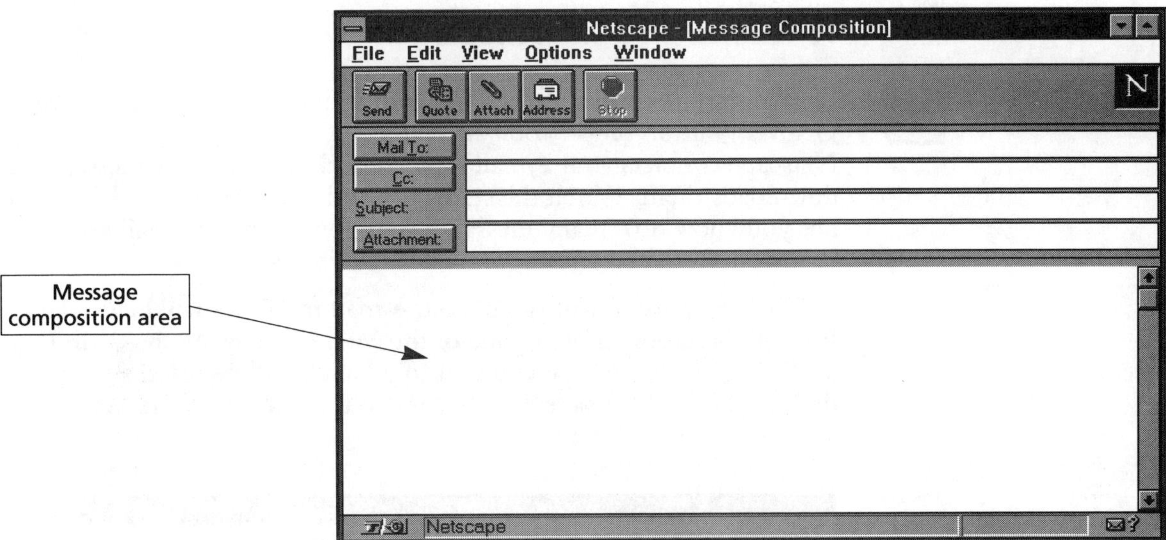

Figure 4.20

3 Enter your e-mail address in the Mail To field.
Yes, this means you will be sending this message to yourself. This is a good way to get acquainted with sending and receiving e-mail messages in one fell swoop! If you prefer, you can enter the e-mail address of one of your classmates who is also working through this project.

4 Press TAB to go to the Cc: field.
The Cc: field is used for sending a copy of your message to someone else. Often, you will want more than one person to get a copy of a message you are sending. This is especially common in business communications.

5 Press TAB to go to the Subject field.
Unlike some e-mail programs, Netscape does not require that you enter a subject, but it will ask you about it if you leave this field blank. It is courteous to enter a subject so that the recipient of your message will have some idea, at a glance, of what the message is about.

6 Enter `My First Message` in the Subject field.

7 Press TAB again to go to the message composition area at the

bottom of the window (pointed out in Figure 4.20).
A blinking I-beam cursor appears in the message composition area, indicating you are ready to type your first e-mail message.

8 Enter some text of your choice, just a few words if you like.
This text is the body of your e-mail message.

To send an e-mail message:

1 When you have finished typing your message, select the Send button on the toolbar.
Netscape contacts your e-mail server and sends the message. The message composition window then disappears.

To receive an e-mail message:

1 A minute or two after sending your first e-mail message, select the Get Mail button on the toolbar.
Netscape contacts your e-mail server, checks for any new messages, and downloads them. Watch the status bar at the bottom of the Mail window. It lets you know how many messages were found on your mail server and will keep you posted on its progress downloading your mail.

Once they are downloaded, your e-mail messages will be displayed as a list in the message header pane of the Mail window. As shown in Figure 4.21, the e-mail message you sent to yourself will be listed and will also be displayed in the message display pane at the bottom of the Mail window.

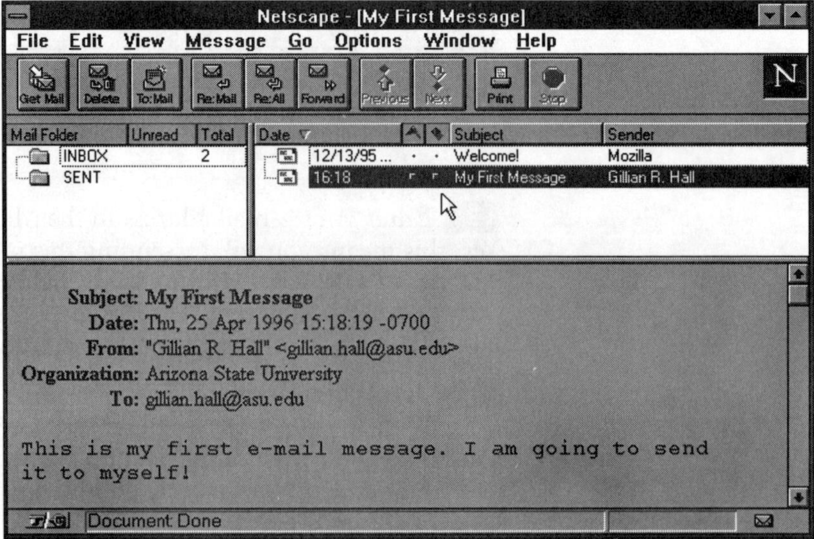

Figure 4.21

Tips If your e-mail message is not listed in the message header pane, wait a few moments and try the Get Mail button again. If your e-mail message is listed but not displayed in the message display pane, click the appropriate message icon in the Sender column.

REPLYING TO AND FORWARDING E-MAIL

Often, you will want to send replies to e-mail messages you receive. To send a reply, you must know the sender's e-mail address. You can find that address in the message header. As shown in Figure 4.10, the header contains the e-mail addresses of both the sender and the recipient of the message (of course, in this case the two addresses are the same).

To reply to a message you could find the sender's address in the header of the message, write it down, select the To: Mail button, enter the address in the Mail To field of the Message Composition window, enter a Subject to jog the memory of the person to whom you are replying regarding the topic of the original message, compose your reply, and send it using the Send button. Sounds like a lot of work, doesn't it? Well, it is. That's why Netscape has kindly provided you with a reply button called the Re: Mail button in the toolbar.

To reply to an e-mail message:

1 In the message header pane of the Mail window, select the message to which you want to reply. In this case, select the message you just received from yourself, if it is not already selected.

2 Select the Re: Mail button from the Mail window toolbar. A Message Composition window appears as shown in Figure 4.22.

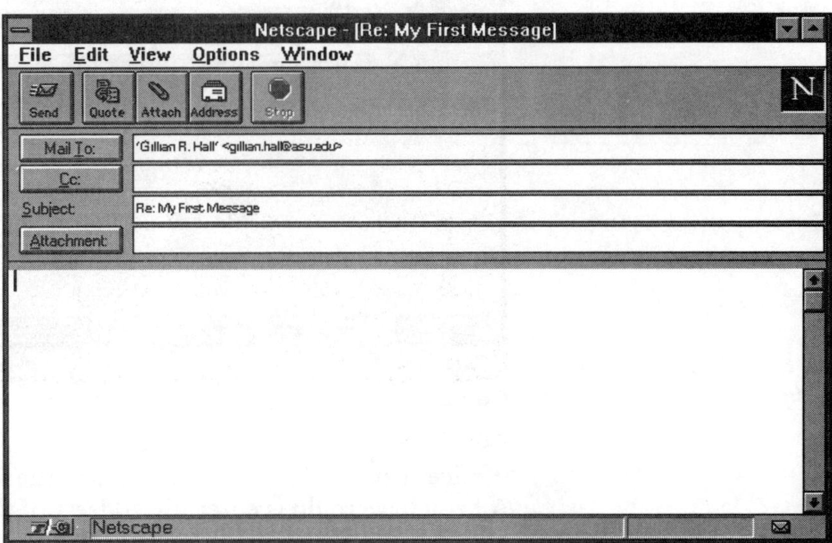

Figure 4.22

Notice that the Mail To and Subject fields are already completed, with the sender's address and a reference to the subject of the original message. All you have to do is type your reply and send the message.

3 Type `My reply to my very first message.` in the message composition area of the Message Composition window.

4 Select the Send button.
That's all there is to it. In a few moments you can use the Get Mail button to view your reply!

In addition to replying to e-mail messages, there may be times when you will want to forward e-mail messages you receive to someone else. This is common in business. For example, if someone sends you information you know a colleague is also interested in, or if you receive an inquiry that would be more appropriately handled by someone else in your organization, you would forward the message to the appropriate person.

Netscape also provides you with a quick and easy way to forward e-mail messages. You don't even want to hear about the hard way to forward a message!

To forward an e-mail message:

1 In the message header pane of the Mail window, select the original message you sent to yourself.

2 Select the Forward button from the toolbar.
The Message Composition window appears as shown in Figure 4.23.

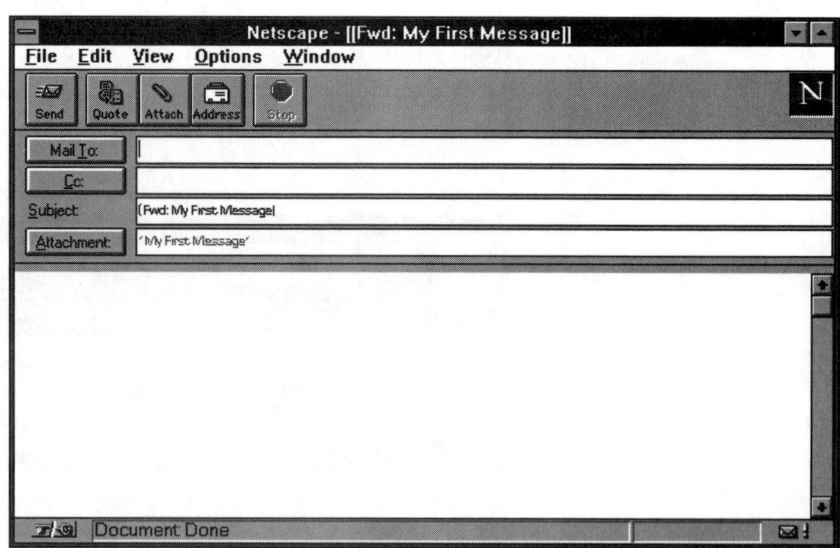

Figure 4.23

Notice that the Subject field contains the subject of the original message. All you have to do is enter the address of the person to whom you would like to forward the message. You can also enter text in the message composition area of the window, telling the recipient why you've forwarded the message.

3 Enter your own e-mail address in the Mail To field to forward the original message to yourself.

4 In the message composition area of the Mail Composition window, type `I thought you might be interested in this message.` This text will precede the forwarded message when you receive it.

5 Select the Send button.
In a few moments you can use the Get Mail button to view your forwarded message. Notice how a forwarded message is formatted. The entire original message is displayed (including the header), preceded by the new header and the text you entered.

DELETING E-MAIL MESSAGES

After you have read an e-mail message, you may wish to delete it. Netscape puts deleted messages into a special ***Trash folder***. Messages are not actually deleted until you "empty the trash." This feature allows you to change your mind about deleting a message before it is really gone!

To put a message in the trash:

1 In the message header pane of the Mail window, select the message from Mozilla.

2 Select the Delete button from the toolbar.
The message from Mozilla disappears. A Trash folder appears in the mailbox pane, as shown in Figure 4.24.

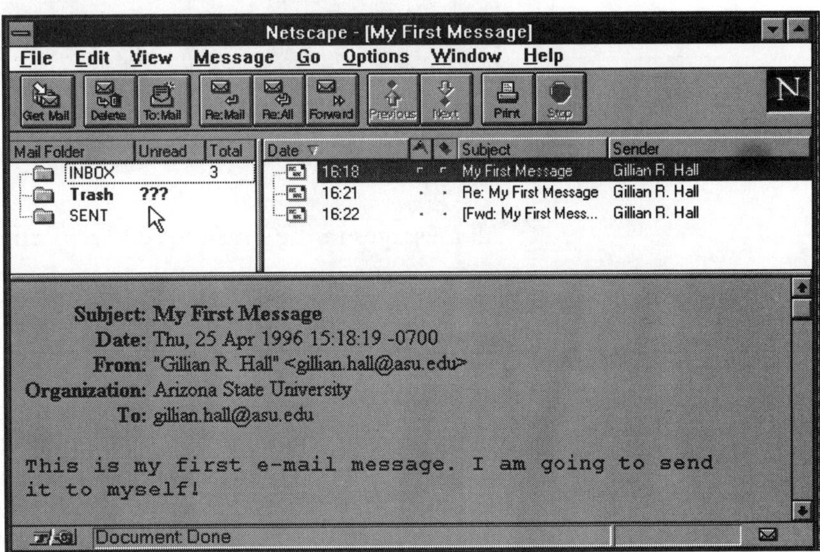

Figure 4.24

> **Tip** There are other ways to select the Delete function. You can select the Delete Message option from the Edit menu, or you can press DEL

If you select the Trash folder, the contents of the trash will be displayed in the message header pane. The message from Mozilla should be there. So by selecting the Delete button, you have really just moved the selected message into the Trash folder. It hasn't been deleted at all! Messages are only permanently deleted when you "empty the trash."

To empty the trash:

1 Choose the Empty Trash Folder from the File menu, as shown in Figure 4.25.

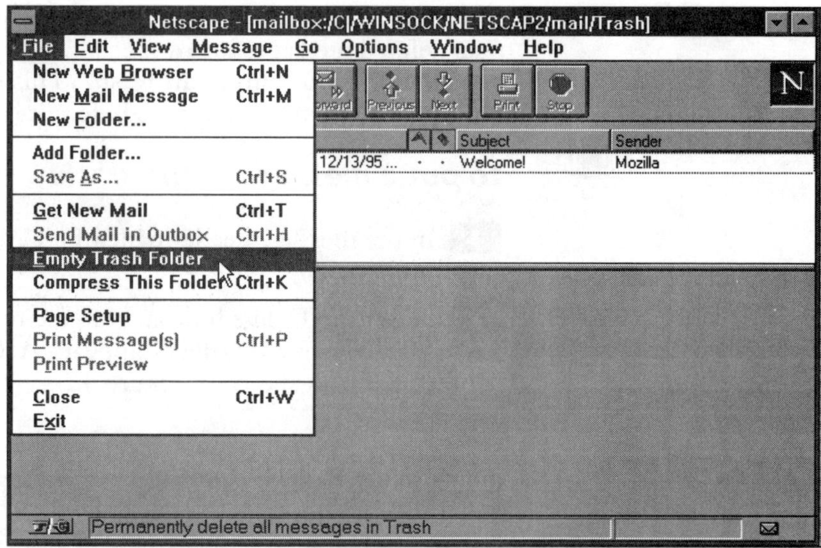

Figure 4.25

All messages in the Trash folder are permanently deleted.

SORTING E-MAIL MESSAGES

As you receive more messages, you may want to organize them in some way. One method of organizing your e-mail is by sorting the list of messages in the message header pane of the Mail window. In this section, you will learn to sort your e-mail messages by sender, subject, and date. You will also learn to change the sort order of your messages.

To sort e-mail messages by sender:

1 Select the Inbox folder in the mailbox pane of the Mail window.

All of the messages you have received are displayed in the message header pane.

2 Select the Sender column header in the message header pane. Your messages are sorted in ascending order (A to Z) by sender or user name.

To sort e-mail messages by subject:

1 If it is not already selected, select the Inbox folder in the mailbox pane of the Mail window.

2 Select the Subject column header in the message header pane. Your messages are sorted in ascending order (A to Z) by subject.

To sort e-mail messages by date:

1 If it is not already selected, select the Inbox folder in the mailbox pane of the Mail window.

2 Select the Date column header in the message header pane. Your messages are sorted in descending order (oldest first) by date.

> ***Tip*** There is another way to sort e-mail messages in the message header pane. Select Sort from the View menu. A list of sort options appears, as shown in Figure 4.26. Notice that the currently selected sort order, by date, is checked.

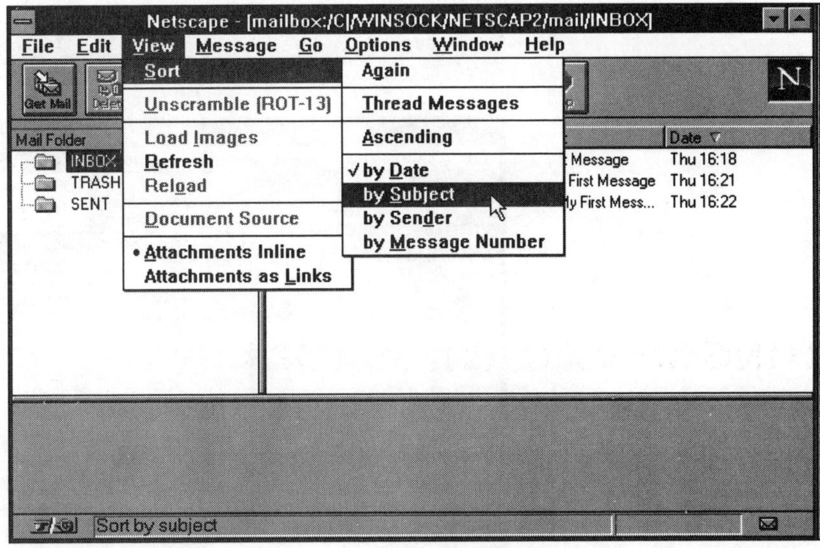

Figure 4.26

Netscape uses default sort orders when sorting by subject, sender, and date, and there may be times when you wish to reverse the sort order. For example, Netscape's default sort order for date is descending (oldest first). This means that if you keep a large number of e-mail messages in your message header pane, you will always have to scroll down to view the new messages, which will be listed last. This can be annoying.

To change the sort order:

1 Choose Sort from the View menu.

2 Select Ascending from the Sort submenu.
The order of the e-mail messages displayed in the message header pane is reversed—the newest message is displayed first and the oldest is last.

WORKING WITH THE ADDRESS BOOK

When you begin receiving and sending e-mail messages on a regular basis, you will find that it becomes tedious to locate and enter the same addresses over and over to people you correspond with often. It is for this reason that Netscape provides you with an e-mail feature called an ***Address Book***. Once you have entered a name and e-mail address in your Address Book, you need never type it again. You will simply click on the appropriate name, and both the person's name and e-mail address are automatically entered in your Message Composition window!

To access the Address Book window:

1 Choose Address book from the Window menu, as shown in Figure 4.27.

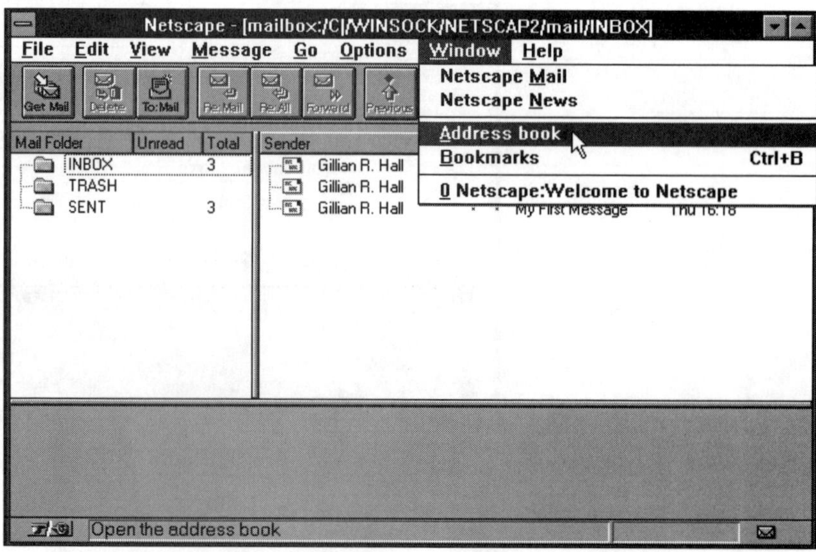

Figure 4.27

The Address Book window appears as shown in Figure 4.28. The Address Book window is functionally identical to the Bookmarks window covered in Project 2. Using this window, you can add, edit, and delete addresses and group addresses into folders (called Mailing Lists).

Figure 4.28

To add an address:

1 Choose Add User from the Item menu, as shown in Figure 4.29.

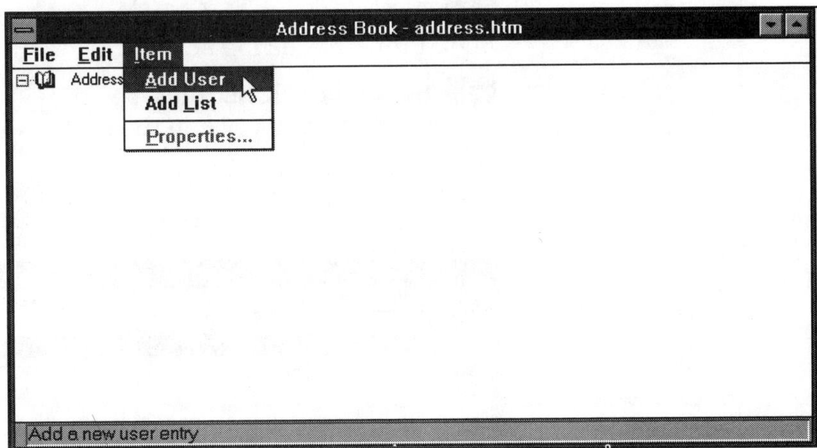

Figure 4.29

The Address Book Properties dialog box appears as shown in Figure 4.30.

Tip The first field on the Address Book properties dialog is called Nick Name. You can use the value entered in this field instead of an e-mail address when you are addressing a new message. Very handy! Take care to use only lowercase letters and no spaces. Otherwise, Netscape will object.

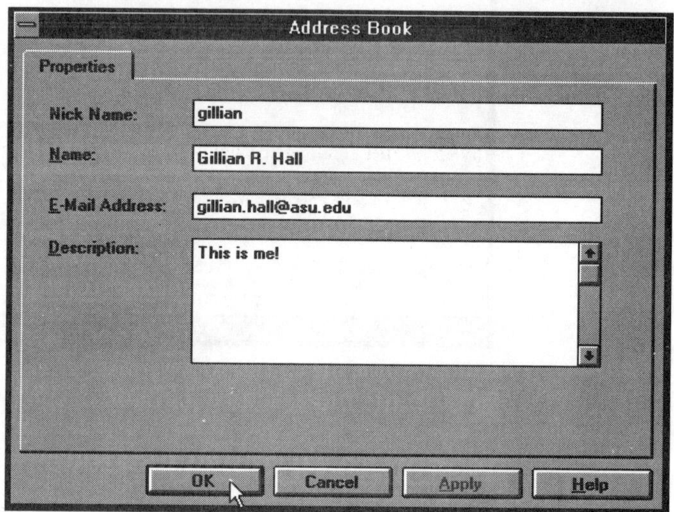

Figure 4.30

2 Enter your own information in the fields provided in the Address Book Properties dialog box.

3 Select the OK button.

The new address appears in the Address Book window, as shown in Figure 4.31.

Figure 4.31

To edit address properties:

1 Select the address entry you just created for yourself.

2 Choose Properties from the Item menu.
The Address Book Properties dialog box appears. You can now modify any of the properties for this entry in your address book.

3 Select the OK button.
Any changes you made to the selected address entry are saved.

To delete an address:

1 Select the address entry you created for yourself.

2 Choose Edit from the Address Book menu bar.
The Delete option on the Edit menu, shown in Figure 4.32, will permanently remove the selected address entries from the Address Book window. For now, *do not* select the Delete option. If you've already done it, that's okay, just add your address entry again and proceed.

3 Click somewhere off of the Edit menu, or press ESC to cancel the Edit menu.

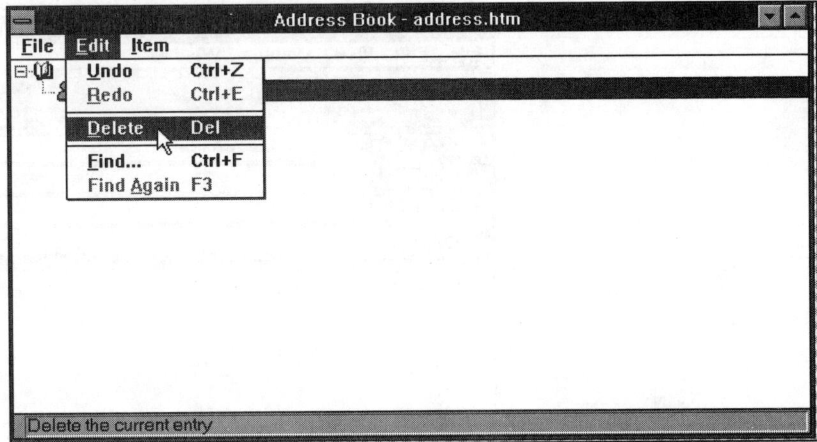

Figure 4.32

> ***Tip*** Another way to delete an address entry from the Address Window is to select the address, and press DEL

To use the Address Book window to begin a new message:

1 Select the address entry you created for yourself.

2 Choose Mail New Message from the File menu, as shown in Figure 4.33.

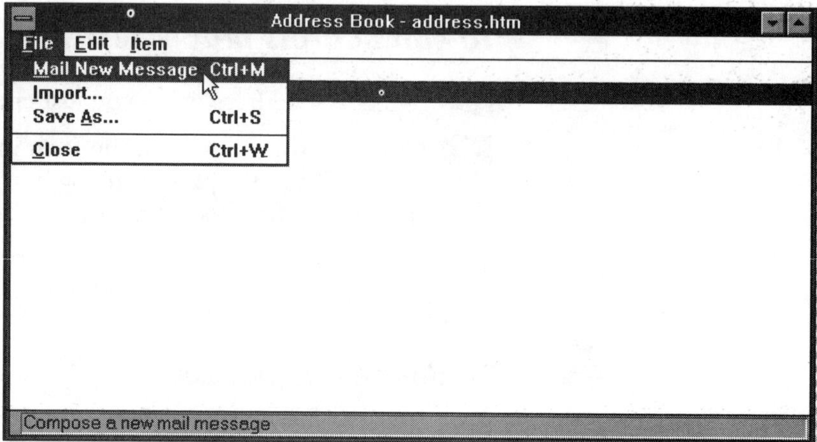

Figure 4.33

A Message Composition window appears as shown in Figure 4.34. Notice that the e-mail address to the recipient has been automatically completed for you!

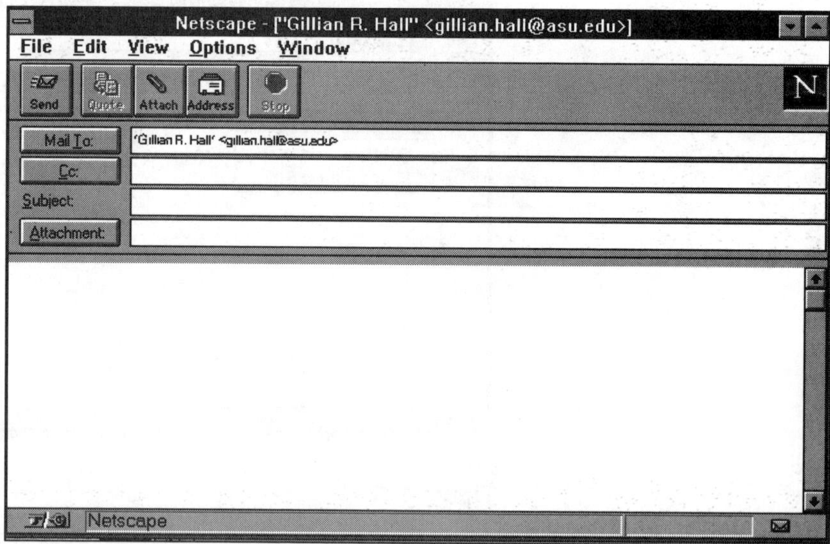

Figure 4.34

> ***Tip*** There are other ways to begin a new message from the Address Book window. You can double-click on the desired address or press CTRL + M

3 Choose Close from the File menu (or double-click on the control menu box in the upper left corner of the window) to close the Message Composition window and cancel the new message.

To select addresses using the Address button:

1 Select the To: Mail button.
A new Message Composition window appears.

2 Select the Address button from the Message Composition toolbar.
The Select Addresses dialog box appears, as shown in Figure 4.35.

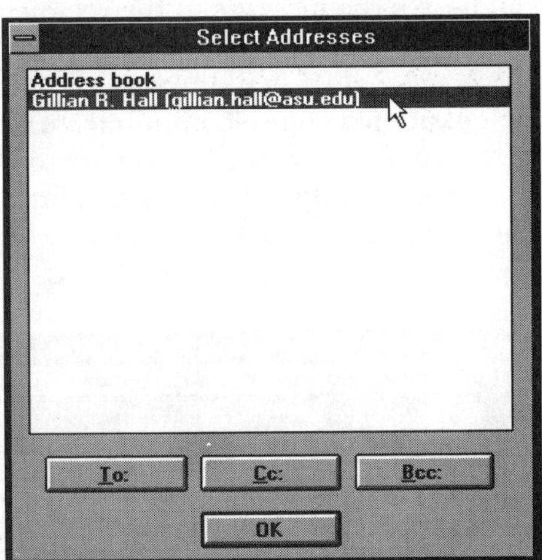

Figure 4.35

3 Select your name from the list displayed in the Select Addresses dialog box.

4 Select the To: button at the bottom of the Select Addresses dialog box.
This means you want your new message to be sent to the selected address.

5 Select the OK button.
Either your name and e-mail address or your nick name (from the Address Book Properties dialog box) is displayed in the Mail To: field of the Message Composition window.

6 Close the Message Composition window to cancel the new message.

> ***Tip*** When using either the Address Book window or the Select Addresses dialog box to address a new message, you can select multiple addresses. Do this by holding down SHIFT while selecting addresses with the mouse. The e-mail message will be sent to all of the addresses selected.

If necessary, you can take a break at this point. If you are working at school, make a note of the Servers settings in the Mail and News Preferences dialog box before you exit Netscape. When you come back, start up Netscape Navigator, re-enter your Servers configuration if necessary, and proceed.

USING E-MAIL LINKS ON WEB PAGES

Once you have configured Netscape for e-mail, you can use the *e-mail links* found on some Web pages. An ***e-mail link*** contains an e-mail address. When clicked, an e-mail link opens a new Message Composition window and addresses the message to the recipient specified in the e-mail link. E-mail links may be particularly useful in your job search, since many employers include e-mail links on their job announcement Web pages to make it easier for you to communicate with them.

As shown in Figure 4.36, it is easy to identify an e-mail link on a Web page. E-mail links look just like text links, except that they are always e-mail addresses.

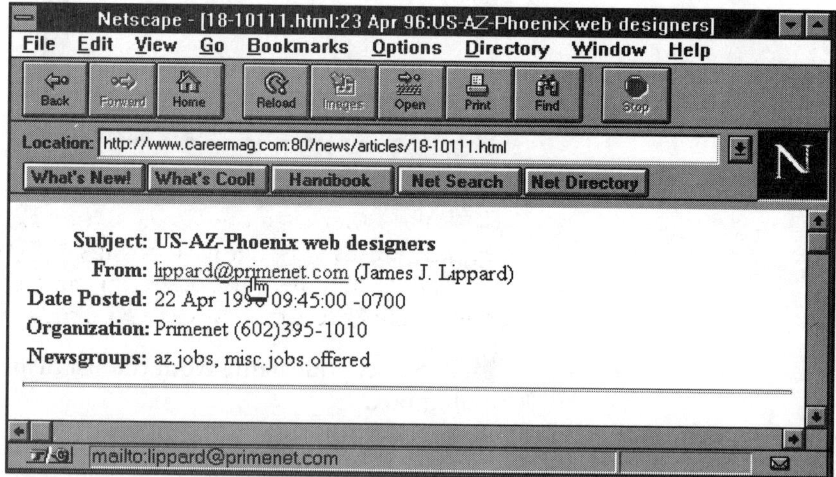

Figure 4.36

When you select an e-mail link, a Message Composition window appears, as shown in Figure 4.37. Notice that the e-mail address shown in the e-mail link is automatically entered in the Mail To field on the Message Composition window.

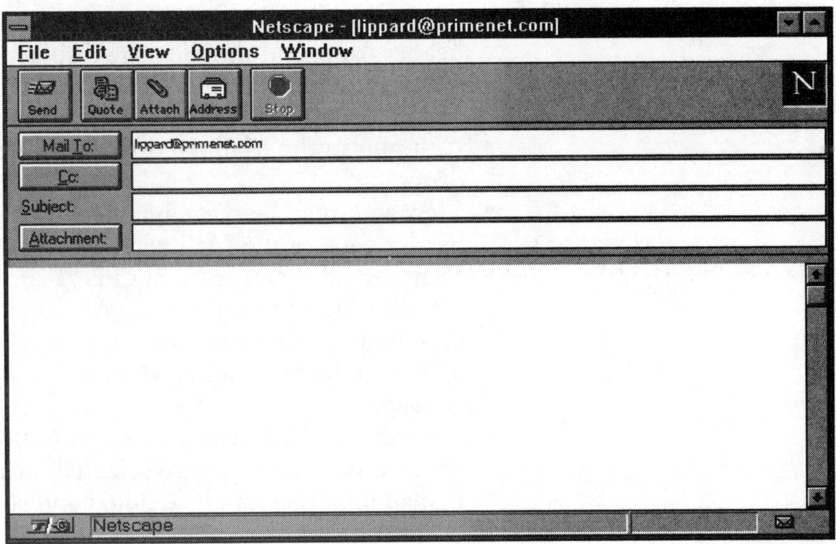

Figure 4.37

THE NEXT STEP

In this project you have learned how to use Netscape Navigator for e-mail. You are now ready to use e-mail to communicate with prospective employers. The next step is to explore sources of information on the Internet other than the Web. In the next project you will learn how to access and use Usenet newsgroups, FTP servers, and Gopher servers.

This concludes Project 4. You can either exit Netscape or go on to work the Study Questions, Review Exercises, and Assignments.

SUMMARY AND EXERCISES

Summary

- Electronic mail (e-mail) is a special way of sending electronic messages from one computer to another.
- An e-mail address is a specially formatted address containing the user name and domain name of the e-mail service provider.
- E-mail messages generally contain three parts: the header, the body, and the signature.
- Netscape must be specially configured for e-mail before you can receive mail with Netscape.
- Use the Servers tab on the Mail and News Preferences dialog box to enter your e-mail address and servers.
- Use the Mail window to access your e-mail.

- The Mail window contains three panes: the mailbox pane, the message header pane, and the message display pane.
- The panes and columns in the Mail window can be resized by dragging and dropping.
- Columns in the Mail window can be rearranged by dragging and dropping.
- View an e-mail message by clicking its message icon in the message header pane of the Mail window.
- Print e-mail messages using File/Print Message(s) in the Mail window.
- The To: Mail button opens a Message Composition window where you can compose an e-mail message.
- The Send button on the Message Composition window sends an e-mail message.
- You can use the Forward and Re: Mail buttons in the Mail window tool bar to forward or reply to selected messages.
- E-mail messages can be deleted and sorted in the message header pane of the Mail window.
- The Address Book allows you to store frequently used e-mail addresses and automatically apply those addresses to new messages.
- You can add, delete, and edit addresses in the Address Book window.
- The Address button on the Message Composition window allows you to select an address from the Address Book.
- You can create a separate signature file using a text editor that you specify in the Identity screen of the Mail and News Preferences dialog box.
- E-mail links are special links that allow you to send e-mail right from Web pages.

Key Terms and Operations

Key Terms

Address Book
body
column
domain name
e-mail
e-mail link
header
mailbox pane
message display pane
message header pane
pane
password
POP server
signature
signature file
SMTP server
Trash folder
user name

Operations

Configure e-mail servers
Configure e-mail identity
Open the Mail window
Resize Mail window panes
Resize Mail window pane columns
Rearrange window pane columns
View e-mail
Preview and Print e-mail messages
Use the Message Composition window
Send e-mail messages
Forward e-mail messages
Reply to e-mail messages
Delete e-mail messages
Sort e-mail message headers
Add addresses to the Address Book
Edit and delete addresses
Send e-mail with the Address Book
Use the Address button
Create a signature file
Use e-mail links to send e-mail from Web pages

Study Questions

Multiple Choice

1. Most e-mail messages are composed of the following three parts:
   a. identity, body, closing.
   b. introduction, text, name.
   c. header, body, signature.
   d. address, body, signature.

2. All e-mail addresses conform to a standard format containing a
   a. user name and address.
   b. identity and location.
   c. identity and domain name.
   d. user name and domain name.

3. The two parts of an e-mail address are separated by a(n) ______.
   a. .
   b. @
   c. &
   d. #

4. The signature portion of an e-mail message generally contains information about the
   a. subject of the e-mail message.
   b. date and time the message was sent.
   c. person who sent the message.
   d. All of the above.

5. The header portion of an e-mail message generally contains information about the
   a. subject of the e-mail message.
   b. date and time the message was sent.
   c. person who sent the message.
   d. All of the above.

6. Before Netscape can be used for your e-mail, you must configure the ______________ screen of the Mail and News Preferences dialog box.
   a. Composition
   b. Organization
   c. Servers
   d. Identity

7. The ______ server handles your outgoing mail, while the ______ server handles your incoming mail.
   a. POP, MAIL
   b. MAIL, SMTP
   c. POP, SMTP
   d. SMTP, POP

8. To access your e-mail, you must provide Netscape with your user name, server information, and
   a. password.
   b. domain name.
   c. protocol.
   d. home page.

9. ________________ is the name of another popular e-mail application.
   a. Eunice
   b. Eugene
   c. Eudora
   d. Unicorn

10. An e-mail link on a Web page looks just like a text link, except it is a(n)
    a. URL.
    b. domain name.
    c. e-mail address.
    d. user name.

Short Answer

1. The ________________ part of your e-mail address identifies the computer which handles your e-mail.
2. Your ______________ should not be shared with anyone.
3. The ____________ portion of an e-mail message is where the actual message appears.
4. You can use ________________ to modify the margins for printing e-mail messages.
5. E-mail messages are displayed by Netscape as _________ documents, just like Web pages.
6. E-mail messages are composed in the ________________ window.
7. When e-mail messages are deleted, they are actually just moved into the ____________________.
8. To permanently delete an e-mail message, you must "________ the ________."
9. A ____________ specified in the Address Book can be used instead of an e-mail address when sending an e-mail message.
10. You can specify your signature file using the __________ screen of the Mail and News Preferences dialog box.

For Discussion

1. Both Web page URLs and e-mail addresses contain domain names. Does *domain name* mean the same thing for both e-mail and Web page addresses?
2. You went to quite a bit of trouble in this project to set up your e-mail preferences using the Mail and News Preferences dialog box. If you are working with a networked version of Netscape, none of your preferences were saved when you exited. If you are using a computer to which others have access, then perhaps you don't want any of your preferences saved (especially your e-mail configuration). Would it be helpful to be able to carry your own Netscape preferences file around with you on a floppy? How might this be useful?

Review Exercises

Give Your Address Book a Workout

1. Add five more addresses to your address book, such as addresses of some of your classmates.
2. Send a message to all five addresses at once, using the Address button on the Message Composition window to select multiple addresses.
3. Send a message to someone, and a copy of the message to yourself using the To and Cc buttons on the Select Addresses dialog box.

Assignments

Finding E-mail Addresses for Your Job Search

Use the Career Magazine Jobline Database to search for jobs in your area. Locate the e-mail addresses of the contact persons for those jobs. (Hint: look for e-mail links.) Add those addresses to your Address Book with descriptions of the jobs advertised.

Creating Mailing Lists

Netscape allows you to create mailing lists with your Address Book. Use the Handbook to find out more about mailing lists, and then create a mailing list containing the addresses of the contact persons you located.

PROJECT 5: USING OTHER INTERNET RESOURCES

Objectives

After completing this project, you should be able to:

- Understand the terms *Gopher*, *FTP*, and *newsgroup*
- Access Gopher servers and search Gopherspace
- Access and use FTP servers
- Configure Netscape's News server
- Participate in newsgroups

CASE STUDY: EXPANDING THE JOB SEARCH

You have come a long way since beginning this book. You are now an accomplished Web surfer. You have organized yourself on the Web with bookmarks, performed Internet searches using a variety of tools, and have even set yourself up to use e-mail with Netscape. These have all been important steps in gearing up for your job search. So far the Internet has provided some very powerful tools for your job search—the World Wide Web and e-mail. But you have learned that the Web and e-mail are just segments of the Internet. Are there other Internet resources out there that you have not yet explored? If there are, could they too be valuable assets in your job search?

An Internet Solution

Now it is time to explore some other Internet resources which might also be useful in your job search. You've heard of these resources—Gopher, FTP, Newsgroups—but do you really know what they are and what they're for? In this project you'll find out!

URLS REVISITED

Remember in Project 1 when we talked about URLs and what the different parts of URLs mean? In that discussion we introduced the idea of a *protocol,* which tells Netscape the document type and how to interpret the document.

So far you have seen only one type of Internet document, a Web page. All Web pages must be interpreted by Netscape using a protocol called HTTP, or Hypertext Transfer Protocol. So the URL of every Web page begins with http: to tell Netscape that the document is a Web page and to interpret it using HTTP.

In Project 1 you also learned that the Web is just one segment of the Internet. As you know, the Internet is much older than the Web, and there is a lot of information on the Internet that is not part of the Web. So what is this other information? You will know it when you see it, because the URL will give it away! As shown in Table 5.1, different types of Internet documents are indicated by different protocols. Web pages use http:, Gopher documents use gopher:, and FTP documents use ftp:.

Table 5.1

Document Type	Protocol and URL Format
FTP	ftp://*domain.name/complete.file.name*
Gopher	gopher://*domain.name:port*
Web pages	http://*domain.name/directory/path/filename.html*

Being able to distinguish different types of Internet documents by their URLs is a good start. Now let's find out just what a Gopher document is and how you can access one.

INTRODUCING GOPHER

We will begin our exploration of other Internet resources with ***Gopher***. The development of Gopher by the University of Minnesota actually laid the groundwork for the philosophy behind the Web—the philosophy of making Internet resources accessible to "the rest of us."

Gopher uses a hierarchical network of menus to guide you to text-based resources located on ***Gopher servers*** all over the world. You can enter ***Gopherspace*** (the world of all Gopher servers) at any level of any Gopher menu and get anywhere—literally. It's just a matter of navigating upward and downward through the great labrynth of menus and submenus sometimes called Gopher burrows.

For many years, Gopher offered the easiest access available to the Internet. However, in recent years Gopher has been left behind by the World Wide Web. The problem is that, while a tremendous amount of information still resides exclusively in Gopherspace, fewer and fewer people are accessing that information because, well… the Web is more fun! In fact, according to some Internet veterans, Gopher is terminally ill. Some say that Gopher is dead, while others insist that Gopher is being reincarnated in the form of super-Web pages. These new Web pages will contain the Web's equivalent of Gopher menus—lists of text links!

What Is a Gopher Server?

Gopher servers are systems made up of hierarchical text-based menus arranged by subject. If you dig deep enough in any of these menus, you'll eventually find text files. Gopher servers are generally maintained by universities and government agencies, and they are good places to find information such as government statistics, large catalogs, and other general information. Gopher servers provide access to both archived (sometimes very old) and relatively current information.

As already noted, however, Internet users are turning away from Gopher servers and looking more to Web sites for information. Existing Gopher servers will gradually begin to disappear, while virtually no new Gopher servers are being brought online, spelling the doom of Gopher. For now Gopherspace still offers a wealth of information not available on the Web. So lets make our first excursion into Gopherspace and burrow a bit!

Using Netscape to Tunnel Through Gopherspace

To access Gopher servers using Netscape, you must have two things: You must have Netscape running, and you need the address (URL) of a Gopher server. So open Netscape (if you need help with this, review the procedure for starting Netscape in the Overview). Since you may not know any Gopher server addresses off the top of your head, we'll give you one. (Let's hope that address is still valid when you read this book!)

To enter Gopherspace:

1 With Netscape running, use the Open button, as shown in Figure 5.1, or the Location field to go to the Arizona State University Gopher Server, whose URL is gopher://gopher.asu.edu

Figure 5.1

Arizona State University's Gopher Menu page is displayed, and will look something like the one shown in Figure 5.2. That's all there is to it. You are now officially in Gopherspace. And from here you can go anywhere else in Gopherspace using the menu items displayed.

Notice that Netscape displays the ASU Gopher Menu page using text links and folder icons. As is the case with Web pages, the Internet (Gopher) document that Netscape has accessed is not nearly as pretty as the one displayed on your screen. Gopher documents are just text—no pretty icons, no colorful menus, just text. Netscape has interpreted the Gopher document in the same way that it interprets Web documents, and displayed it as you see it on your screen. Not bad.

Notice the different types of icons in the Gopher Menu page. The document icon (▤) indicates a link to a text-based document, the folder

( ) icon indicates a link to yet another Gopher Menu page, and the icon shaped like a pair of binoculars ( ) indicates a link to a Gopherspace index or search tool.

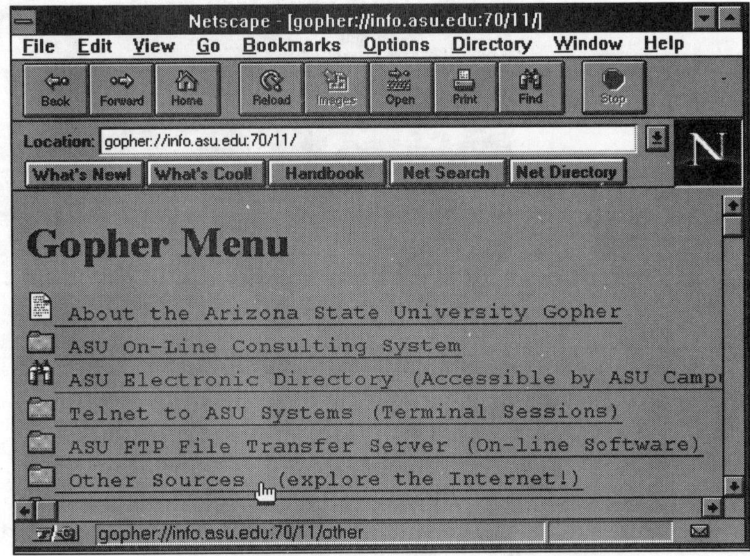

Figure 5.2

2 Scroll through the Gopher Menu page to view all the subjects available on ASU's Gopher server.
The Other Sources (explore the Internet!) menu item (text link) will take you downward in the hierarchy of Gopher menus at ASU, so let's try it.

To tunnel through Gopherspace:

1 Select Other Sources (explore the Internet!), as shown in Figure 5.2. Another Gopher Menu page appears as shown in Figure 5.3. You have just tunneled a little deeper into ASUs Gopherspace.

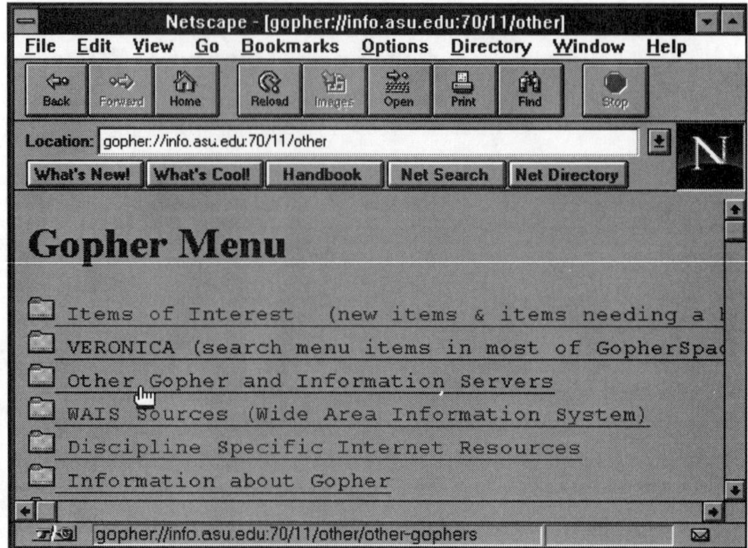

Figure 5.3

2 If it is an available menu item, select Other Gopher and Information Servers from this new Gopher menu, as shown in Figure 5.3.
Yet another Gopher Menu page appears. This time it should look something like Figure 5.4. This page is your gateway to Gopher servers all over the world!

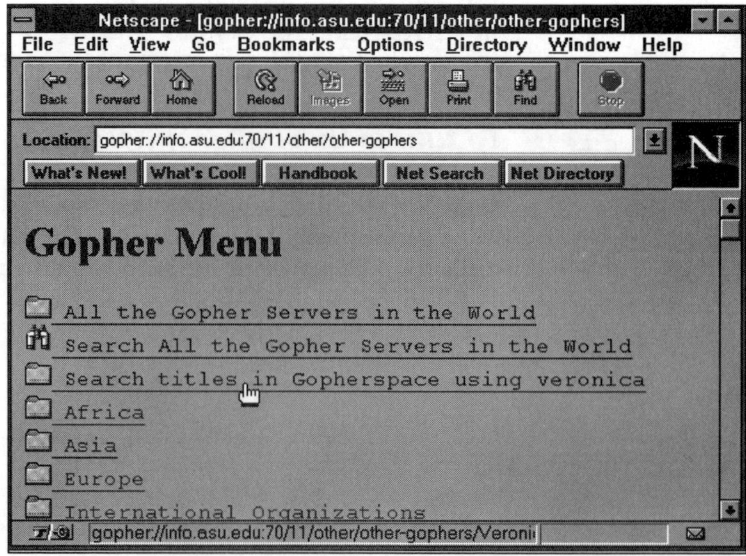

Figure 5.4

Searching Gopherspace Using Veronica

Veronica is a program that indexes Gopher menus. It is used to locate specific information on Gopher servers. Because it has become so popular for searching Gopherspace, there are many Veronica search engines operating on a number of Gopher servers all over the world. In fact, you will find menus on any Gopher server containing options for accessing Veronica.

> ***Tip*** There are a number of stories behind the selection of the name Veronica for this Gopher search engine. One story is that the name is an acronym for Very Easy Rodent-Oriented Netwide Index of Computerized Archives. Another story points out that Veronica is the name of Archie's girlfriend in the classic comic strip. Since Archie is the name of another Internet search system (for FTP servers and documents), that explanation makes sense also.

To access a Veronica search engine:

1 Select Search titles in Gopherspace using veronica (or any menu item suggesting a search using something called Veronica), as shown in Figure 5.4.
Another Gopher menu page appears, like the one shown in Figure 5.5. This menu provides a number of options for searching Gopherspace.

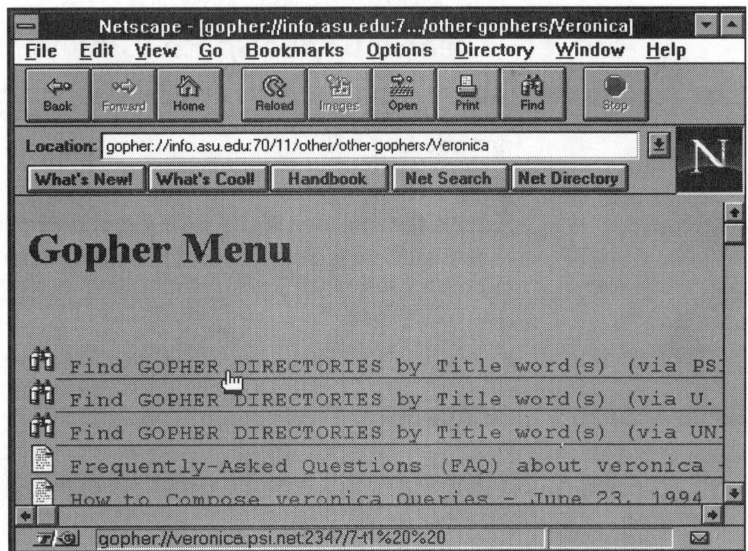

Figure 5.5

2 Select one of the menu options beginning Find GOPHER DIRECTORIES by Title word(s)..., as shown in Figure 5.5.

A Veronica Gopher Search screen appears as shown in Figure 5.6. Notice that the address (URL) of the Veronica Gopher Search engine you have accessed is displayed as part of the title. This is just how Netscape interprets Gopher Search pages like this one.

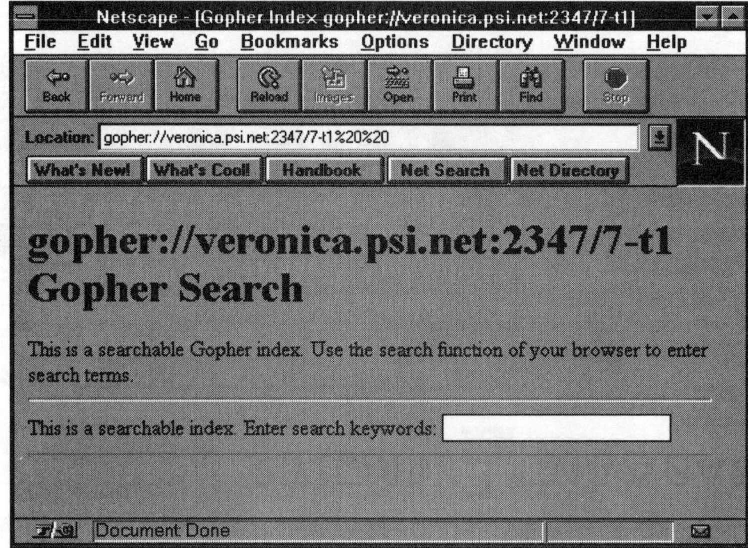

Figure 5.6

To search Gopherspace using Veronica:

1 On the Gopher Search page type **`employment`** in the keywords field provided.

2 Press (ENTER) to begin your search.
After a few moments, a list of Gopher directories (from all over the world) that match your search will be displayed on the screen, something like that shown in Figure 5.7.

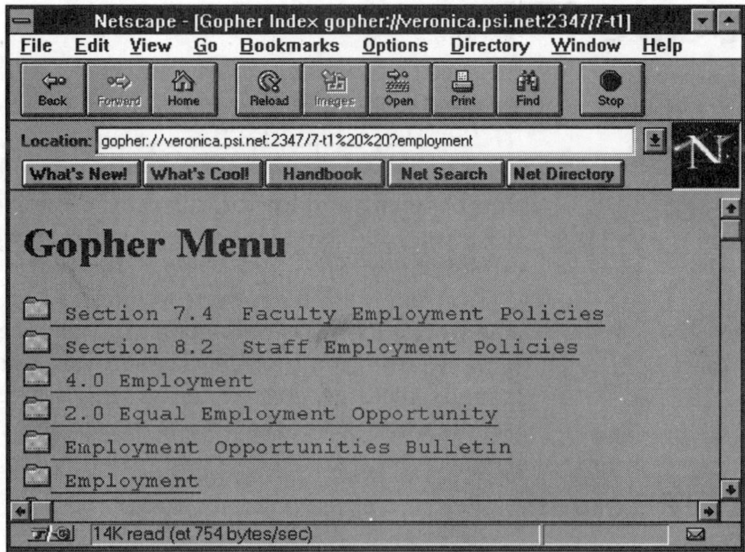

Figure 5.7

3 Scroll through this list of Gopher directories that match your request. At the end of the list, you'll see a statement that there are more indexed Gopher directories that match your request (That number may be VERY large!).

4 Explore other Gopher directories by selecting them. Look for useful sources of information for your job search.
Notice the status bar as you pass your mouse over each directory. The URL displayed in the status bar is for the link over which you are passing. It will give you a clue as to the location of the given Gopher directory.

> ***Tip*** Use the Back and Forward buttons to navigate up and down through menus you have visited.

You may notice that many of the Gopher directories you visit appear to be "empty" when you visit them. Remember all the talk at the beginning of this project about the decline and fall of Gopher? Well, when you encounter an empty Gopher directory, you're experiencing it first hand.

> ***Tip*** Place a bookmark on any Gopher documents or directories you encounter that may be useful in your job search. Yes, you can bookmark any kind of Internet document, not just Web pages.

EXIT If necessary, you can take a break at this point. When you come back, just start up Netscape Navigator and proceed.

INTRODUCING FTP

Now we will shift gears and go from Gopher to ***File Transfer Protocol (FTP)***. Very simply, FTP is a means by which computers communicate with one another and exchange files. At one time, long ago, FTP involved lots of typing and lots of frustration. Luckily for all of us, those days are long past, and Netscape now provides one of the easiest FTP interfaces around.

You can use FTP to retrieve files and transmit files virtually anywhere in the world. FTP has revolutionized the ease with which we can obtain goodies from the Internet like software updates, shareware programs, sounds, pictures, government forms, movies, and so on. FTP has also made sending files easier than it has ever been before.

What Is an FTP Server?

Unlike Gopher servers, FTP servers are a thriving dynamic force on the Internet. Companies and even individuals are setting up FTP servers at the pace fax machines were being set up in the 1980s. FTP servers allow companies to provide customers with all kinds of documentation online. They also facilitate data sharing between individuals. For example, the authors and publishers of this book utilized FTP constantly, passing projects back and forth between Arizona, Oregon, and California for revisions and review. The only printouts we made were for our own reference. When it came to sharing the latest version of the latest project, we sent the files electronically, using FTP.

FTP servers are computers on the Internet set up to send and receive files using the File Transfer Protocol. FTP server administrators, select which directories can be accessed, which files can be downloaded, and into which directories users can upload files. Some FTP servers require special passwords for either download or upload access. All of these issues are determined by the FTP server administrator.

Using Netscape to Access FTP Servers

To access FTP servers, you need an FTP server address. Once again, we will provide you with an address, but you won't get as much mileage out of it as you did the Gopher address. Unlike Gophers, FTP servers contain no links to other FTP servers. Each FTP server is basically on its own. You can get to it if you know the address or stumble upon a link to it on a Web page. But once you get to an FTP server, you can only poke around on that FTP server. You cannot jump to some other FTP server unless you know its address too.

To access an FTP server:

1 Use the Open button, as shown in Figure 5.8, or the Location field to go to the FTP server of (oh dear) the IRS. It is located at ftp://ftp.fedworld.gov

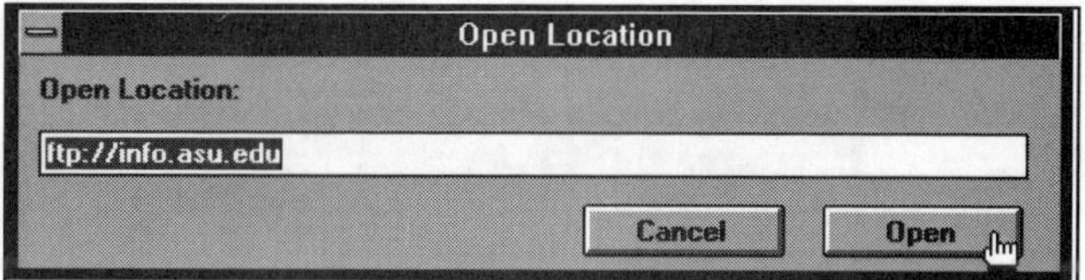

Figure 5.8

The IRS FTP server directories are displayed, similar to Figure 5.9.

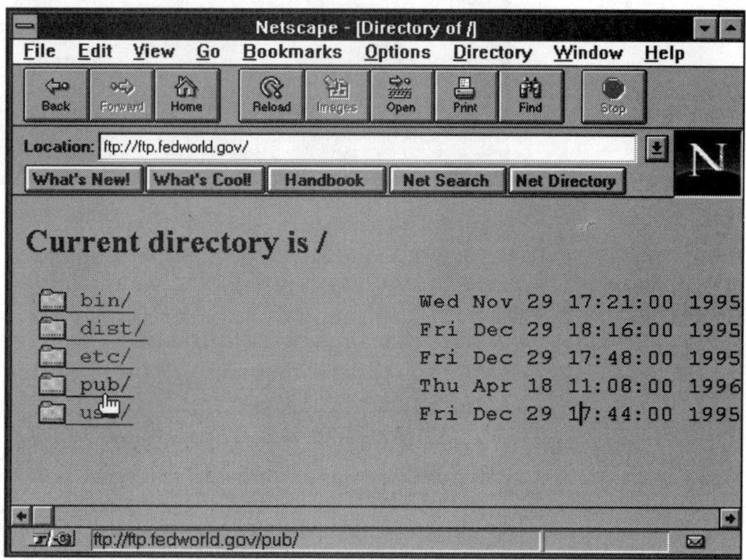

Figure 5.9

It doesn't get much easier than that. You have officially arrived at your first FTP server. From here you can explore the resources the IRS has put at your disposal.

Notice that Netscape displays the FTP server using folder icons ( ) for directories. There are also special icons for documents and executable files (programs), which you will see shortly. The names of directories are displayed as text links. When you select one of these text links, the contents of the directory will be displayed.

To get around on an FTP server:

1 Select the pub/ text link on the IRS FTP server as shown in Figure 5.9.

Most FTP servers have a pub directory that normally stores interesting information. The contents of the pub directory are displayed as shown in Figure 5.10

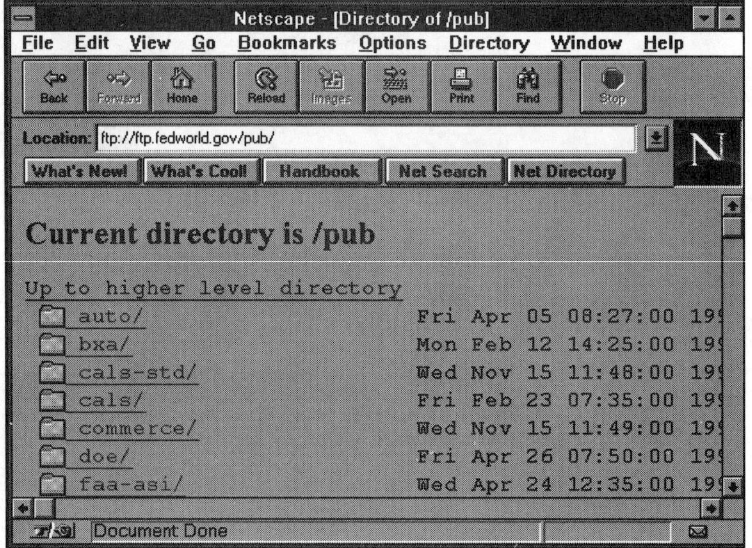

Figure 5.10

Notice that the current directory name (and its path) are always displayed at the top of the screen as the title. Notice too that you can go back up the hierarchy of directories using the Up to higher level directory text link. These are standard features of FTP servers when they are displayed using Netscape.

2 Scroll down through the list of directories displayed, and select the irs-ps/ directory when you come to it, as shown in Figure 5.11.

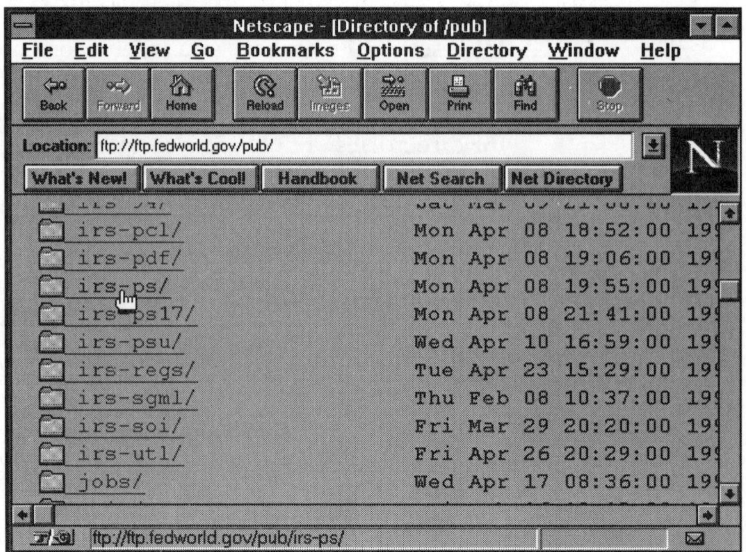

Figure 5.11

The pub/irs-ps directory of the IRS FTP server is displayed, as shown in Figure 5.12. Notice that program files and text files are displayed with special icons.

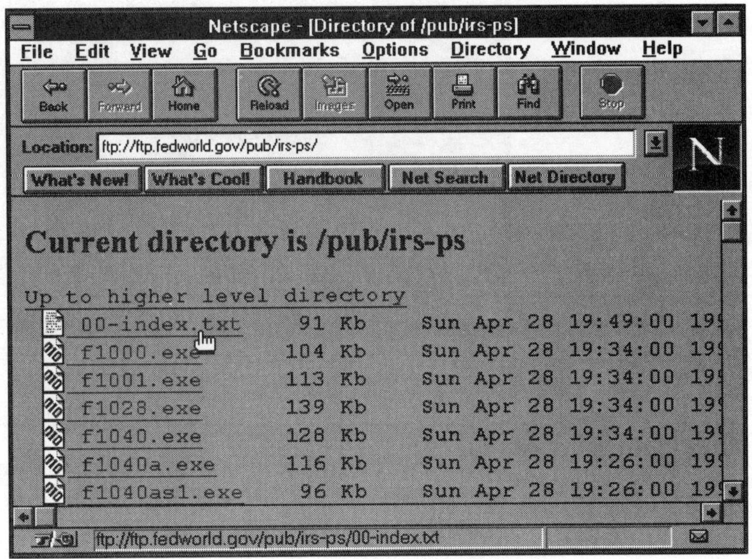

Figure 5.12

Care to guess what types of files this directory contains? That's right, tax forms. This is a useful FTP site around tax time. Rather than running to your local government office, fighting crowds, and standing in lines, you can download all the tax forms you've ever dreamed of using the IRS FTP server. Let's first have a look at the index for this directory.

To view a file on an FTP server:

1 In the pub/irs-ps directory, select the file called 00-index.txt, as shown in Figure 5.12.
The file called 00-index.txt is displayed on your screen, as shown in Figure 5.13. This file contains a listing of the contents of the pub/irs-ps directory and a brief description of each file.

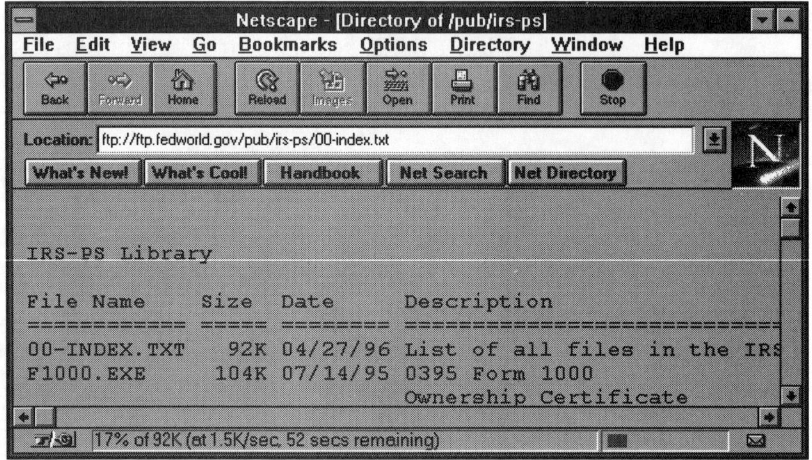

Figure 5.13

2 Scroll down through the index file until you find the description of the 1040EZ form (the description should read something like "199X Form 1040EZ"). Look at the file name corresponding to the description—probably F1040EZ.EXE.

3 Use the Back button to return to the pub/irs-ps directory.

To download a file from an FTP server:

1 Scroll down through the contents of the pub/irs-ps directory until you come to f1040ez.exe.

2 Select the file f1040ez.exe.
The standard Windows Save As dialog box appears as shown in Figure 5.14. You have just initiated your first FTP file transfer. You are now going to *download* an electronic version of the 1040EZ tax form. ***Downloading*** a file means copying it from a remote computer to a disk on your computer.

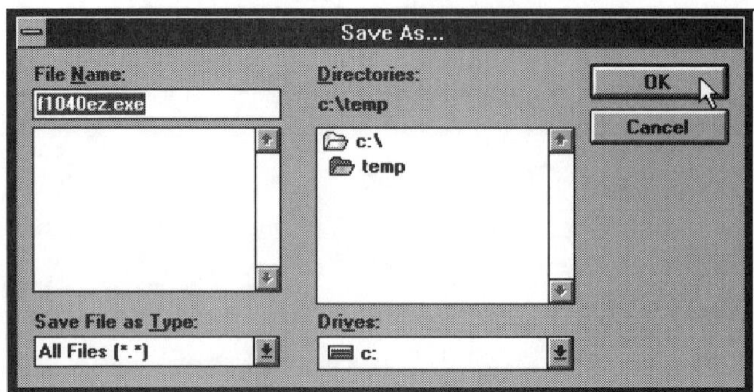

Figure 5.14

3 Using the Drives and Directories lists in the Save As dialog box, select a location to save the file f1040ez.exe, as shown in Figure 5.14.

4 Select the OK button.
The Saving Location dialog box appears, and the FTP file transfer begins, as shown in Figure 5.15.

Figure 5.15

The Saving Location dialog box tells you the name of the file being downloaded, the location where it is being saved, the size of the file, the elapsed time, and the estimated time for completing the download. When the download is complete, this dialog box will disappear.

The file you just downloaded from the IRS FTP server is in a special format. It is ***archived***, or ***compressed***, to make it faster to download. Archived files are generally what we call ***self-extracting***. This means that the instructions needed for decompressing the file have been included with the file itself. When opened, a self-extracting archived file will write a decompressed version of the file to the same directory where the archived file resides. Receiving archived or compressed files is almost standard in the world of FTP. No one wants to wait twice as long to download a file that could have arrived in half the time if it had been compressed.

To use a downloaded file:

1 Open the File Manager in Windows, and locate the downloaded file. Ask your instructor for assistance if you need help with this step.

2 When you have located the downloaded file, as shown in Figure 5.16, double-click it.

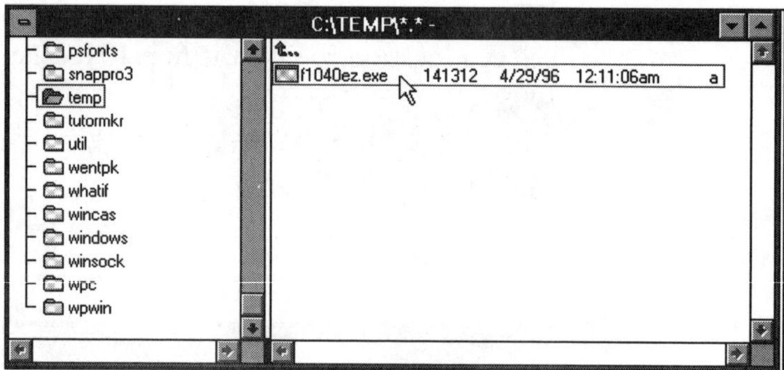

Figure 5.16

The file automatically extracts or decompresses. The decompressed file is written to the same location as the downloaded file and is called f1040ez.ps. The .ps file extension indicates the file type. In this case, the file is in a special format called PostScript (.ps). If you would like, you can now print the file using a DOS command.

3 Double-click the MS-DOS Prompt (located in the Windows Program Manager Main program group). Again, ask your instructor for help if necessary.

To print the downloaded Postscript file, your computer must be connected to a Postscript printer. To print the file, you will use a DOS command in the following format: copy *filename printer*, where *filename* is the path and name of the file (e.g., c:\temp\f1040ez.ps), and *printer* is the name of the port to which the desired printer is connected (e.g., lpt1).

In this case, the DOS command will be copy c:\temp\f1040ez.ps lpt1. Your instructor can help you with this step if you need assistance.

4 At the DOS prompt type `copy c:\temp\f1040ez.ps lpt1`
Confirm the printer port (lpt1) with your instructor. If instructed to do so, you may need do substitute lpt1 with another port (e.g., lpt2).

5 Press (ENTER)
The file is sent to the printer, and in a few moments you will be in possession of an official 1040EZ tax form.

6 After the form has printed, type `exit` at the DOS prompt to return to the Program Manager, then return to Netscape.

Searching FTP Servers Using Archie

You just successfully downloaded a file from an FTP server, decompressed it, and printed it. This is quite an accomplishment. But how would you have found the IRS FTP server if we had not supplied the address (URL)? And how do you find other resources like programs, information, pictures, sounds, and movies that are also available on FTP servers all over the world?

Earlier in this project, you had the opportunity to search Gopherspace using a system called Veronica. As we mentioned, Veronica has a counterpart in the world of FTP named ***Archie*** (perhaps a pet name for archival retrieval system). Archie is designed to maintain a continually updated database of files stored on ***anonymous*** FTP servers. In this case anonymous means FTP servers that do not require special permission and passwords for outsiders (like you) to log on. Netscape attempts to log you on as an anonymous user (automatically entering "anonymous" as your user name and your e-mail address as your password).

Because there are so many anonymous FTP servers around the world and they contain so many files, Archie servers must work day in and day out. They are constantly searching the FTP sites in their geographical areas, updating their databases, and sharing their data with other Archie servers.

As was the case with the Veronica search engine you used to search Gopherspace, you must first find an Archie server before you can use it to find FTP files. Table 5.2 lists a few Archie server addresses in the U.S. that will get you started. You can easily find an Archie server on your own, too. Using an Internet search service, as you did in Project 4, you can search for Archie FTP and come up with a long list of Archie servers all over the world.

Table 5.2

Archie server URL	Location
hoohoo.ncsa.uiuc.edu/archie.html	Illinois
archie.unl.edu	Nebraska
archie.internic.net	New Jersey
archie.rutgers.edu	New Jersey
archie.ans.net	New York
archie.sura.net	Maryland

To access an Archie server:

1 Use the Open button or the Location field to go to the following address: **`hoohoo.ncsa.uiuc.edu/archie.html`**
Netscape loads the Archie Request Form shown in Figure 5.17.

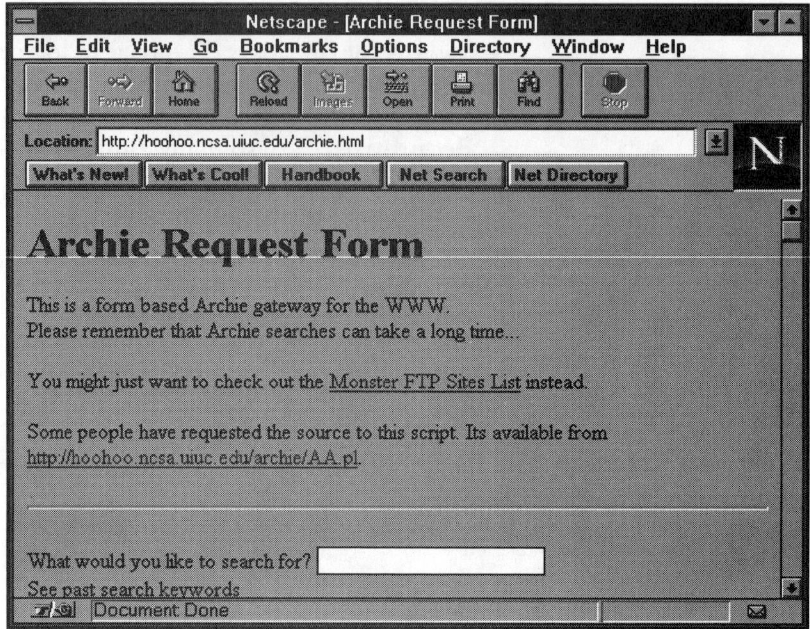

Figure 5.17

2 Scroll down to view the entire page.
A description of Archie appears at the bottom of the page.

3 Read the description, and then scroll back to the top of the page.

To perform an FTP search using Archie:

1 In the field labeled What would you like to search for? on the Archie Request Form, type **`pk204g.exe`**
This is the archived version of PKZIP, a very common file compression utility for the PC.

2 Scroll down to the menu labeled There are several types of searches, and if it's not already selected, select the option Case Insensitive Substring Match.
This will give you the broadest search possible.

3 Select By Host in the field labeled The results can be sorted by.

4 Scroll down to the menu "The impact on other users can be".
This menu allows you to select the priority for your search. The priority you select affects the speed of searches others are performing on the same Archie server. Menu options range from "very nice" to "not nice at all". The bottom line is that the "meaner" you are, the faster you will get your search results, while others' searches will be slowed down.. Select the option that satisfies your conscience.

5 Scroll down to the menu Several Archie Servers can be used.
From this menu you will select the Archie server that will be accessed for your search. Selecting a server on your continent usually speeds up the search results considerably.

6 Select University of Nebraska.

7 In the field labeled You can restrict the number of results returned, type **10**
This means that only the first ten matching files will be displayed.

8 Select the Submit button to begin your search.
Archie searches tend to take a while, so sit back and be patient while you wait for the results to be displayed. An example is shown in Figure 5.18.

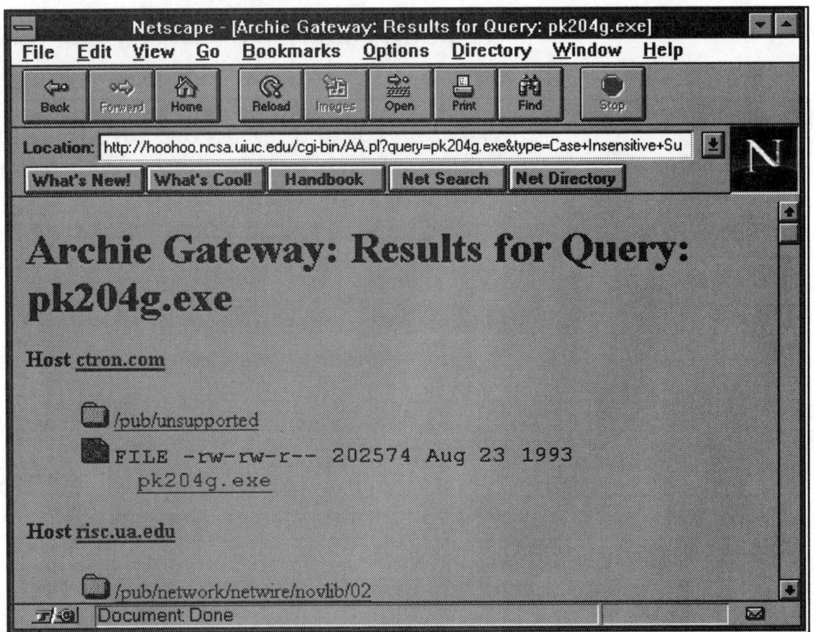

Figure 5.18

On the Archie Request Form, you can select text links to the Host or the FTP server on which the matching file resides, and Netscape will take you to that FTP server. You can also select a text link to the specific directory on that host where the file is located. Or, you can select a link to the file itself. In doing so the process of downloading the file will begin.

Limitations of Using Archie for FTP Searches

There are a few noteworthy disadvantages associated with using Archie to locate files on FTP servers. First, Archie searches are often very slow. Second, you must know the name of the file for which you are searching. Because most files on FTP servers are archived, they often have rather obscure names. For example, if you are looking for a copy of PKZIP, a very common file compression utility available on most FTP servers, you will probably have no luck using PKZIP as your search parameter on an Archie server. That's because PKZIP is archived using other file names like pk204g.exe. But why would you know the archived file name? The answer is that you probably wouldn't. The third major disadvantage with using

Archie is that, while we are told these databases are updated "constantly," Archie servers are often way out of date. The IRS tax form you just downloaded is a good example. At the time this book was written, the file f1040ez.exe was nowhere to be found using any Archie server in North America. Finally, Archie is useful only for finding files on FTP servers. You cannot use it directly to find the servers themselves. For example, searching for IRS using Archie will not turn up the IRS FTP server. It will only turn up files archived on FTP servers with names containing or exactly matching IRS.

Searching for FTP Servers Using the Web

These days the Web is really the best choice if you want to search for resources on the Internet. Archie is rapidly being abandoned in favor of friendlier, faster, easier methods for performing FTP searches. In fact, you can easily locate FTP servers for most organizations by locating Web pages for those organizations. Those Web pages generally contain links to their FTP servers or to specific files or directories on those servers. For example, while you may not be able to locate the IRS FTP server using Archie, you can easily locate it using any of the Web search services discussed in Project 3 (like Yahoo!, Magellan, or Infoseek Guide) with search parameters such as Internal Revenue Service, Department of Revenue, or US Government. Once you have found the Web page, the FTP server won't be far off.

Most anonymous FTP servers are accessed through the Web. People surfing the Web often stumble upon an interesting Web page with a tantalizing link that says "Click here to download some cool stuff," and off you go into the wonderful world of FTP without even trying!

Tip You can place a bookmark on any FTP servers (or even files or directories located on FTP servers) you encounter that may be useful in your job search. Yes, you can bookmark any kind of Internet document, not just Web pages!

If necessary, you can take a break at this point. When you come back, just start up Netscape Navigator and proceed.

INTRODUCING USENET NEWSGROUPS

Usenet is a term that is actually older than the Internet itself. ***Usenet*** refers to an earlier system of interconnected mainframe computers that used standard telephone lines and early versions of desktop modems. Articles for discussion were transferred from one computer to another using this system. The term *Usenet* has persisted over the years, but newsgroups (the way in which the Usenet is organized) have come a long way both in the technology used to support their communications and in popularity.

Newsgroups are electronic discussion groups, where people with an interest in common can carry on virtual conversations with each other. Each newsgroup generally limits the discussion to just one topic, but there are literally thousands of newsgroups on the Internet discussing everything from motorcycles to breast cancer to alien encounters to Buddhism to finding a job!

As with e-mail, Netscape must be configured to access newsgroups. Before you can begin configuring Netscape for newsgroups, you must first start Netscape, so go ahead and do that now.

To access news preferences:

1 Select Mail and News Preferences from the Options menu, as shown in Figure 5.19.

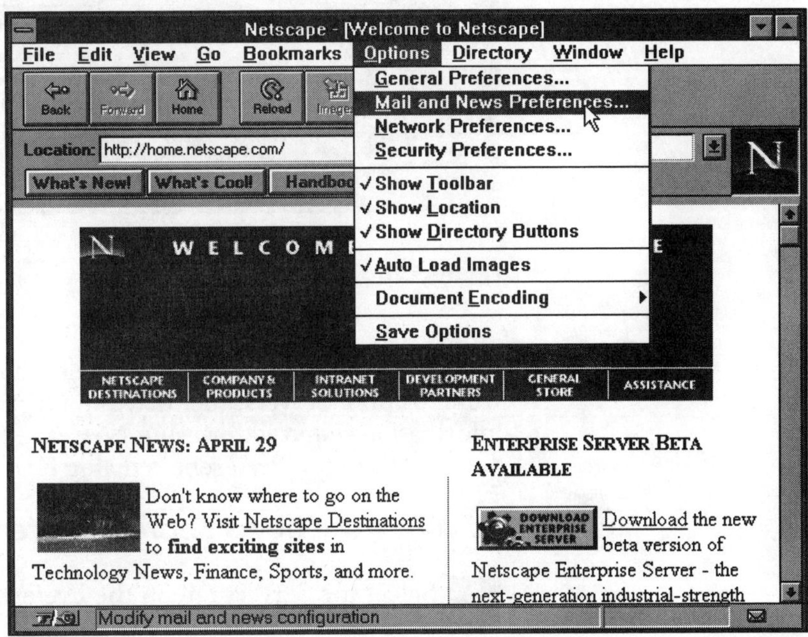

Figure 5.19

The Preferences dialog box used for configuring Netscape for newsgroups appears as shown in Figure 5.20. This dialog box should look very familiar. You saw it in Project 4 when you configured Netscape for e-mail.

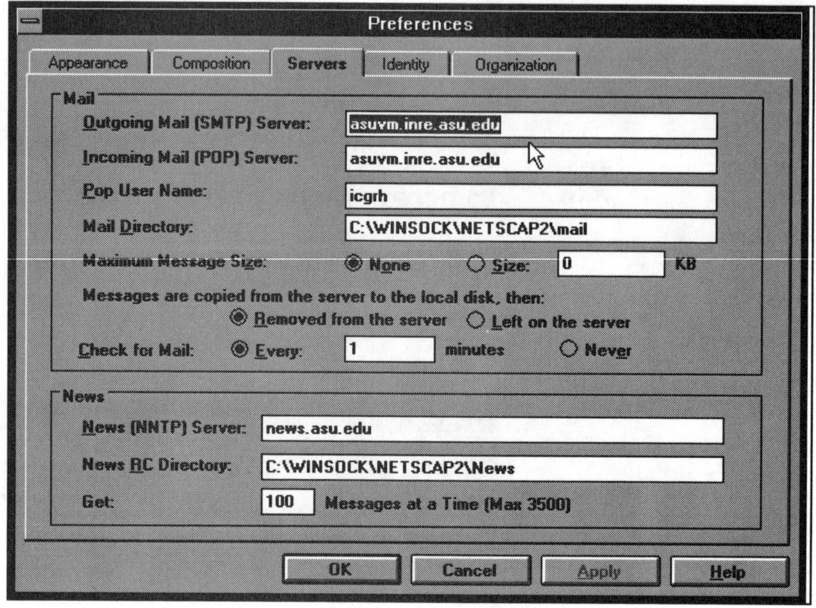

Figure 5.20

Notice the tabs at the top of the dialog box labeled Appearance, Composition, Servers, Identity, and Organization. As with e-mail, the information required for using Netscape for newsgroups is listed under the Servers tab in the Preferences dialog box.

To configure news Servers preferences:

1 Select the Servers tab on the Preferences dialog box, as shown in Figure 5.20.

The same Servers preferences screen you used to specify e-mail configuration also allows you to specify your news server configuration. As you continue through the following numbered steps, we will describe the fields in the News section of the Servers screen.

News (NNTP) Server: Netscape must connect to the appropriate news server in order to interact with Usenet newsgroups. To do this, Netscape needs the domain name of your NNTP server. Your instructor will tell you if the default is correct or what address to enter if not.

2 With your instructor's help enter the address of your news server in the News (NNTP) Server field.

> ***Alert!*** The information shown in Figure 5.20 is only an example. You must enter your own news server address. The one shown here won't do you any good at all!

News RC Directory: This field should contain the name of the folder (or subdirectory) where Netscape will keep your newsgroup subscription and information files. Netscape may display a default here. Your instructor will help you to determine if the default is appropriate, of if you should designate a folder in your computer account at school.

3 With your instructor's help enter the path and name of your news directory in theNews RC Directory field.

Get: This simply allows you to limit the number of messages you can transfer from the server in one block. The larger the number, the longer it takes to transfer each block of messages. This may be useful later on if you subscribe to a number of newsgroups, some of which send a large number of messages per day. For now just stick with the default, 100.

4 Select the OK button.

Accessing Newsgroups Using Netscape

Now that you have Netscape configured for newsgroups, you are ready to open the News Window. You will use this window to interact with newsgroups.

To open the Netscape News window:

1 Choose the Netscape News from the Windows menu, as shown in Figure 5.21.

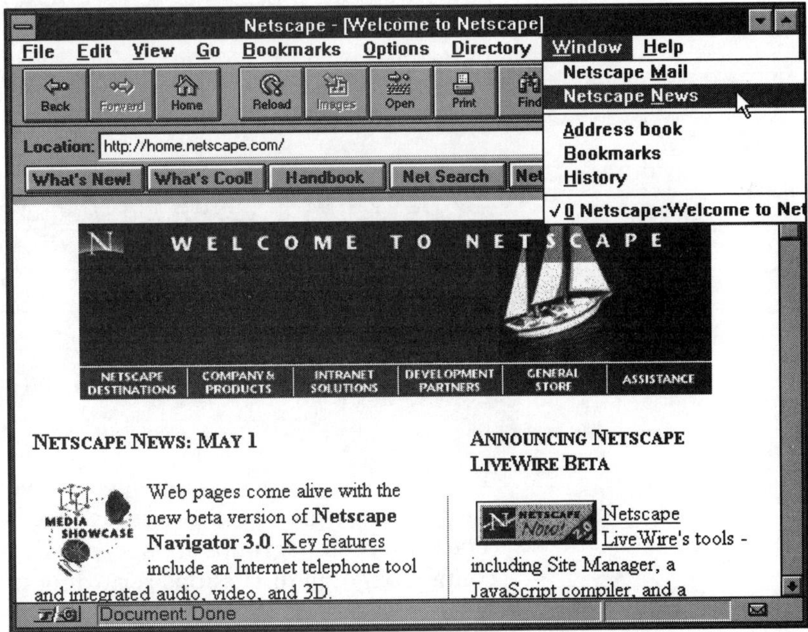

Figure 5.21

The Netscape News window appears as shown in Figure 5.22. Notice that the News window is very much like the Mail window for using e-mail. Like the Mail window, the News window contains a message header pane, message display pane, and, in place of the e-mail mailbox pane, a ***news server pane***. The news server pane contains news servers and newsgroups to which you are connected.

In Project 4 you learned to resize and move Mail window panes and column headers. You can use these same skills to manipulate the News window.

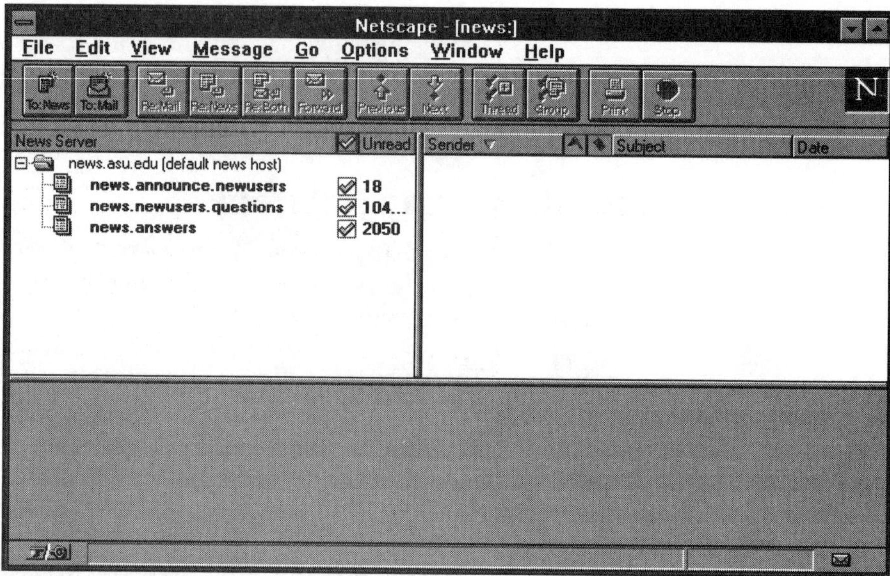

Figure 5.22

Don't Panic If there is something wrong with your News Servers configuration, you will get some sort of error message regarding Netscape's ability to communicate with your news server. If this happens, go back to the Servers Preferences screen, and get your instructor to help you track down the problem. It is probably just a typo, so don't worry.

The first time you access newsgroups, you are automatically subscribed to the three newsgroups shown under the News Server header in Figure 5.22. These three newsgroups are specifically for new newsgroup users and contain ongoing discussions regarding using Usenet newsgroups.

To browse newsgroup categories:

1 To see other newsgroups (besides the three to which you are currently subscribed), choose Show All Newsgroups from the Options menu, as shown in Figure 5.23.

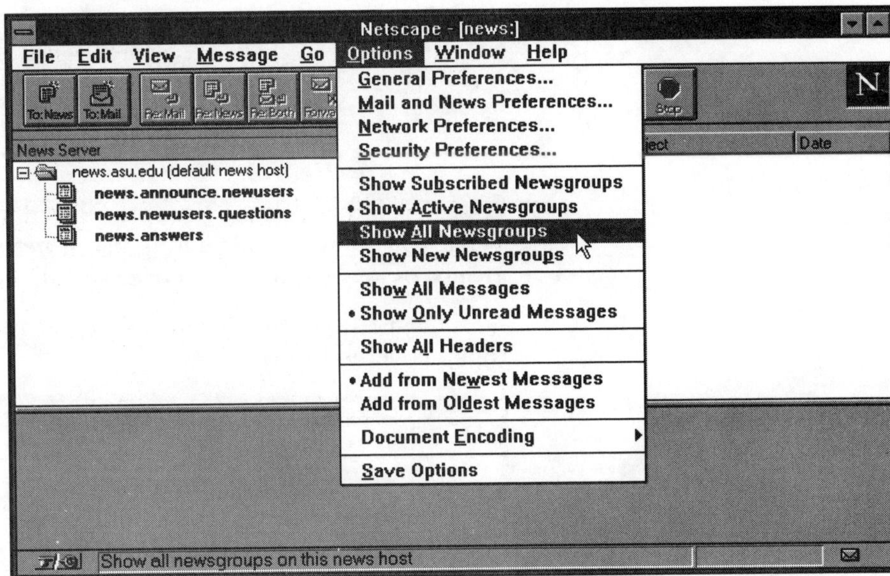

Figure 5.23

As shown in Figure 5.24, all the newsgroups kept on your news server will be displayed under the New Server header.

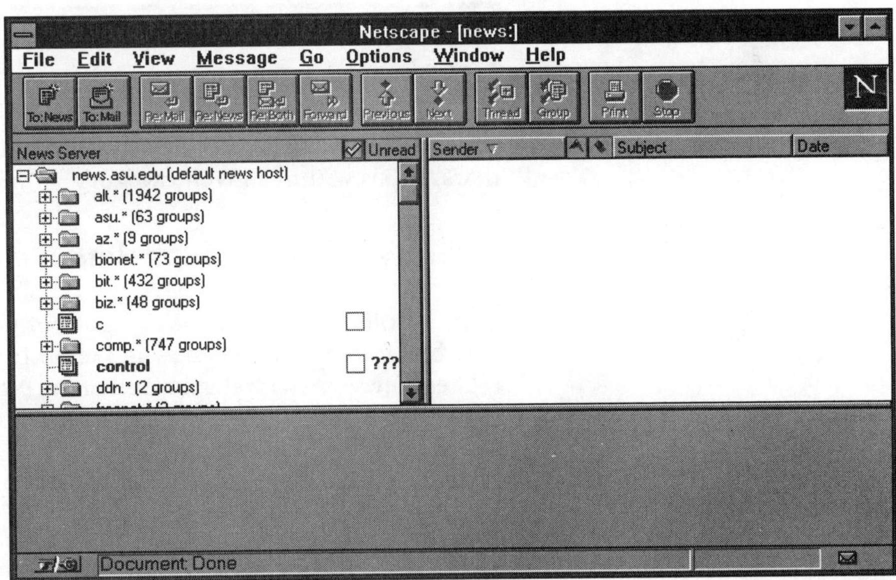

Figure 5.24

Don't Panic if the newsgroups listed on your screen are different than those displayed in Figure 5.24. There is no standard list of newsgroups, and the list is always changing.

2 Scroll through the list of displayed newsgroups.
What you see is actually a long list of ***newsgroups categories***, which are groups of newsgroups that cover specific topics.

Table 5.3 lists just a few of the major newsgroup categories and the topics covered by each.

Table 5.3

Category	Topic
alt.	Alternative—topics outside the mainstream; sometimes very controversial
biz.	Business—topics related to the business world
comp.	Computers—topics concerned with computers
rec.	Recreational—topics related to recreational interests
sci.	Science — focuses on scientific issues
soc.	Social—focuses on debate over social issues

The number of newsgroups currently within each category is listed next to the category name in the News window. You can view a list of the newsgroups within a given category.

To browse newsgroups within a category:

1 Scroll down to the biz category of newsgroups and double-click it.
The biz. folder icon opens as shown in Figure 5.25 and the list of business-related newsgroups is displayed below. Notice that there are subcategories of biz. These are folders within the biz category folder.

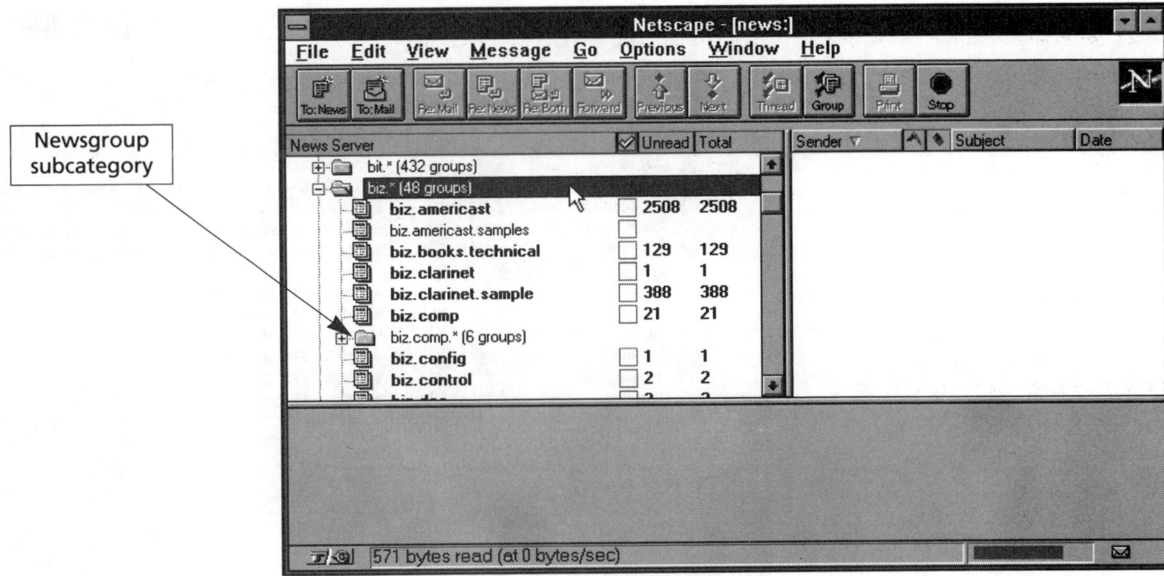

Figure 5.25

2 Scroll through the list of biz newsgroups to find a newsgroup related to jobs or employment.
Notice that the number of messages associated with each newsgroup appears under the Unread and Total column headers. (You may need to size the mailbox pane or the column headers for better viewing.)

To browse a newsgroup's messages:

1 If you find it displayed in your list of biz newsgroups, select the newsgroup called biz.jobs.offered. Otherwise, select any newsgroup that sounds like it might be useful in your job search.
All of the messages from the selected newsgroup are displayed in the message header pane of the News window.

2 Resize the panes and columns of the News window to view the list of message headers better, as shown in Figure 5.26. (Refer to Project 4 if you need a refresher on resizing parts of a window.)

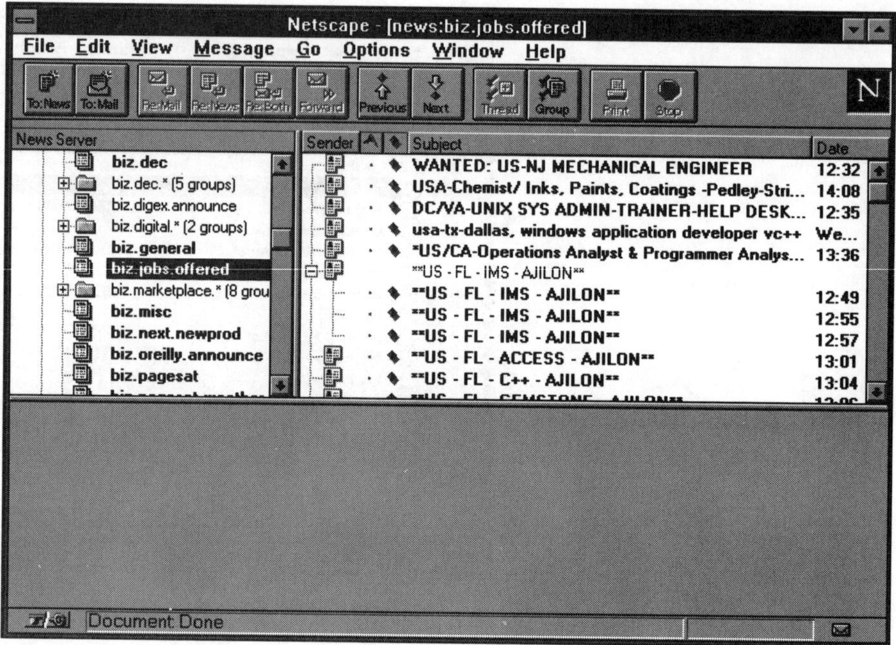

Figure 5.26

To view a newsgroup message:

1 Scroll through the list of messages displayed in the message header pane of the News window. Look for something that peaks your interest.

2 When you find a job announcement that appeals to you, select it. The selected message will appear in the message display pane of the News window as shown in Figure 5.27. You may wish to resize the message display pane for a better look at the body of the message.

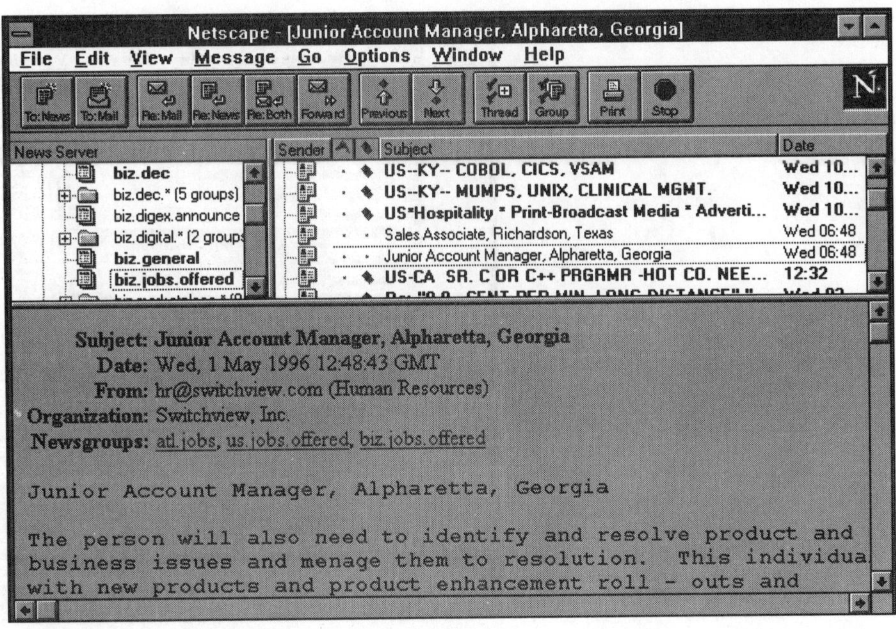

Figure 5.27

3 Use the scroll bar to view the entire message.
Notice that you may reply to this message using the same Re: Mail button on the toolbar that you use to reply to e-mail. So if this job sounded good, you could just select the Re: Mail button and request an application packet from the company!

Once you have identified newsgroups like this one that have information in which you are interested, you may wish to subscribe. Subscribing to a newsgroup does not put you on any mailing lists nor does it make you the member of any group. A newsgroup subscription is simply a way for you to keep better track of the goings on in that newsgroup.

To subscribe to a newsgroup:

1 Click in the check box opposite the name of the displayed newsgroup (biz.jobs.offered), as shown in Figure 5.28. You may have to change the size of the news server and message header panes to see the subscription check boxes. That's all there is to it. You have just subscribed to the biz.jobs.offered newsgroup!

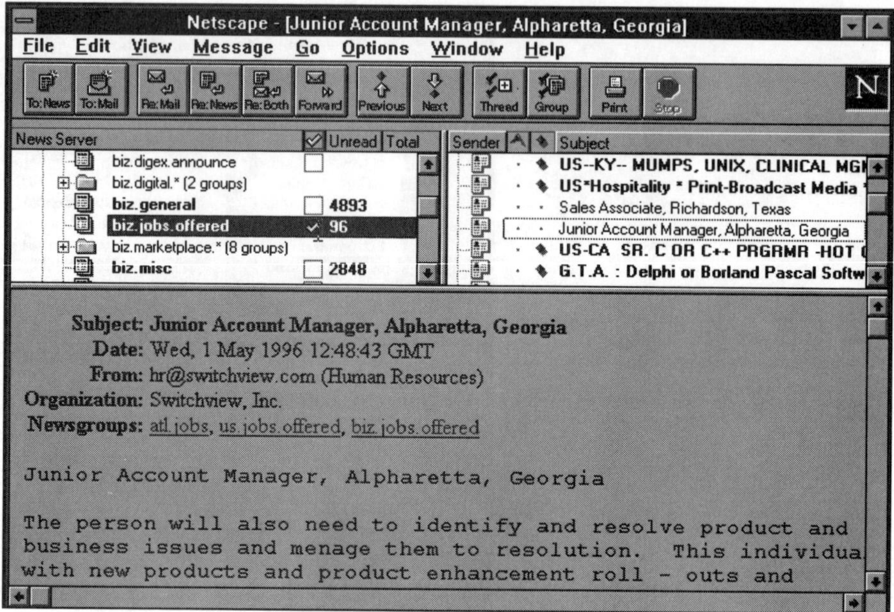

Figure 5.28

2 Choose Show Subscribed Newsgroups option from the Options menu.

As shown in Figure 5.29, biz.jobs.offered has been added to your list of subscribed newsgroups.

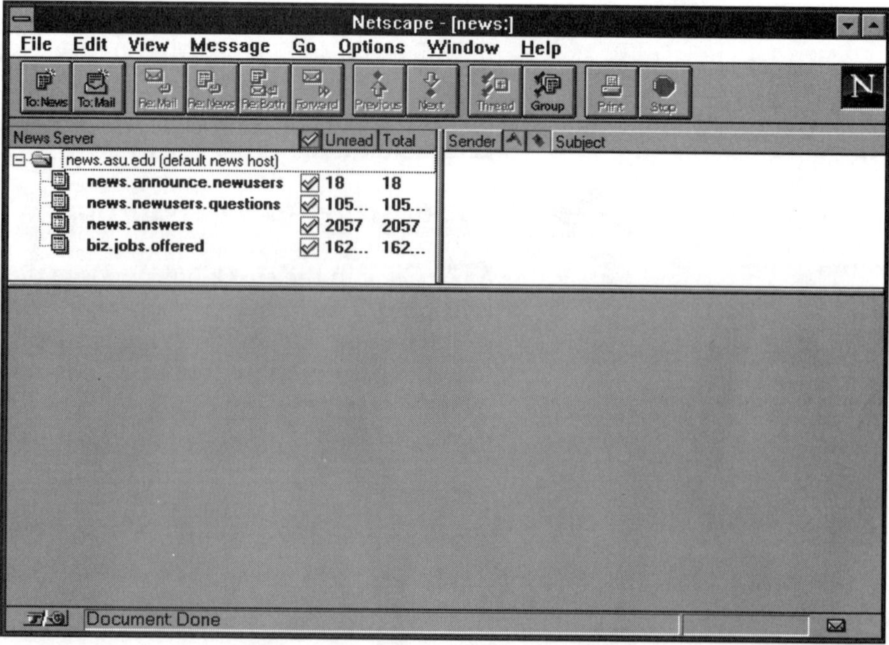

Figure 5.29

> ***Tip*** To cancel your subscription to a newsgroup, click the check box to the right of the newsgroup name.

THE NEXT STEP

In this project you have learned about a few more resources available to you on the Internet: Gopher, FTP, and Usenet newsgroups. You also learned how to use Netscape to access, search, and utilize these valuable resources.

This concludes Project 5. You can either exit Netscape or go on to work the Study Questions, Review Exercises, and Assignments.

SUMMARY AND EXERCISES

Summary

- Like Web pages, FTP and Gopher resources have special URL protocols — ftp: and gopher:, respectively.
- Gopher uses a hierarchical network of menus to guide you to text-based information resources on Gopher servers all over the world.
- Gopherspace is the complex network of interconnected Gopher menus.
- Many Gopher resources are being transferred to the Web due to its growing popularity.
- To access a Gopher server, you need to know its address (URL).
- Gopher menus are displayed in Netscape using menus of text links and icons indicating the types of links.
- Veronica is a popular search engine used to search Gopherspace for specific resources.
- File Transfer Protocol (FTP) is a means of passing from one computer to another.
- An FTP server is a computer that has made certain files available for downloading and certain directories available for uploading files.
- You can access an FTP server by using its URL or by selecting a link to an FTP server from a Web page.
- Netscape displays FTP servers using directory and file icons and text links to guide you through the hierarchy of directories.
- FTP servers provide many types of files, including graphics, programs, sounds, movies, text files, and more.
- Most files available on FTP servers are archived or compressed.
- Archie is a popular database system used to search all known FTP servers for specific files.
- Usenet newsgroups are electronic discussion groups.
- In order to access newsgroups using Netscape, you must configure a news server.
- You can view all newsgroups served by your news server using the News window in Netscape.

- Newsgroups are organized into categories and subcategories by discussion topics.
- You can subscribe to a newsgroup by selecting the Subscribe check box.
- You do not need to subscribe to a newsgroup to participate in its discussions.

Key Terms and Operations

Key Terms

anonymous
Archie
archived file
category
compressed file
download
File Transfer Protocol (FTP)
Gopher
Gopher server
Gopherspace
newsgroup
news server pane
self-extracting file
Usenet
Veronica

Operations

Navigate Gopher menus
Use Veronica
Navigate FTP directories
Download a file
Use Archie
Configure News Servers
Open the New Window
Browse newsgroup categories
Browse newsgroups
Browse newsgroup messages
View a message
Subscribe to a newsgroup

Study Questions

Multiple Choice

1. The protocol portion of an URL tells you the __________ of the Internet document.
   a. size
   b. age
   c. type
   d. location

2. Gopher uses a hierarchical network of __________ to access resources.
   a. categories
   b. servers
   c. locations
   d. menus

3. When you are exploring the complex network of interconnected menus that make up the collection of Gopher servers, you are said to be tunneling through
   a. a rabbit warren.
   b. Gopherspace.
   c. a worm hole.
   d. cyberspace.

4. Gopher servers are currently ______________ in number due to the growing popularity of the Web.
   a. increasing
   b. decreasing
   c. not changing
   d. exploding

5. Many resources that have previously been available on gopher servers are being migrated over to
   a. FTP servers.
   b. mainframe computers.
   c. the Web.
   d. CD-ROMs.

6. The popular search engine used to search Gopherspace is called
   a. Archie.
   b. Magellan.
   c. Yahoo!.
   d. Veronica.

7. FTP stands for
   a. File Transfer Paradigm.
   b. File Transfer Protocol.
   c. File Type Protocol.
   d. Fiberoptical Transfer Packet.

8. You ____________ a file from an FTP server to a storage device on your local computer.
   a. translate
   b. download
   c. upload
   d. encrypt

9. A Usenet newsgroup is an electronic
   a. magazine.
   b. news program.
   c. discussion group.
   d. e-mail clearing house.

10. Newsgroups are organized into ____________ based on the ____________ of discussion for that newsgroup.
    a. categories, rating
    b. topics, length
    c. topics, subcategories
    d. categories, topic

Short Answer

1. ____________ describes the complex interconnected network of Gopher menus on Gopher servers all over the world.
2. Veronica is a ____________ used for searching Gopher menus.
3. Gopher menus are organized by ____________.
4. You do not need a special password to log on and access a(n) ____________ FTP server.
5. The directory in which most of the interesting files are kept on an FTP server is generally called ________.
6. In Netscape, you can begin downloading a file from an FTP server simply by ____________ its icon.
7. To view a text file on an FTP server, without initiating the download process, you can ____________ it.
8. Archie searches all known FTP servers for a specified ______ name.
9. You can keep better track of the discussion going on in a newsgroup by ____________ to that newsgroup.
10. Before Netscape can access newsgroups, you must configure your ____________ server.

For Discussion

1. Why are resources previously available on Gopher servers migrating to the Web?
2. What is the difference between Gopher and FTP? Give an example of information or resources you would consider looking for using each.

3. Describe Veronica and Archie. What are they and what is the difference between them?

Review Exercises

Using Gopher to Visit the World

Visit Gopher servers in Africa, Asia, and Europe. Navigate using the Gopher menus alone.

Downloading an Application

Download a copy of PKZIP from an FTP server. Remember to search for the file name pk204g.exe.

Browsing Newsgroup Messages

View the messages in the three newsgroups related to new users to which you were automatically subscribed when you configured Netscape for news. Read any messages that interest you, and then take yourself off of these three newsgroups.

Assignment

Finding Job-Related Newsgroups

Locate five more newsgroups that provide a forum for jobs offered. Use your Internet search services (try Yahoo!) or just explore the newsgroup categories. Subscribe to the newsgroups you find.

Project 6: Creating Your Own Web Page

Objectives

After completing this project, you should be able to:

- Design and develop a simple Web page
- Use HTML tags to format a Web page
- Insert graphics and links in a Web page
- Open and view your Web page using Netscape
- View the HTML source code for any Web page

Case Study: Managing the Job Search

You are rapidly approaching graduation and for the past few weeks have been busily learning how to use Netscape to access valuable job search resources on the Internet. In fact, you have probably spent more time recently learning about the Internet than you have polishing your resume. Never fear! Your big chance to show off your resume in its best light may be coming up soon!

Actually, you have been hearing a lot of talk around campus about "my home page" this and "her home page" that. All this home page stuff sounds both intriguing and intimidating at the same time. But now that you have a solid foundation with the Internet using Netscape, you're beginning to wonder if creating your own Web page is really all that mysterious and difficult. After all, could it be much harder than, say, configuring e-mail servers?

An Internet Solution

A personal Web page can be very useful in your job search. Imagine prospective employers visiting a professionally created Web page where you present, your resume, a brief biography, and an e-mail link. Would you be impressed if you were an employer? Maybe. By the end of this project you will have the skills necessary to put together just such a Web page. But first you will be guided through the process of creating a Web page to organize the employment resources you have located during your travels on the Internet. If nothing else, when you finish this project, you'll be able to say, "Been there, done that," the next time someone tries to impress you with their Web mastery by telling you that they have their own Web page.

INTRODUCING THE HYPERTEXT MARKUP LANGUAGE

As we pointed out in the beginning of this book, the Hypertext Markup Language (HTML) is a simple programming language used to create Web pages. If you are a die-hard fan of early word processors like WordPerfect and WordStar for DOS, then HTML will suit you nicely. But if you always thought typing "bold" before words you wanted bold in your word processing documents was irritating and archaic, then welcome to your worst nightmare, because in this project, that's the kind of thing you'll be doing!

Basically, HTML involves using *markup tags* (very much like old-time word processor formatting tags) to enclose text you want your Web browser to interpret and display in a particular way. These markup tags fall into four general categories: technical tags, formatting and style tags, logical tags, and attribute tags. Some of these tags are very simple. Some are not so simple. The good news is that the language has a small number of tags, and we will give them all to you here along with examples of how to use them.

With all that said, let's get started developing your first Web page. You won't be needing Netscape for awhile, so if it's not open now, don't bother. Instead, we'll begin by using the Windows text editor, Notepad.

LAYING OUT THE STRUCTURE OF YOUR WEB PAGE

All HTML documents have a few things in common. The basic layout is pretty simple and involves a few markup tags that, with one exception, all HTML documents must contain. These tags are called ***technical tags*** and are used to structure your HTML document.

To begin creating an HTML document:

1 Press (ALT) + (ESC) to go to the Windows Program Manager window.

2 Open the Accessories application group.

3 Double-click the Notepad icon in the Accessories application group to open the Notepad application.

> ***Tip*** You can use any text editor or word processor. We suggest using Notepad for this project because it is probably available to you. Also, it saves documents as text (no formatting). If you use a word processor (like MS Word), you will have to take care to save your document in text format.

Table 6.1 provides a summary of all the HTML technical tags. They include a tag that indicates the document is an HTML document (<HTML>), a tag indicating the ***header*** of the document (<HEAD>), a tag for indicating the text that should appear in the title bar when the document is displayed (<TITLE>), and a tag indicating the ***body*** portion of the document (<BODY>). All of these tags occur in pairs, enclosing some portion of the HTML document, and they are nested in the following fashion: The <HTML> tag encloses the <HEAD> and <BODY> tags, and the <HEAD> tag encloses the <TITLE> tag. Confused? Don't be. We'll go through it step by step.

Table 6.1

Technical tags	Description
<HTML> *document* </HTML>	Encloses entire HTML document
<! *comments* >	Encloses each comments line
<HEAD> *header* </HEAD>	Encloses document header, contains title and optional comments
<TITLE> *title* </TITLE>	Encloses document title displayed in window title bar
<BODY> *body* </BODY>	Encloses body of document

To indicate the document type:

1 Type **<HTML>** on the first line of your Notepad document.
The <HTML> tag indicates that this is the beginning of an HTML document. This is important because all Web browsers know how to interpret HTML documents.

2 Press (ENTER) a few times.

3 Type **</HTML>**
The </HTML> tag indicates the end of an HTML document. As shown in Figure 6.1, you now officially have an HTML document displayed in your Notepad window. It's a pretty simple document—in fact it will be completely blank if you look at it with Netscape, but it's an HTML document nonetheless.

> ***Tip*** HTML tags are not case sensitive. This means that it does not matter whether you type tags as <HTML> or <html>. Typing tags in uppercase letters is simply a convention used by many HTML authors. It makes finding the tags in a document much easier.

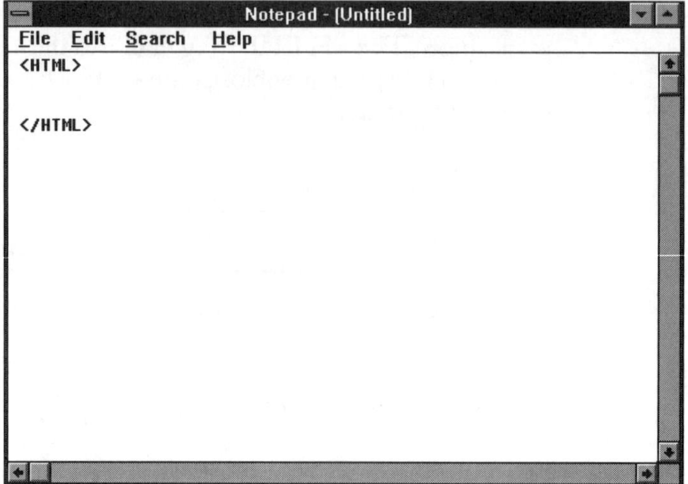

Figure 6.1

To insert some comments about your document:

1 Position the insertion point two lines below the <HTML> tag in your Notepad document.

2 Type `<!`
The <! tag indicates the beginning of a line of *comments*. You can use ***comments*** to describe the document and its contents "silently." Your comments will not be displayed when the document is viewed with a Web browser. Comments give a professional touch to Web pages.

3 Type **`This is a job search resources Web page developed at >`**

4 Press (ENTER)

5 Type `<!` ***`your school's name`*** **`by`** ***`your name`*** `>`

6 Press (ENTER)

7 Type `<!` **`on`** ***`today's date.`*** `>`

You have just coded three lines of comments in HTML. Your Notepad document should now look something like Figure 6.2 (Note that you should have entered your own school, name, and the current date). You can insert any other comments you want. Just remember that each line of comments must begin with <! and end with >

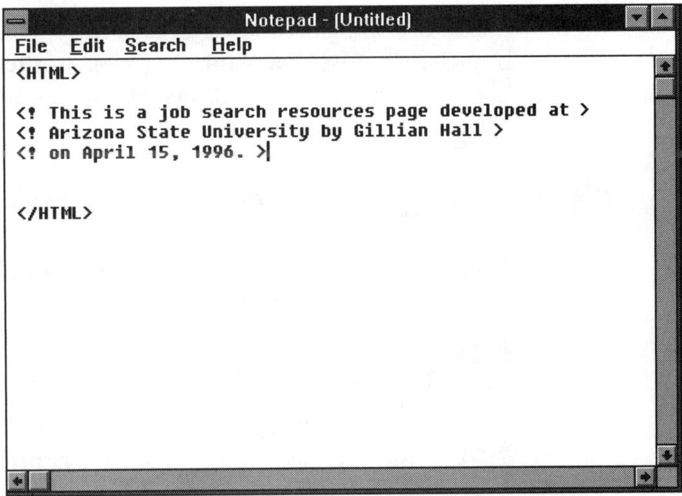

Figure 6.2

The <HEAD> tag comes next. This tag indicates to your Web browser the portion of the HTML document that is the header.

To designate the header portion of your document:

1 Position the insertion point two lines below the last comment line in your Notepad document.

2 Type **<HEAD>**
The <HEAD> tag indicates the beginning of the header portion of your HTML document.

2 Press (ENTER) two times.

3 Type **</HEAD>**
The </HEAD> tag indicates the end of the header portion of the document. Your HTML document should now look similar to Figure 6.3.

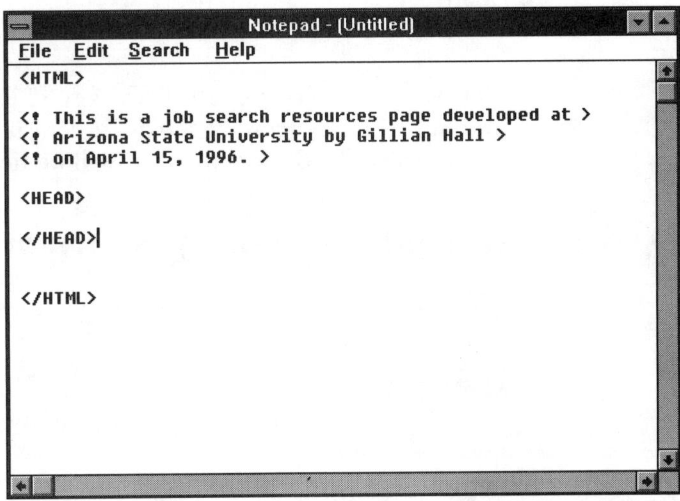

Figure 6.3

Next we will insert the <TITLE> tag. This tag indicates to your Web browser the text you want to appear in the title bar when the document is displayed. Because the title is part of the document header, it will be nested within the <HEAD> tag.

To indicate text for display in the title bar:

1 Position your insertion point on the line below the <HEAD> tag in your Notepad document.

2 Type **<TITLE>**
The <TITLE> tag indicates the beginning of the title bar text for your HTML document.

3 Type **Job Search Resources </TITLE>**
The </TITLE> tag indicates the end of the title bar text for your HTML document. What you have just done is indicate that when your document is displayed by a Web browser, the title bar should read, Job Search Resources. Your HTML document should look similar to Figure 6.4.

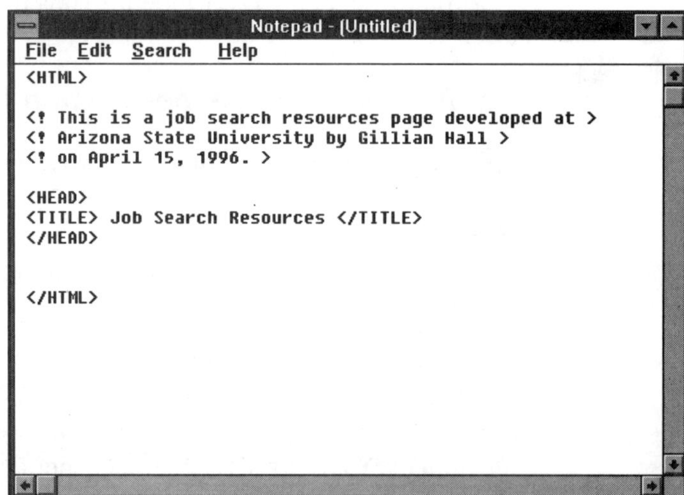

Figure 6.4

Next we will insert the <BODY> tag. This tag indicates to your Web browser which portion of the document is the body. Because the body is part of the HTML document, it will be nested within the <HTML> tag.

To designate the body portion of your document:

1 Position the insertion point two lines below the </HEAD> tag in your Notepad document.

2 Type **<BODY>**
The <BODY> tag indicates the beginning of the body portion of your HTML document.

3 Press (ENTER) twice.

4 Type **`This is the body of my job search Web page.`**

5 Press **W** twice.

6 Type **</BODY>**
The </BODY> tag indicates the end of the body portion of your HTML document.

7 Press **W**
Your HTML document should look similar to Figure 6.5.

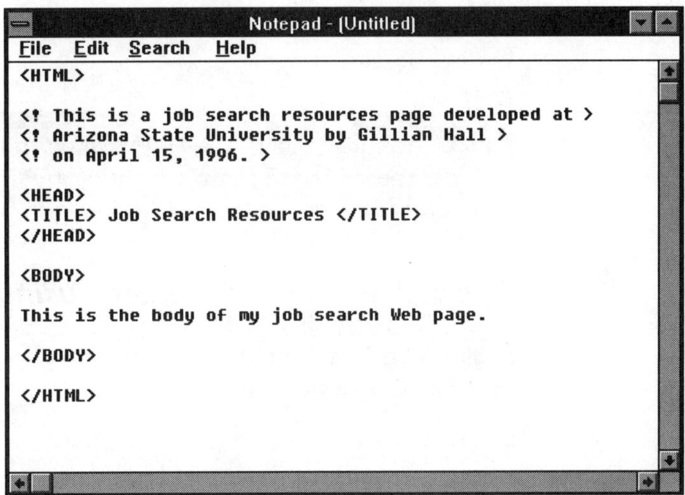

Figure 6.5

You now have a complete Web page. It has all the necessary components. It is properly formatted, and it is ready to be displayed using Netscape. Of course, you have not yet inserted some of the fancy features like text links, picture links, graphics, sounds, or movies (not to mention meaningful content), but you do have before you a legitimate HTML document. So let's save your work and have a look at your document using Netscape.

To save a file using Notepad:

1 Choose Save As from the Notepad File menu.

2 Save your document as MYPAGE.HTM, as shown in Figure 6.6. You may save it on a floppy disk, to your computer account, or to the hard drive on the computer you are using. Ask your instructor which location is best.

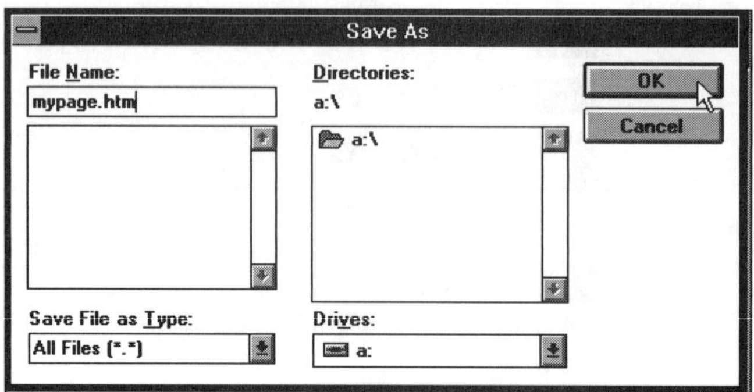

Figure 6.6

> ***Tip*** Be sure to save your HTML document using .htm as the file type. This is the standard file type used (on PCs) for HTML source code documents.

To open an HTML document using Netscape:

1 Open Netscape if necessary, and choose Open File from the File menu as shown in Figure 6.7.

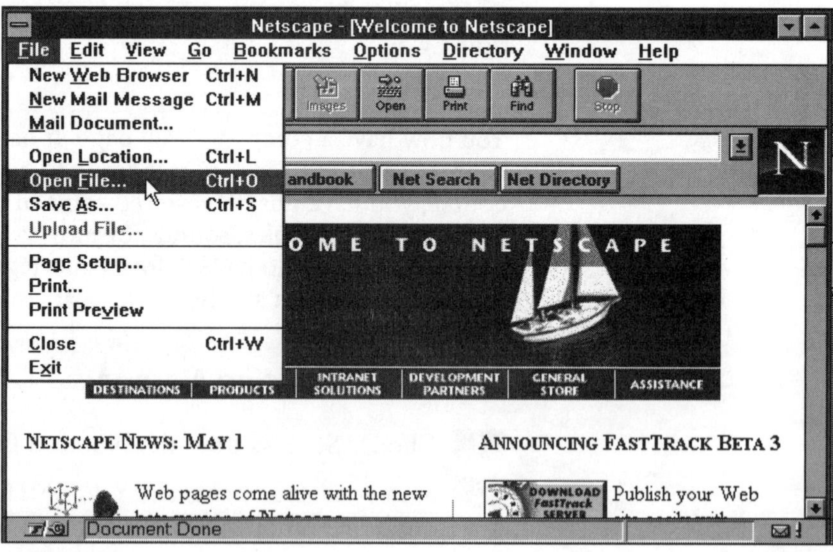

Figure 6.7

> ***Tip*** You can also open a document in Netscape by pressing CTRL + O

2 Select your MYPAGE.HTM file using the Open dialog box, as shown in Figure 6.8.

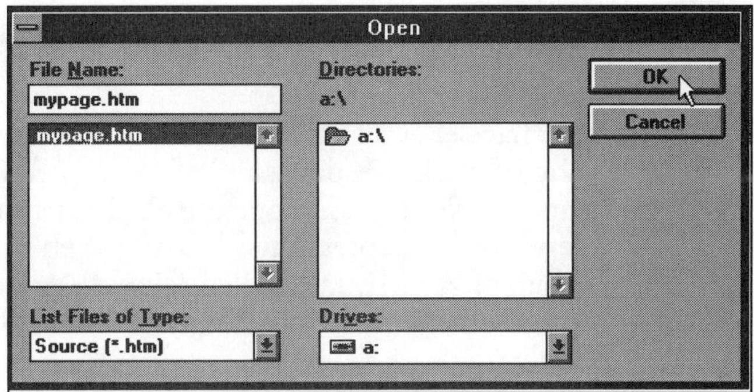

Figure 6.8

3 Select the OK button in the Open dialog box to open your file. Your HTML document is displayed, as shown in Figure 6.9. Notice that the title bar displays the text you entered. The body of the document is a bit short now, but it's exactly what your HTML code says it should be. Let's move on and expand it.

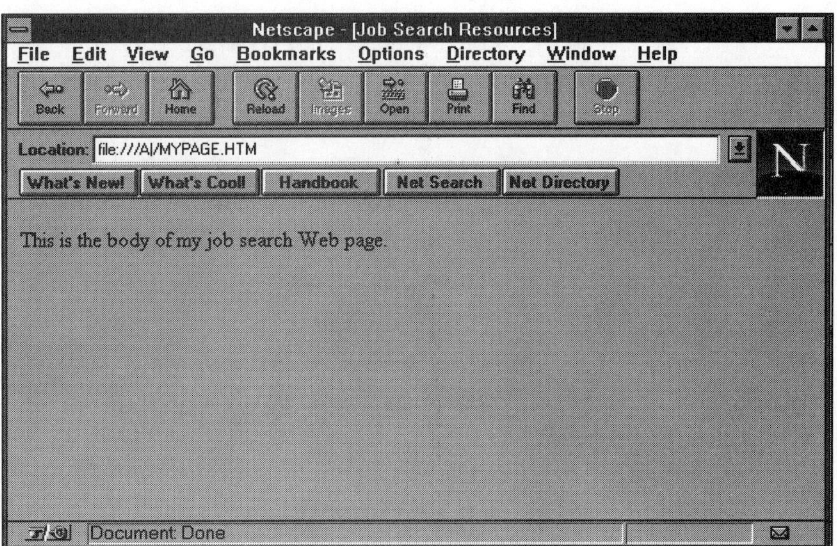

Figure 6.9

EXIT If necessary, you can take a break at this point. When you come back, just use Notepad to open your HTML document, MYPAGE.HTM, and proceed.

FORMATTING THE BODY OF YOUR WEB PAGE

You have created an HTML document (an actual Web page), but you have a bit of work ahead of you before it will look like some of those fancy Web pages you've seen in your travels through the Internet. The next step in developing a professional-looking Web page involves the use of another group of HTML tags called ***formatting and style tags***. These tags are used to lay out and format the body of your HTML document, as described in Table 6.2.

Table 6.2

Formatting and Style Tags	Description
<H1> *heading* </H1>	Encloses largest heading
<H6> *subheading* </H6>	Encloses smallest heading
<P> *paragraph* </P>	Encloses a paragraph
 	Creates a line break
<HR>	Creates a line and paragraph break
<PRE> *formatted text* </PRE>	Encloses text that should appear as formatted
<BLOCKQUOTE> *text* </BLOCKQUOTE>	Encloses a block of text that should be indented
<ADDRESS> *e-mail address* </ADDRESS>	Normally found at the end of the page and holds contact information
<UL> *bulleted list* </UL>	Encloses an unnumbered list (bulleted list)
<OL> *numbered list* </OL>	Encloses an ordered (numbered) list
<LI> *list item*	Precedes an item in a list
<DL> *glossary* </DL>	Encloses a glossary of terms
<DT> *glossary term*	Precedes the term to be defined in a glossary
<DD> *glossary definition*	Precedes the definition of a term in a glossary (block indented)

There are a lot more formatting and style tags than there are technical tags. Don't let that worry you. You won't have to memorize or even use them all in this project. Once you have used a few of them, though, you will have no trouble using Table 6.2 to find others that peak your interest.

To begin formatting the body of your job search Web page, let's add a heading at the top of the page in big bold letters.

To add a heading to your document:

1 If it is not already open and displayed in the Notepad window, open your HTML document called MYPAGE.HTM.

2 Delete the line of text you typed earlier in the body portion of the page: This is the body of my job search Web page.

3 Type **<H1>** two lines below the <BODY> tag.
This is a heading tag. Heading tags are numbered H1 through H6, where H1 indicates the largest heading and H2, H3, and so on indicate subheadings, each one smaller than the last. For the main heading of your Web page, therefore, you are using the largest heading tag, H1.

4 Type **Job Search Resources </H1>** and press ENTER twice.

You have just added a major heading to your Web page. Your document should now look similar to Figure 6.10.

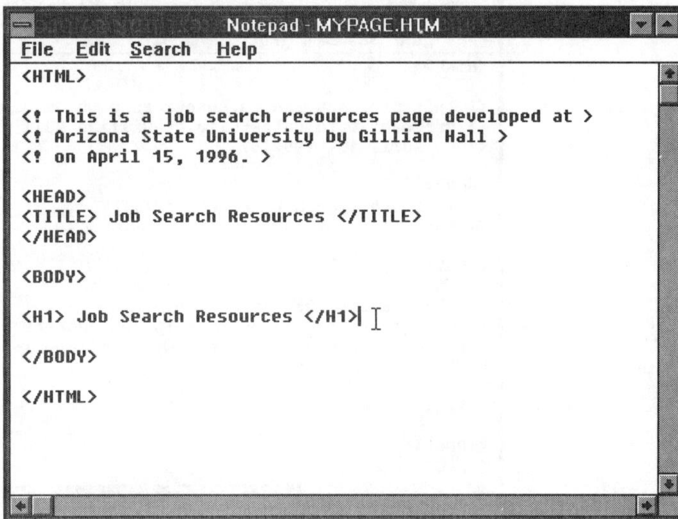

Figure 6.10

To add some text to the body of your document:

1 Position the insertion point on the line below the heading tag.

2 Type **This page was developed to help job hunters locate** and press ENTER

3 Type **the hottest sources of employment information available** and press ENTER

4 Type **on the Internet today!**

> ***Tip*** Your Web browser will completely ignore any carriage returns inserted in your text. It only acknowledges tags that indicate a carriage return. So all those (ENTER) key presses were just to make your Web page easier to read in the Notepad window.

To add a line to the body of your document:

1 Position the insertion point on the line below the text you just entered and press (ENTER)

2 Type **<HR>**
The <HR> tag creates a paragraph break and inserts a line, as stated in Table 6.2.

3 Press (ENTER)
Your HTML document should now look similar to Figure 6.11.

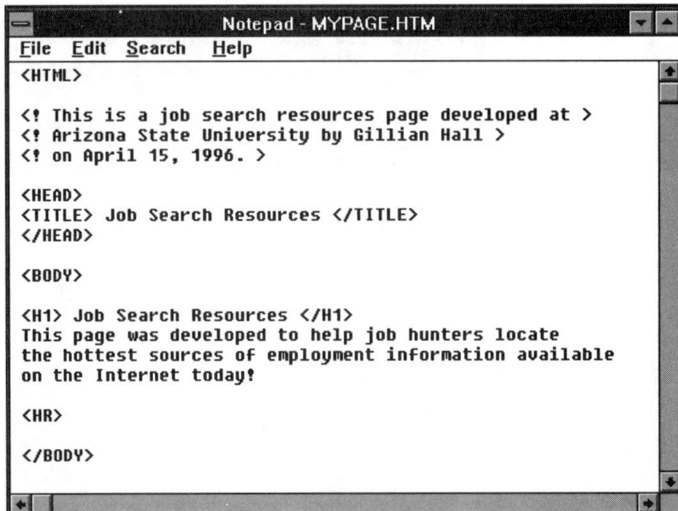

Figure 6.11

To add a subheading to your document:

1 In the Notepad window, scroll down until just the body portion of your HTML document is displayed.

2 Position the insertion point on the line below the <HR> tag and press (ENTER)

4 Type **`<H2> Great Employment Web Sites </H2>`**
The H2 tags enclose a subheading. You will list some Web sites that you have found helpful under this subheading later in this project.

5 Press (ENTER) twice.

To add a bulleted list to your document:

1 Position the insertion point on the line beneath the subheading you just added.

2 Type **<UL>**
As described in Table 6.2, the <UL> tag is used to begin a bulleted list of items. This is just one of several types of list tags available in HTML.

3 Press (ENTER) twice and type **</UL>**
The </UL> tag marks the end of a bulleted list.

5 Press (ENTER)

Your document should now look similar to Figure 6.12.

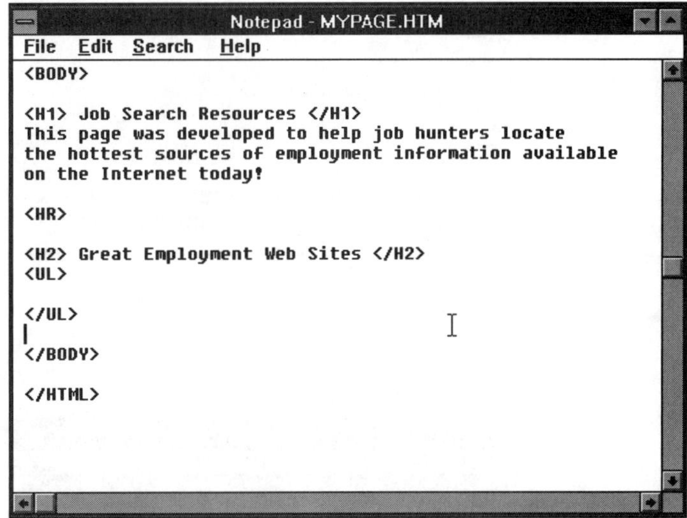

Figure 6.12

To add items to a bulleted list :

1 Position the insertion point on the line beneath the <UL> tag you just added.

2 Type **<LI> Web site**
As described in Table 6.2, the <LI> tag precedes each item in a list. You are using it here to add an item to your bulleted list. Unlike other tags you have encountered so far, <LI> does not have a pair (there is no </LI>). You simply use this tag in front of text that is to be an item in a list. <LI> tags must be enclosed within some type of list tags, however, or they are not valid.

3 Press (ENTER)

4 Repeat steps 2 and 3 two times so that your document looks similar to Figure 6.13.

5 Save your document.

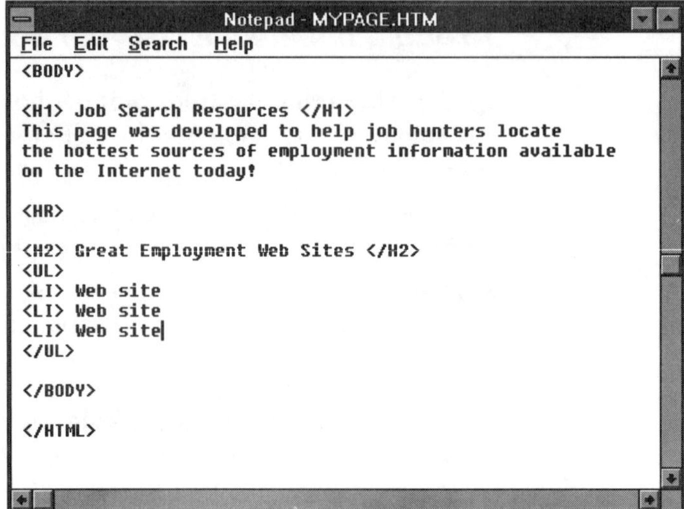

Figure 6.13

Before moving on to the next section, you may want to view your Web page again using Netscape. Follow the same procedure described earlier in this project for opening an HTML document using Netscape. When viewed with Netscape, your Web page should now look similar to Figure 6.14.

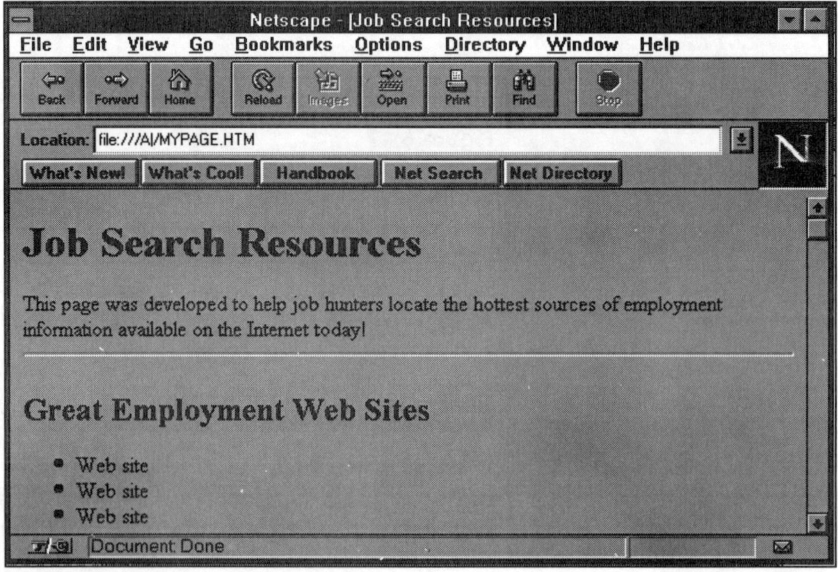

Figure 6.14

MODIFYING TEXT ATTRIBUTES THE RIGHT WAY

Another class of markup tags in HTML is known as ***logical tags***. Logical tags get their name from the concept of using "logical" descriptions of how text will be used (such as strong, emphasis, keyboard input, or definition), rather than describing the physical attributes of text on a Web page (such as bold, italic, underline, etc.). So, rather than dictating specifically how you want to format the text, you state what characteristics you want selected (tagged) text to convey, allowing Netscape to interpret how to display it.

The idea of describing specific physical text attributes defeats one of the main purposes HTML is designed to accomplish. HTML is a language that is understood and interpreted by all Web browsers. However, the same HTML document may be displayed very differently by different Web browsers. For example, recall from the Overview that you can customize the Netscape Window, selecting the fonts and colors you want displayed in Web pages. Because of all this potential variation between display preferences, HTML was designed as generically as possible.

So when you want some text emphasized on a Web page, you don't use physical descriptors like **bold**. You use logical descriptors, like **emphasis**. This means that rather than giving specific instructions, you ask each Web browser to do whatever it normally does to emphasize text on a Web page (be it italics, bold, larger font, different color, or whatever).

All this is not to say that there are no physical tags in HTML. There are many. We're not going to tell you what they are, though, because there is really never a good reason to use physical tags. In this section we will only show you how to modify text attributes using the logical tags listed in Table 6.3.

Table 6.3

Logical tags	**Description**
<STRONG> *text* </STRONG>	Strong emphasis, usually bold
<EM> *text* </EM>	Emphasis, usually italics
<STRIKE> *text* </STRIKE>	Strike-out character displayed through text
<SAMP> *text* </SAMP>	Computer status messages, usually fixed-width font
<KBD> *text* </KBD>	Keyboard input, usually plain or bold fixed-width font
<DFN> *text* </DFN>	Word definitions, usually italics
<CODE> *text* </CODE>	Computer code, usually fixed-width font
<CITE> *text* </CITE>	Book, film, etc. citations, usually italics

To emphasize text strongly:

1 In the Notepad window, position the insertion point just in front of the word *hottest* in the text below the heading.

2 Type **<STRONG>**

3 Move your insertion point to the end of the word *hottest.*

4 Type **</STRONG>**
You have just added a logical tag to your Web page. Instead of dictating a specific physical attribute to use, you have allowed Web browsers to interpret your code based on their own preferences and configurations. Your document should now look similar to Figure 6.15.

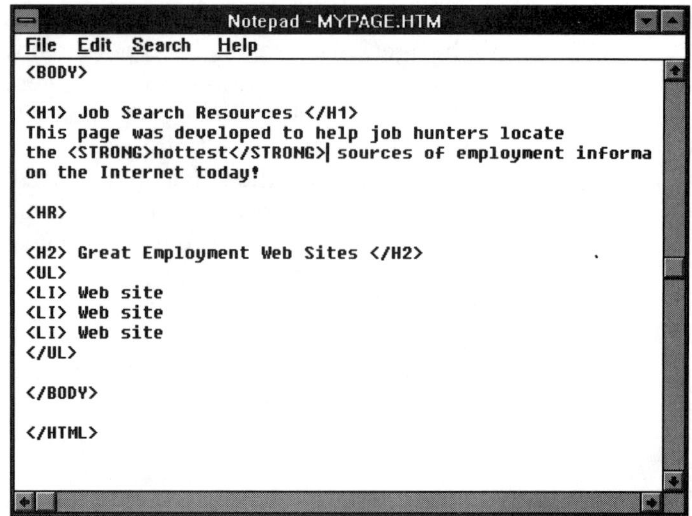

Figure 6.15

ADDING LINKS TO YOUR WEB PAGE

Now it's time to get to the really fun part of writing an HTML document—creating links to other documents. In this section we will cover only text and e-mail links. In the next section, after you learn how to include a graphic in your Web page, you will create a picture link.

So far you have created a Web page with a bulleted list. You entered dummy text, Web site, for each item in the bulleted list, but now it's time to actually list those great employment sites you found in your travels and to provide links to them!

To create links in HTML, you will have to gain some understanding of the fourth and final class of HTML markup tags called ***attribute tags***. There are two types of attribute tags, an ***anchor tag*** (<A>...</A>) and an ***image tag*** (<IMG>). We will go through a couple of examples of anchor tags in this section. We'll wait to attack image tags in the next section when we deal with graphics.

Let's jump right in and use an anchor tag to link your Web page to one of the employment Web pages you found in Project 3. This is where HTML gets a little confusing and convoluted, but far from impossible.

To add a text link to another Web page:

1 If it is not already open and displayed in the Notepad window, open your HTML document, MYPAGE.HTM.

2 Delete the dummy text, *Web site*, from the first item in your bulleted list.

3 Position the insertion point after the first <LI> tag.

4 Type **<A HREF = "http://www.careermag.com/">NCS Career Magazine</A>**
Congratulations! You have just added an anchor tag. Your HTML document should look similar to Figure 6.16.

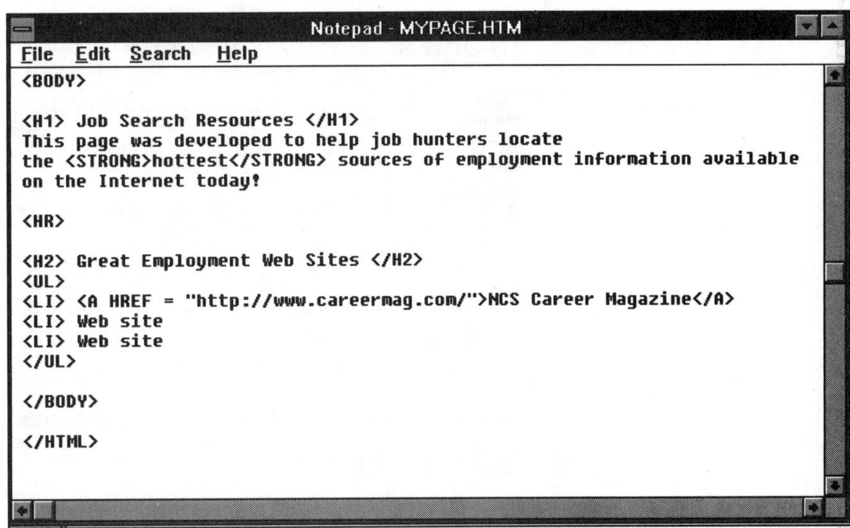


```
<BODY>

<H1> Job Search Resources </H1>
This page was developed to help job hunters locate
the <STRONG>hottest</STRONG> sources of employment information available
on the Internet today!

<HR>

<H2> Great Employment Web Sites </H2>
<UL>
<LI> <A HREF = "http://www.careermag.com/">NCS Career Magazine</A>
<LI> Web site
<LI> Web site
</UL>

</BODY>

</HTML>
```

Figure 6.16

The anchor created by the anchor tag jumps you from your Web page to another document with a click of the mouse. The anchor is displayed on the Web page as a text link. Like other tags you have used, an anchor tag encloses the portion of text in your document that you want to affect—the text you want to make into an anchor or a hypertext link. In this case the enclosed text is "NCS Career Magazine," because this text falls between the initial tag (<A>) and the closing tag (</A>).

Each component of the anchor tag is listed and its function is described in Table 6.4. In plain English this anchor tag says the following: "Make this text, NCS Career Magazine, into the anchor for a text link to another document called http://www.careermag.com/." In other words, when your Web page is displayed, what you will see is a bullet that reads "NCS Career Magazine." This bullet will be displayed as a text link. When you click it, you will jump to http://www.careermag.com/ (which just happens to be the NCS Career Magazine page).

Table 6.4

Tag component	Function
<A	Says that you are creating an anchor tag
HREF	The type of attribute involved (HREF is a hypertext document reference attribute)
=	Assigns a value to the attribute, HREF
"http://www.careermag.com/"	The value being assigned to the HREF attribute
>	Closes the initial part of the anchor tag
NCS Career Magazine	The affected text (the anchor or link)
</A>	Closes the anchor tag

To add an e-mail text link:

1 Position the insertion point two lines below the </UL> tag.

2 Press (ENTER) and type **Contact**

3 Press (ENTER) and type **<A HREF = "mailto:*your e-mail address*"> *your e-mail address* </A>**
This anchor tag should look at least a little familiar. This time, instead of referencing a Web page, you have referenced an e-mail address. Notice that "mailto:" precedes your e-mail address. This tells Netscape to open its message composition window and enter your address in the Mail To field.

4 Press (ENTER) and type **with comments and suggestions.**

5 Press (ENTER)
Your document should look similar to Figure 6.17. One notable difference is that *your* e-mail address, not the one shown here, should be used in the e-mail tag.

6 Save your document.

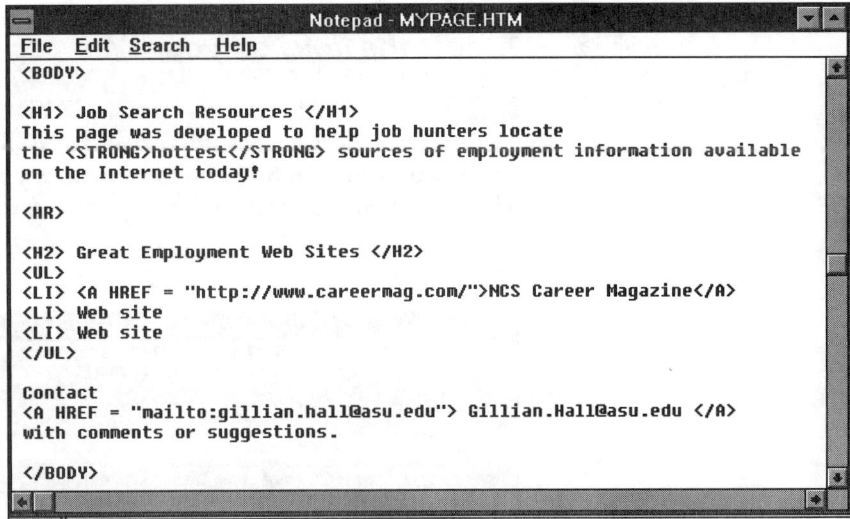

```
<BODY>

<H1> Job Search Resources </H1>
This page was developed to help job hunters locate
the <STRONG>hottest</STRONG> sources of employment information available
on the Internet today!

<HR>

<H2> Great Employment Web Sites </H2>
<UL>
<LI> <A HREF = "http://www.careermag.com/">NCS Career Magazine</A>
<LI> Web site
<LI> Web site
</UL>

Contact
<A HREF = "mailto:gillian.hall@asu.edu"> Gillian.Hall@asu.edu </A>
with comments or suggestions.

</BODY>
```

Figure 6.17

Are you ready to have a look at your handiwork and try out your links? Follow the same procedure described earlier in this project for opening an HTML document using Netscape. When viewed with Netscape, your Web page should now look similar to Figure 6.18.

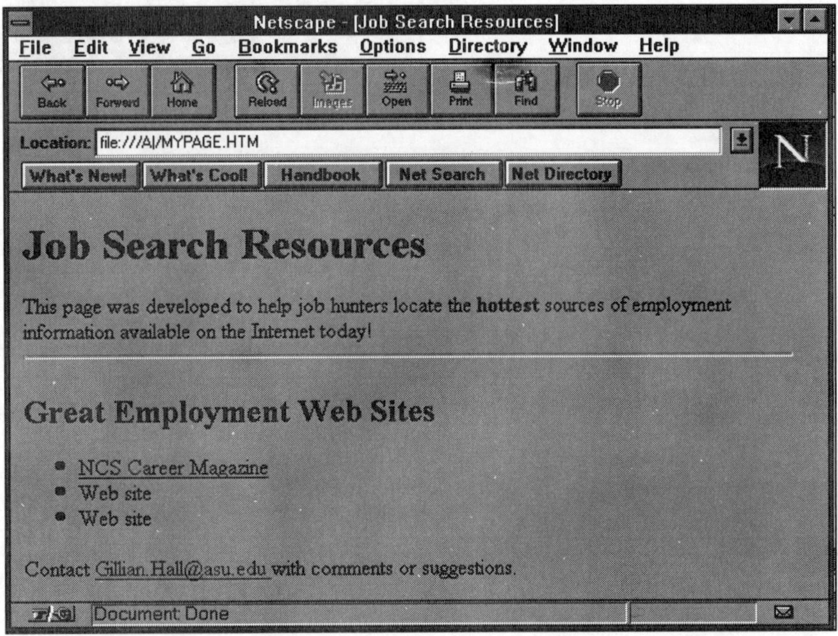

Figure 6.18

To test the links on your Web page:

1 With your HTML document, MYPAGE.HTM, displayed in the Netscape window, select the text link, NCS Career Magazine.
As shown in Figure 6.19, Netscape takes you to the address you associated with this anchor in the anchor tag, http://www.careermag.com.

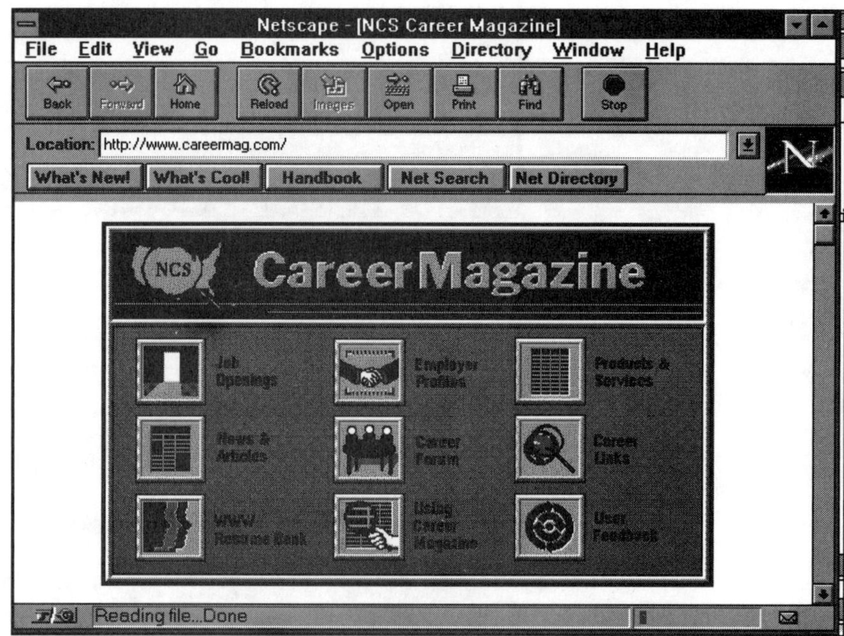

Figure 6.19

2 Select the Back button on the toolbar to return to your Web page.

3 Select the e-mail link at the bottom of the page.
As shown in Figure 6.20, Netscape displays the message composition window, complete with your e-mail address in the Mail To field.

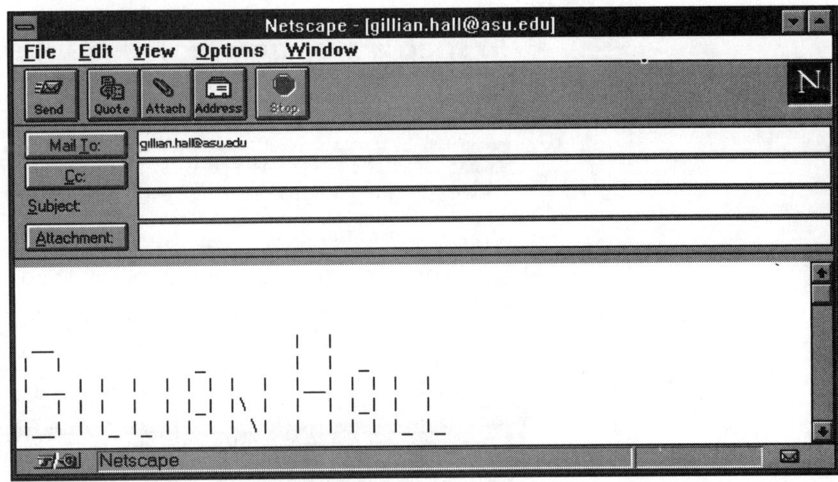

Figure 6.20

4 Close the message composition window by selecting Close from the File menu or by double-clicking the control-menu icon in the upper-left corner of the window.

Congratulations! You have created a fully functional Web page complete with two hypertext links.

If necessary, you can save your document and take a break at this point. When you come back just use Notepad to open your HTML document, MYPAGE.HTM, and proceed.

ADDING GRAPHICS TO YOUR WEB PAGE

One of the most engaging features of Web pages (despite their slow downloading speed) is the graphics. When used properly, graphics can add tremendously to the professionalism and overall appeal of your Web page. Before we get into actually adding graphics, however, please bear in mind how frustrating it can be to wait for massive graphics to load when you visit a new Web site. Don't do this to yourself or to those who stumble upon your Web page in their travels. Use graphics sparingly! Everyone will love you for it.

To use graphics in Web pages, you must learn how to use another type of attribute tag, the image tag (<IMG>). Image tags can be used alone to place graphics in a Web page. Image tags can also be imbedded in anchor tags to create picture links. In this section we will insert a graphic and also create a picture link

Before we can begin adding graphics to this Web page, however, we must find some graphics to use. So the first thing we must do is to search for some nice graphics to use in your Job Search Resources Web page.

To snag a nice graphic from another Web page:

1 If it is not already running, open Netscape.

2 Use the Location field or the Open button to go to the following address: www.contrib.andrew.cmu.edu/~ender/ergraph.html

Netscape loads the page at this address, as shown in Figure 6.21. This Web site provides some cool graphics for Web page developers like yourself. You will find backgrounds, icons, buttons, lines, and bullets available at this site.

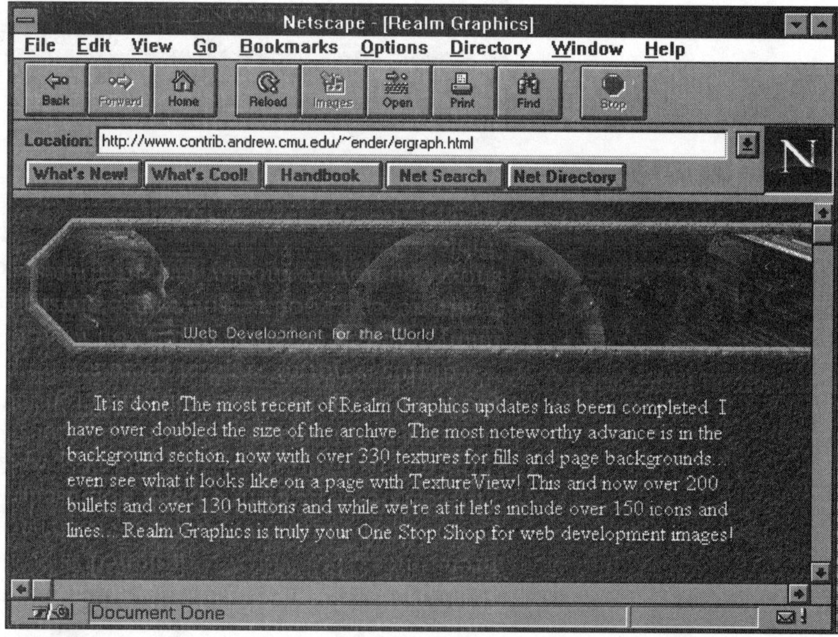

Figure 6.21

3 Scroll down the page until you find a list of the types of graphics available. Use the Icons text link to browse the available icon graphics.

4 Find a small brightly colored graphic among the icons provided by this service. Also find a graphic that would intuitively suggest that, if you clicked on it, you would access e-mail.

5 For each graphic you decide to use, select the graphic with the right mouse button to access its pop-up menu.

6 Select the Save this Image As option from the pop-up menu, as shown in Figure 6.22.

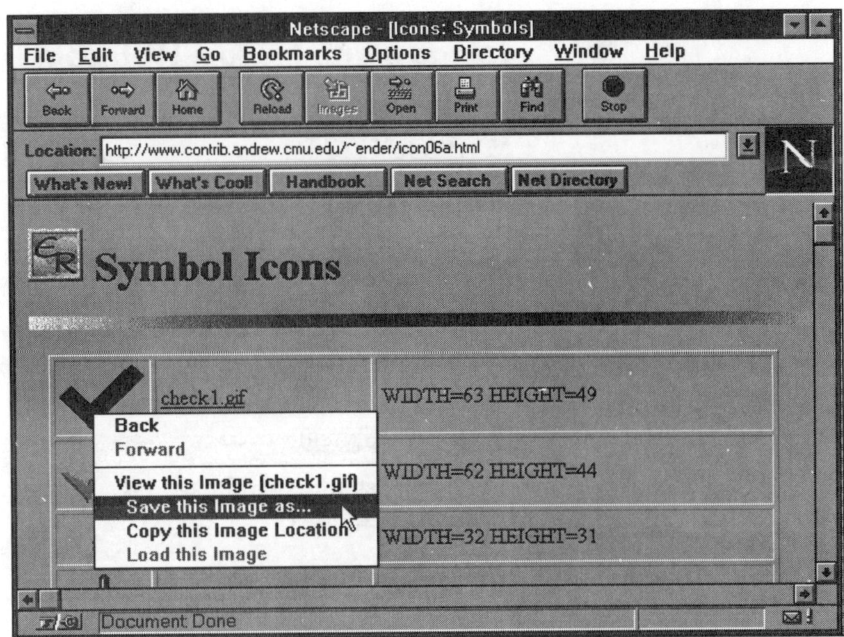

Figure 6.22

7 Use the Save As dialog box to save the image file to a floppy, as shown in Figure 6.23. Later you can copy the file to your computer account or some other more permanent location if you like. Netscape will download the picture and save it to the location specified.

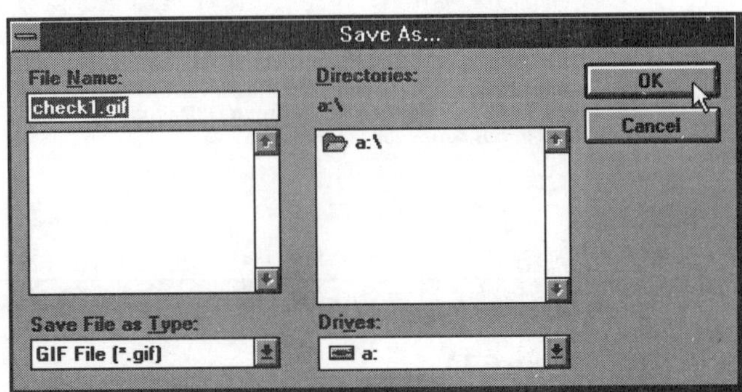

Figure 6.23

> ***Tip*** You can download graphics from any Web page in this same way. We have sent you to this particular Web site to hunt for graphics because these are advertised as free, public domain graphics.

Now you are ready to incorporate these graphics into your Web page.

To add a graphic to a Web page:

1 If it is not already open and displayed in the Notepad window, open MYPAGE.HTM.

2 Scroll down so that just the body portion of the document is displayed.

3 Position the insertion point right after the <H1> tag.

4 Type **<IMG SRC = “file:///A|*filename*“ ALIGN = BOTTOM>**
For filename, enter the name of a graphic you downloaded. For example, <IMG SRC = “file:///A|check1.gif“ ALIGN = BOTTOM>.

5 Press ENTER

You have just added an image tag. Your document should now look similar to Figure 6.24.

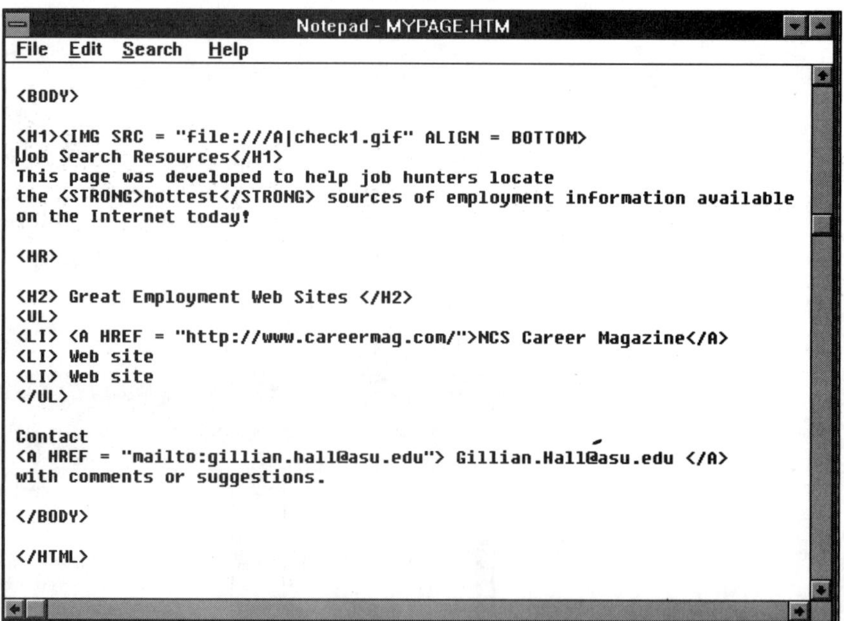

Figure 6.24

An image tag simply tells Netscape where to find the image file, where to put it on your Web page, and how to align with adjacent text. Each component of this image tag and its function is described in Table 6.5. In plain English, this image tag says the following: “Get the graphic file called *filename* located on drive A, put it in the heading of this document, and align the heading text at the bottom of the graphic.” So when your Web page is displayed, you will see the graphic specified in front of the heading text.

Table 6.5

Tag component	Function
<IMG	Says that you are creating an image tag
SRC	The type of attribute involved (SRC); used to define the filename of the source (in this case the graphics file)
=	Assigns a value to the attribute SRC
"file:///A|*filename*"	The value being assigned to the SRC attribute; the file name and location
ALIGN	An attribute used to position text adjacent to the image
=	Assigns a value to the attribute ALIGN
BOTTOM	The value being assigned to the ALIGN attribute
>	Closes the image tag

To add a picture link:

1 In the Notepad window delete the line of text near the bottom of the document that reads "Contact."

2 On that same line, type `Click to send comments or suggestions...`

3 Position the insertion point immediately after the <A...> tag.

4 Delete the text between the <A...> and </A> tags (Your e-mail address).

5 Press (ENTER)

6 Type **<IMG SRC = "file:///A|*filename*" ALIGN = BOTTOM>**
For filename, enter the name of a graphic you downloaded. For example, <IMG SRC = "file:///A|enve.gif" ALIGN = BOTTOM>.

7 Press (ENTER)

Check that your document now looks like the example in Figure 6.25. You have just added a picture link. This link will function in exactly the same way as the e-mail link you created, except now you will click on a graphic rather than text.

```
Notepad - MYPAGE.HTM
File  Edit  Search  Help
<BODY>

<H1><IMG SRC = "file:///A|check1.gif" ALIGN = BOTTOM>
Job Search Resources</H1>
This page was developed to help job hunters locate
the <STRONG>hottest</STRONG> sources of employment information available
on the Internet today!

<HR>

<H2> Great Employment Web Sites </H2>
<UL>
<LI> <A HREF = "http://www.careermag.com/">NCS Career Magazine</A>
<LI> Web site
<LI> Web site
</UL>

Click to send comments or suggestions...
<A HREF = "mailto:gillian.hall@asu.edu">
<IMG SRC = "file:///A|enve.gif" ALIGN = BOTTOM></A>

</BODY>

</HTML>
```

Figure 6.25

You are probably anxious to have a look at the graphics in your Web page. Save your document in Notepad, then follow the same procedure described earlier in this project for opening an HTML document using Netscape. When viewed with Netscape, your Web page should have graphics positioned in the same places as those in the example in Figure 6.26.

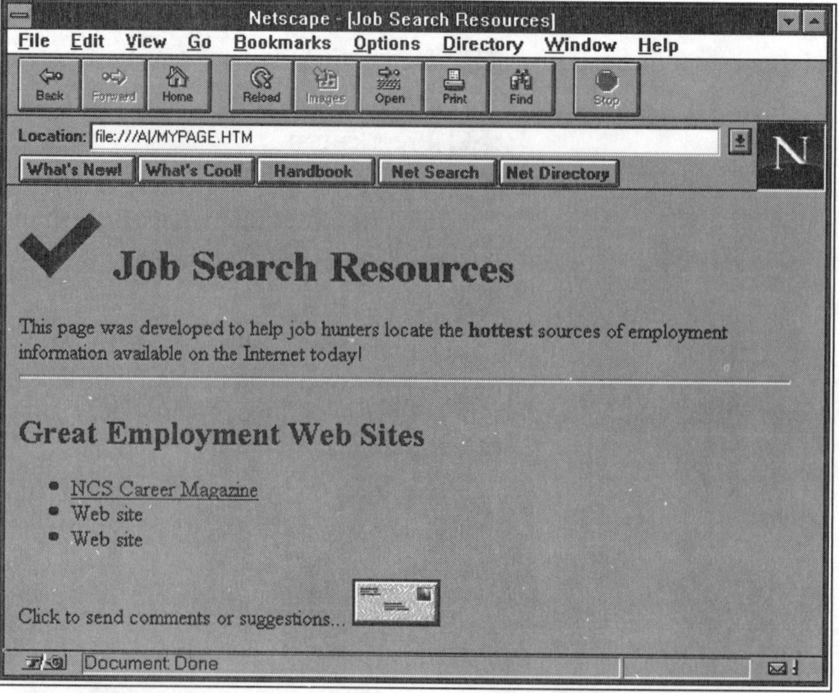

Figure 6.26

TAKING LESSONS FROM THE PROS

One of the best ways to learn new skills is by example, and Netscape provides budding HTML authors such as yourself with the source code for every Web page you view. This means that if you ever find yourself looking at a particularly nifty feature on a Web page and asking yourself, "I wonder how they did that?", the answer is at your fingertips. The answer is called Document Source. There is no better way to get good ideas for Web pages than surfing the Web. Similarly, there is no better way to learn how to implement those good ideas than by looking at the HTML ***source code***.

To view Web page source code:

1 With your Job Search Resources page displayed in the Netscape window, select Document Source from the View menu, as shown in Figure 6.27.

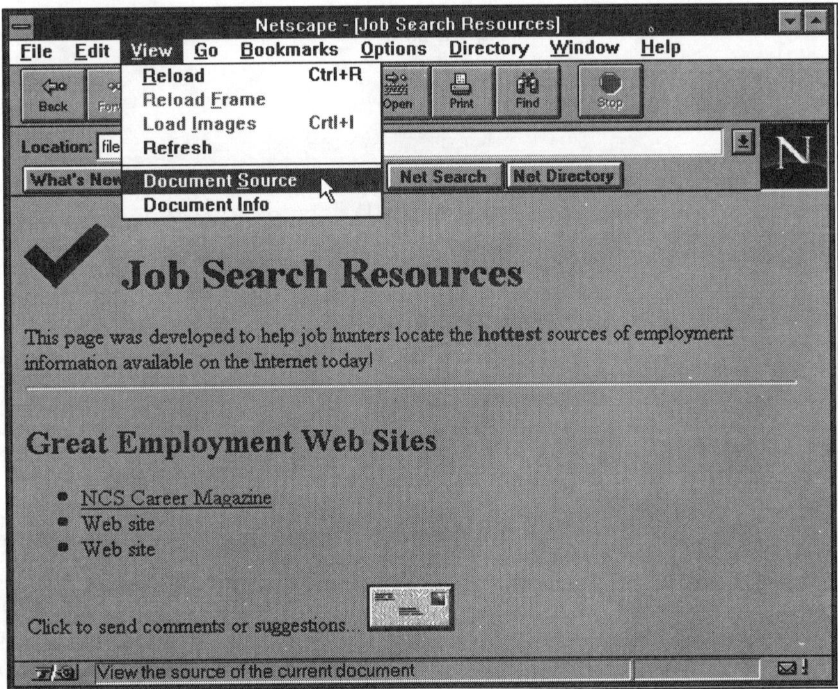

Figure 6.27

The Netscape Source window appears as shown in Figure 6.28.

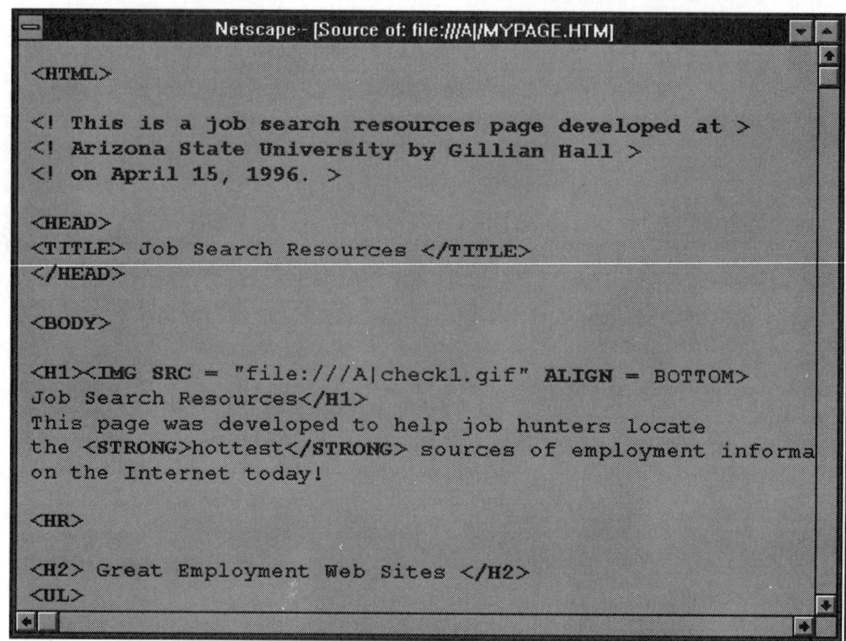


```
<HTML>

<! This is a job search resources page developed at >
<! Arizona State University by Gillian Hall >
<! on April 15, 1996. >

<HEAD>
<TITLE> Job Search Resources </TITLE>
</HEAD>

<BODY>

<H1><IMG SRC = "file:///A|check1.gif" ALIGN = BOTTOM>
Job Search Resources</H1>
This page was developed to help job hunters locate
the <STRONG>hottest</STRONG> sources of employment informa
on the Internet today!

<HR>

<H2> Great Employment Web Sites </H2>
<UL>
```

Figure 6.28

2 Scroll through the Source window to view all of the source code for your HTML document.

3 Close the Source window by selecting Close from the File menu or by double-clicking the control-menu icon in the upper-left corner of the window.

PUBLISHING YOUR WEB PAGE

You may have heard the term *publishing* used in conjunction with the Web. ***Publishing*** on the Web simply means making some information resource you have created available on the Web. The Web page you have created is not published and cannot be accessed by others until you find it a permanent home. At universities many people put their Web pages in their computer accounts on campus. Other people must use commercial Internet service providers to publish Web pages.

If you are at a college or university and you have a computer account there (by computer account we mean some space on a hard drive somewhere that has been assigned to you with a user name and password), then you can now copy your HTML document and the two graphics into that account. This means you will have to change the addresses for the graphics you just added. If the graphics are kept in the same directory as the HTML document, you can simplify the address of the graphics files in the <IMG> tags to filename, and delete everything else (such as "file:///A|").

Once your HTML document and its associated graphics files have been copied into your school computer account, people from all over the world will be able to access your Web page, assuming they know its URL. If you do decide to publish your Web page, you can ask your instructor or computer services staff for assistance in determining your Web page's URL.

THE NEXT STEP

In this project you have learned to create a Web page using HTML. You made excellent progress toward building a Job Search Resources Web page including text links, picture links, and graphics. The next step is to complete the Job Search Resources Web page. This will give you the opportunity to practice skills you have learned in this project and to expand those skills. You will add more bulleted lists and more links to the Job Search Resources page in the Assignments at the end of this project.

This concludes Project 6. You can either exit Netscape or go on to work the Study Questions, Review Exercises, and Assignments.

SUMMARY AND EXERCISES

Summary

- The Hypertext Markup Language (HTML) is the programming language used to write Web documents.
- Markup tags are used to enclose and designate text that you want the Web browser to interpret and display in a particular manner.
- Markup tags fall into four general categories: technical tags, formatting and style tags, logical tags, and attribute tags.
- Technical tags are used to define the structure of a Web document.
- You can use any text editor or word processor to compose HTML documents.
- All Web documents contain tags designating the document type, the header, and the body of the document.
- An HTML document can be viewed using the Open File option on the File menu.
- Formatting and style tags are used to lay out and format the body of an HTML document.
- Logical tags allow each Web browser to interpret text attributes based upon their individual configurations and preference settings.
- The two types of attribute tags are anchor tags and image tags.
- Anchor tags are used to create text and graphic anchors that, when displayed with a Web browser, are text and picture links.
- You can download graphics from other Web pages by using the pop-up menu for the graphic item.
- To add a graphic to a Web page, you must use image tags.
- Picture links are created by embedding an image tag within an anchor tag.

- You can view the source code for any Web page by using the Document Source option on the View menu.
- To publish a Web page, it must be placed on a computer connected to the Internet.

Key Terms and Operations

Key Terms	Operations
anchor tag	Open Notepad
attribute tag	Use markup tags
body	Save a file with Notepad
comment	Open an HTML file with Netscape
formatting and style tag	View HTML document source
header	
image tag	
logical tag	
markup tag	
publishing	
source code	
technical tag	

Study Questions

Multiple Choice

1. HTML is an acronym for
   a. Hypertalk Mirror Language.
   b. Helpertext Monitor Language.
   c. Hypertext Markup Language.
   d. Helpertalk Monitor Language.

2. The four general categories of HTML tags are
   a. attribute, logical, font, structure.
   b. structure, formatting and style, logical, attribute.
   c. logical, formatting and style, attribute, technical.
   d. technical, structural, logical, attribute.

3. The <HTML>, </HTML> tag is used to indicate the document
   a. type.
   b. size.
   c. location.
   d. header.

4. The <TITLE>, </TITLE> tags are nested directly within the
   a. header tag.
   b. body tag.
   c. attribute tag.
   d. image tag.

5. HTML documents written on PCs are generally given the file extension
   a. .gif
   b. .txt
   c. .htm
   d. .doc

6. The tag that identifies the end of the HTML document is
   a. <HTML>
   b. </HTML>
   c. </END>
   d. <EXIT>

7. A graphic file format frequently used in Web pages is
   a. .htm
   b. .xbd
   c. .grf
   d. .gif

8. A logical tag used to emphasize text is
   a. <EMPH>
   b. <BLD>
   c. <STRONG>
   d. <BOLD>

9. All good Web pages should contain
   a. links to related documents.
   b. many large graphic files.
   c. None of the above.
   d. Both a and b.

10. A tag used to create a bulleted list is
   a. <OL>
   b. <UL>
   c. <DL>
   d. <HR>

Short Answer

1. ________________ are used to enclose text that you want Web browsers to interpret and display in a particular manner.

2. The ______________ tag designates the header portion of the document.

3. The title tag indicates text for display in the ________________ when the document is viewed using a Web browser.

4. HTML files should be saved using the _________ file extension.

5. Formatting and style tags are used for laying out and formatting the ____________ of the document.

6. Of the six types of heading tags, <H1>, </H1> is displayed in the _______________ font size and <H6>, </H6> is displayed in the _______________ font size.

7. The _________ tag precedes line items in bulleted lists.

8. _____________ tags are different from ______________ tags in that they do not prescribe specific physical text attributes.

9. __________ tags are used to insert graphics into an HTML document.

10. A Web page is considered to be _________________ when everyone on the Internet can access it with its URL.

For Discussion

1. What advantages does HTML provide for viewing documents on the Internet?

2. Wouldn't it be nice if there was a way to "draw" a Web page, using some graphical user interface, instead of typing in all of the tags and text. Have you heard of any such software tools?

Review Exercises

Finishing the Employment Resources Web Page

1. Add at least two more links to employment-related Web sites in the bulleted list of Great Employment Web Sites.
2. Add another subheading with a bulleted list, just like you did for the subheading Great Employment Web Sites. Call this subheading Job Postings Through Newsgroups. Insert at least three bullets into the list. Each bullet must be a text link to a newsgroup that offers job postings. (Hint: The format for a newsgroup address is as follows: news:category.subcategory.group.name)
3. Add a line between the two subheadings and between the last subheading and the e-mail link.

Assignments

Your Bio and Resume Online!

Build a new Web page from scratch. This page must contain a heading of your choosing, an introduction including a brief biography, your resume (formatted nicely when viewed with Netscape), an e-mail link to your e-mail address, and a text link to your Job Search Resources Web page.

Netscape's Personal Workspace

Netscape has created a tool for helping you build a personal workspace page. Work through the entire tutorial provided online beginning at http://home.netscape.com/custom/index.html, as shown in Figure 6.28.

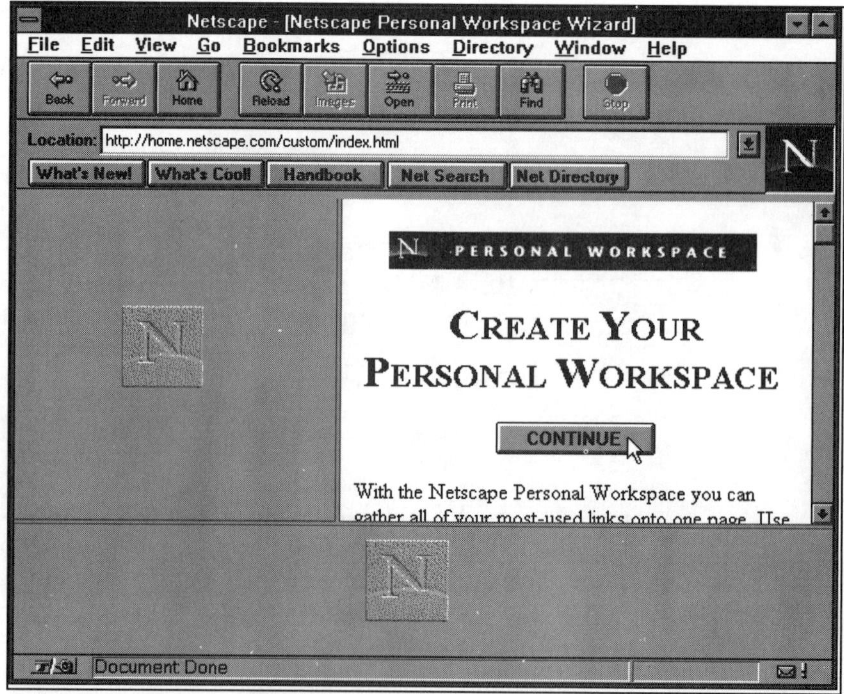

Figure 6.28

Operations Reference

FILE

Button	Menu Item	Keyboard	Description
	New Web Browser	CTRL + N	Opens a new Netscape window.
	New Mail Message	CTRL + M	Opens a Mail Composition window.
	Mail Document		Opens a Mail Composition window in which the currently displayed Internet document is listed as an attachment.
	Open Location	CTRL + L	Opens the Internet document at the address specified.
Open	Open File	CTRL + O	Opens an existing document (e.g., picture, HTML, movie, or sound file)
	Save As	CTRL + S	Saves the currently displayed document to disk.
	Upload File		Selects a file to upload to the FTP server specified by the current URL. Active only when the displayed page is an FTP site
	Page Setup		Edits page orientation, treatment of headers and footers, and other print options.
Print	Print		Selects print options and output currently displayed document to a printer.
	Print Preview		Previews the printed page on screen.
	Close	CTRL + W	Closes Web browser window. Exits Netscape if only one browser window is open.
	Exit		Exits to Windows.

EDIT

Button	Menu Item	Keyboard	Description
	Undo	CTRL + Z	Undoes the last operation.
	Cut	CTRL + X	Cuts selected text and stores on clipboard.
	Copy	CTRL + C	Copies selected text and stores on clipboard.
	Paste	CTRL + V	Pastes from clipboard to insertion point location.
	Select All	CTRL + A	Selects entire document.
Find	Find	CTRL + F	Specifies and locate occurrences of text in currently displayed document.
	Find Again	F3	Finds next occurrence of specific text in displayed document.

VIEW

Button	Menu Item	Keyboard	Description
Reload	Reload	CTRL + R	Loads a fresh copy of the currently displayed document and replaces copy originally loaded.
	Reload Frame		Reloads displayed document into a single frame on a Netscape page containing frames.
Images	Load Images	CTRL + I	Loads and displays embedded images for the currently displayed document.
	Refresh		Replaces currently displayed document with a fresh copy from local memory.
	Document Source		Opens a View Source window with HTML code for current page.
	Document Info		Shows information about currently displayed document.

GO

Button	Menu Item	Keyboard	Description
Back	Back	ALT + ←	Displays the previous page in the history list.
Forward	Forward	ALT + →	Displays the next page in the history list.
Home	Home		Displays the home page whose location is specified in the General Preferences Appearance panel.
Stop	Stop Loading	ESC	Stops loading the current document.
	various history items		There will be at least one Internet document listed representing all the sites visited during the current session.

BOOKMARKS

Button	Menu Item	Keyboard	Description
	Add Bookmark	CTRL + D	Adds currently displayed document to the list of sites in the Bookmarks window.
	Go to Bookmarks	CTRL + B	Displays the Bookmarks window.
	various bookmark items		The Bookmarks you choose are displayed in the bookmarks menu for easy reference.

Options

Button	Menu Item	Keyboard	Description
	General Preferences		Selects preferences for display fonts, colors, formatting, etc.
	Mail and News Preferences		Selects preferences for e-mail and newsgroups such as servers, identity, appearance, etc.
	Network Preferences		Sets network preferences.
	Security Preferences		Sets security feature preferences.
	Show Toolbar		Displays the toolbar (toggle).
	Show Location		Displays the Location field (toggle).
	Show Directory Buttons		Displays the Directory buttons (toggle).
	Auto Load Images		Automatically loads embedded document images if checked.
	Document Encoding		Selects character set for document encoding.
	Save Options		Saves currently selected options.

Directory

Button	Menu Item	Keyboard	Description
	Netscape's Home		Go to the Netscape home page.
What's New!	What's New!		Go to Netscape's What's New! page.
What's Cool!	What's Cool!		Go to Netscape's What's Cool! page.
	Netscape Galleria		Go to Netscape's Galleria page of showcasing Internet innovators.
Net Directory	Internet Directory		Go to Netscape's Net Search page, a collection of Internet search services.
Net Search	Internet Search		Go to Netscape's Net Search page.
	Internet White Pages		Go to Netscape's People page, a collection of search services for people on the Web.
	About the Internet		Go to Netscape's About the Internet page.

Window

Button	Menu Item	Keyboard	Explanation
	Netscape Mail		Opens the Mail window.
	Netscape News		Opens the News window.
	Address book		Opens the Address Book window.
	Bookmarks	CTRL + B	Opens the Bookmarks window.
	History	CTRL + H	Opens the History window.
	Window items		The selected window item is the active window. Each open window is listed as a menu item.

Help

Button	Menu Item	Keyboard	Description
	About Netscape		Gets version, license, and copyright information about Netscape Navigator.
	About Plug-ins		Presents information on currently installed plug-in modules. Plug-in modules are software programs that extend the capabilities of Netscape.
	Registration Information		Displays registration information about the running copy of Netscape.
	Software		Displays upgrade information.
Handbook	Handbook		Displays on-line documentation for Netscape Navigator software.
	Release Notes		Displays new feature information.
	Frequently Asked Questions (FAQs)		Displays answers to frequently asked questions on a variety of Netscape topics.
	On Security		Displays questions and answers about Netscape's security features.
	How to Give Feedback		Displays a feedback form.
	How to Get Support		Displays information about Netscape support programs and relevant e-mail addresses.
	How to Create Web Services		Displays links to help you learn more about authoring and publishing Web documents and services.

Glossary

address book An e-mail facility in Netscape used for storing and retrieving frequently used e-mail addresses.

anchor tag An HTML tag which creates a clickable object on a Web page—hypertext or hypermedia.

anonymous An anonymous FTP server allows any Internet user to download files.

Archie A keyword search service that searches directory and file titles of all indexed FTP servers.

archived file A computer file or collection of files which have been compressed and stored for future retrieval, usually on an FTP server.

ARPAnet A computer network designed by the U.S. Defense Department in 1969 to ensure that its computers could communicate with one other.

attribute tag An HTML tag, such as an Anchor tag or an Image tag, that requires an attribute to tell it exactly what to do.

backbone One of the many massive communication lines that connects major portions of the Internet.

body (e-mail) The part of an e-mail message which contains the message itself.

body (HTML document) The portion of an HTML document contained between the <BODY> and </BODY> tags.

bookmark A Netscape tool for permanently marking favorite places on the Internet.

cache Netscape uses RAM and harddrive memory to store copies of HTML pages retrieved from the internet. This often permits faster loading of pages previously retrieved and stored in local memory.

category Usenet newsgroups are organized into major categories (e.g., biz., alt., rec., comp.), some of which are further organized into subcategories.

column The Netscape Mail and News windows are organized into panes which are further divided into labeled columns (e.g., date, subject,sender).

comment HTML used to provide a description of the document. Comments are not interpreted by Web browsers.

compressed file A computer file which has been subjected to a compression routine rendering it smaller and more efficient to archive and transmit.

digital lines Communication lines between computers using digital signals. Digital communication is much easier and more effective for computers because all data stored and used internally is in digital format.

directory A topic-driven search service provided on the Internet.

directory buttons Netscape buttons which access Netscape Web pages containing links to search services, cool and new Web sites, and the Netscape Handbook.

document display area The portion of the Netscape window in which an Internet document is displayed.

domain name The unique name given to each computer on the Internet. These names are translated into unique domain addresses by domain servers.

download To copy a file from a computer on the Internet to a local storage device (e.g., diskette, hard drive) on your computer, usually via FTP.

e-mail Short for electronic mail, e-mail is the most popular use of the Internet. It allows you to send messages and files to other Internet users.

e-mail link A Web page link which, in Netscape, opens an addressed Message Composition window.
E-mail links provide a short-cut for sending e-mail directly from Web pages.

file name The portion of an Internet address which designates a specific file (in a specified directory on a specified computer).

File Transfer Protocol (FTP) One of the original protocols on the Internet that provides efficient file transfer between computers.

folder (bookmark) A method used by Netscape to organize bookmarks into groups.

followed link A text link on a Web page which has already been clicked. Netscape displays followed links in a different color from other links.

formatting and style tags HTML tags used to lay out and format the body of an HTML document.

gateway A device which connects two networks whose communication protocols are different.

Gopher A method of indexing and navigating Internet files. Gopher-based files are said to exist in "Gopherspace."

Gopher server Computer systems running Gopher software allowing file access through hierarchical text-based menus arranged by subject.

Gopherspace The collection of Gopher servers available on the Internet.

header (e-mail) The portion of the e-mail message containing the components such as date, time, sender name and address, and subject.

header (HTML document) The portion of an HTML document enclosed by the <HEAD> and </HEAD> tags, usually the document title.

history Netscape's method of keeping track of where you've been on the Internet during the current session.

home page A starting point (URL) for Web browsers to contact a person's, company's, or organization's information on the Web.

hypermedia links Web page links to text, graphic, movie, and sound files.

hypertext links Connect multiple files together via Web page links to create a single virtual document.

Hypertext Markup Language (HTML) The formatting system that turns ordinary text files into Web pages.

image tag An HTML attribute tag used to insert inline images and picture links into an HTML document.

Internet The vast system of interconnected computers that Netscape navigates.

Internet Protocol (IP) IP allows long data streams to be divided into small chunks that can be serialized, addressed and sent to locations by different routes where they are reassembled into the original data stream.

link An element on the Web that connects one part of a document to another part of that same document, or to another document or file. Links can connect files located on the same computer or on different computers connected to the Internet.

Location field In Netscape, the Location field displays the Internet address of the currently displayed document. It is also used to enter the address of a document you wish to display.

logical tag A type of HTML tag which specifies the logical description of text (e.g., emphasis) rather than the physical characteristics (e.g., bold) of text, thereby allowing different Web browsers to interpret and display the same HTML document differently.

mail button The envelope icon starts Netscape's e-mail application. A question mark (?) near the mail icon means that Netscape cannot automatically check for mail on your server. An exclamation point (!) means that you have mail on your server.

mailbox pane The portion of the Netscape Mail window that displays folders containing sent mail, received mail, trash, and any other mail folders created by the user.

markup tag Tags used in writing HTML documents. HTML is composed of several types of tags which define the structure, layout, and formatting of an HTML document. *See also hypertext markup language.*

menu bar The part of an MS Windows application window displaying drop-down menus.

message display pane The portion of the Netscape Mail window that displays the selected e-mail message.

message header pane The portion of the Netscape Mail window that displays the headers of all e-mail messages contained in the selected folder.

multitasking A computer which is performing a number of different tasks at once (often in different applications) is said to be multitasking.

Netscape Navigator A popular graphical front-end, Web browser, for accessing and exploring the Internet. *See also Web browser.*

newsgroup One of thousands of discussion groups on the Usenet where people with a common interest share information.

news server pane An area of the Netscape News window indicating the news servers to which you are registered and the newsgroups to which you subscribe.

online Help A Netscape facility which provides users with a complete tutorial, a reference, and access to frequently accessed questions about Netscape via the Internet.

pane Part of a Netscape Mail or News window that generally has its own vertical and horizontal scroll bars.

password A secret set of numbers and letters you use to gain access to your computer account.

picture link A link on a Web page whose anchor is a graphic.

POP server POP stands for Post Office Protocol. This is the e-mail system that handles your incoming mail.

protocol A set of rules by which computers communicate with each other.

publishing In regard to Web pages, publishing refers to making a Web page available to others on the Internet.

scroll bar A special type of control that allows the user to easily navigate through a long list of information. There are vertical and horizontal scroll bars.

search engine A keyword Internet search tool.

search parameter Keywords or other user input used by search engines to search for documents on the Internet.

search strategy The way in which a search service functions (e.g., keyword search, topic search).

security indicator Netscape uses a security system provided by a third party (RSA Data Security, Inc) that allows for secure messaging between an Internet server and client. The security indicator icon is a graphical indicator of the security level of the currently displayed document.

self-extracting file A compressed file that can decompress itself without requiring a separate utility application to do so (such as PKUNZIP or UnStuffIt).

separator A line used to divide the Netscape Bookmarks menu and to organize bookmarks.

signature The portion of an e-mail message containing information about the sender. A signature sometimes includes an e-mail link or a trademark phrase.

signature file A file from which Netscape will retrieve e-mail signature information.

SMTP server SMTP stands for Simple Mail Transport Protocol. This is the e-mail system that handles your outgoing mail.

source code The actual characters input by a programmer in a specific programming language. HTML document source code can be viewed in Netscape using the Document Source option on the View menu.

status bar The bar at the bottom of the Netscape window which displays the application's current communications status.

technical tag A type of HTML tag used to lay out the structure of an HTML document.

text link A link on a Web page whose anchor is text.

title bar The part of an MS Windows application window containing the name of the window or of the document displayed in the window.

toolbar The row of buttons in the Netscape window which provides shortcuts for accessing frequently used menu options.

topic Internet directories perform searches by topic. The user selects a topic from the top level of the directory, then selects a subtopic from each successive list of subtopics until a list of matching Internet documents is reached.

Trash folder When e-mail messages are deleted, Netscape moves them to the Trash folder where they stay until the user empties the trash. Only then are they permanently removed.

Uniform Resource Locator (URL) The unique address assigned to every document accessible on the Web.

upload To copy a file from your local computer to a computer on the Internet, usually via FTP.

Usenet A world-wide network exchanging information grouped under subject categories called newsgroups.

user name The name assigned to an account on a computer on a local network or on the Internet. Usually, both the user name and password are necessary to access a computer account.

Veronica A search tool used to find documents in Gopherspace.

Web browser An application used to access the World Wide Web. Netscape is a graphical Web browser.

Web page A document written in HTML which is readable by a Web browser. *See also hypertext markup language (HTML).*

World Wide Web An arrangement of Internet-accessible resources interconnected through hypertext and hypermedia and addressed by URLs. Also referred to as the Web.

Index